IF I WERE GOD...
THE WORLD WOULD GET A SWIFT KICK IN THE BUTT

WITTY INSIGHTS AND RANTS ON SERIOUS ISSUES
AND OTHER THINGS THAT JUST PISS US OFF

P A BROOK

If I Were God (The World Would Get a Swift Kick in the Butt)
Copyright © 2019 by P A Brook

All characters and events in this book, other than those clearly in the public domain, are fictitious and any resemblance to real persons, living or dead, is purely coincidental.

All rights reserved. No part of this publication may be reproduced, distributed, or transmitted in any form or by any means, including photocopying, recording, or other electronic or mechanical methods, without the prior written permission of the publisher, except in the case of brief quotations embodied in critical reviews and certain other noncommercial uses permitted by copyright law.

For permission requests: https://pabrook.com/

Ordering Information: https://pabrook.com/

Editing by The Pro Book Editor
Design by IAPS.rocks

ISBN: 978-0-9984304-3-0
        Main category—HUMOR/General
           Other category—HUMOR/Adult
First Edition

FOR MORE LAUGHS

VISIT:

https://pabrook.com/if-you-dare/

OTHER TITLES

Oh Shit! I'm Over 50 and Single

(A Guide for Newly Single Mature Men and the Women Who Want to Understand Them)

Real Places You're Glad NOT to Call Home

TABLE OF CONTENTS

For More Laughs iii
Other Titles iv
Note From the Author 9
LIFE 15
    Chapter 1: *Automated Customer Service*
    (Press 7 to Kill Myself) 17
    Chapter 2: *Junk Mail* (Making Beavers Happy) 23
    Chapter 3: *Tits on a Bull*
    (Like Studying Quail Sex-Useless) 33
    Chapter 4: *Pocket Change*
    (Rolling a Joint Is a Lot More
    Fun than Rolling Pennies) 51
    Chapter 5: *Taking a Seat* (It's Not Gay) 68
    Chapter 6: *Rude People*
    (Do Unto Others as You Would Have
    Them Do Unto Your Bitchy Ex-Wife) 73
    Chapter 7: *Addictions*
    (When Fun Turns into FUBAR) 85
    Chapter 8: *The Self-Inflicted*
    (Hey, Have Another Cookie) 93
    Chapter 9: *End-of-Life Suicide*
    (They Don't Hang Dead Men) 98

Chapter 10: *Handicap Parking* (Limp at Your Own Risk) 106

LIBERTY 109

Chapter 11: *Punitive Damages* (When Really Good Lawyers Meet Really Dumb Judges) 111

Chapter 12: *Frivolous Lawsuits* (Suing God Because You Got Sunburned) 115

Chapter 13: *Punishment that Fits the Crime* (One Way to Stop Sodomy…or Maybe Not) 128

Chapter 14: *Jury of Your Peers* (Or If You Are Lucky, Jury Consultant Groupies) 136

Chapter 15: *The Fourth Amendment* (What Many Internet Dates Need) 142

Chapter 16: *Constitutional Amendments According to Social Media* (#MyKindofInalienableRight) 146

Chapter 17: *Gun Control* (Is That an AK-47 Under Your Hat or Are You Just Happy to See Me?) 178

Chapter 18: *Parents Punished for Crimes Committed by Their Children* (Sharing a Jail Cell with Junior) 189

Chapter 19: *Insanity Defense* (If You Are Full of Shit, You Must Acquit) 204

THE PURSUIT OF HAPPINESS 223

Chapter 20: *Golf* (Is It Really a Sport?) 225

Chapter 21: *Newborns* (The In-Alien-able Right to Be Ugly) 233

Chapter 22: *Now, That's What I Call Free Speech* (Shit Is Gluten Free) 238

Chapter 23: *Legalizing Drugs*
(We-ed Shall Overcome) 253

Chapter 24: *Legalizing Prostitution*
(The Pimp and the Pauper) 265

Chapter 25: *Citizenship Without English*
(Needing an Interpreter for
the Pledge of Allegiance) 278

Chapter 26: *Government Waste*
(It's Fun Spending Other People's Money) 286

Chapter 27: *My Travel Ban*
(Give Me Your Tired, Your Poor, Your Huddled Masses
Yearning to Breathe Free and Throw the Smelly Ones
the Fuck Overboard) 299

Chapter 28: *Medical Research*
(Funding Nurture vs. Nature) 307

Chapter 29: *Getting Lucky with the Teacher*
(When Algebra Was Fun) 318

Chapter 30: *Making It Personal*
(It Is My Book, You Know) 331

Chapter 31: *Pontiff-ication*
(A God's Gonna Do What a God's Gotta Do) 335

For More Laughs 367
Other Titles 368
Meet the Author 369

NOTE FROM THE AUTHOR

Did you ever think about what you would do if you were God? I am not talking about world peace or the New York Jets winning a Super Bowl. I'm trying to keep this to the realm of the possible. What would you do about the annoying things? The idiotic that need only have some common sense applied? The ridiculous that could easily be adjusted to the betterment of everyone by simply removing the greed factor, or the idiotic? How would you fix what ails the world?

Would you start small? For example, anyone yapping away on their cell phone on a bus gets electric shock therapy. Whoever invented junk mail can only eat Walmart flyers from now on. The fat guy who spreads out like a Playboy centerfold next to you on the plane is forever banned from eating Twinkies. And buying Playboy.

And gets all your junk mail.

I'm sure you have observed many injustices in your life. The proverbial bad things happening to good people. Or just bad people getting away with shit. And you wanted to do something about it. Reward the good person, take away the hurt, something to make it right. Punish the bad guy.

If only you were God, then you could do something about it.

During the course of my life, I have said on many occasions

when witnessing something that did not feel right, "If only I were God...I would do something about it." Obviously I am not God and never could be, so I'm doing the only thing I can: writing about the things that we should seriously question, if for nothing else than to create a little happiness for our fellow men and women. Some of them you will agree with; some you will not. In my perhaps warped sense of right and wrong, I believe all of them. In doing some research for this book (which I tried to keep at a minimum), I actually changed my opinion on a couple of topics, and for others, realized that God had already done some work in that area.

But I need to be careful as I use God liberally throughout this book. Since I am agnostic by faith, one of the things I would do if I were God is eliminate organized religion. That could qualify me to go to hell.

Mmm, my first dilemma.

So I have to admit that God did a pretty good job on his first try, and His intentions were in the right place. He just decided that He did not want to micromanage man. I wish my wives had come to the same decision before hiring a lawyer to exert their demands. But He did leave just a little to be desired.

To put God into the modern technological vernacular, He was beta testing. And with every beta test, the results provide insights about changes for the better.

And here I am. Ready to roll out a blueprint for God 2.0.

I initially wanted to thank all the bad people who gave me the idea to write this book by their insensitive and even criminal actions, but realized that I might have become one of them if it weren't for my parents. So I wish to thank Mom and Dad for making me a good person, for knowing the difference between right and wrong, and for caring enough to say something about it. One thing they did not

IF I WERE GOD

instill in me, however, is a filter. I used to care about what people thought, but I am way too old for that now, so this manuscript contains what many would consider politically incorrect views and opinions (and desires).

As I said in my first book, if you want politically correct, watch fucking *Oprah* reruns.

But my lack of a filter allows me to express thoughts and opinions that I know many people have but are afraid to express to avoid offending anyone. Not because what is said is, in and of itself, offensive, but because people take things too personally. And when people think others will react a certain way, things automatically become taboo. Perhaps not the best example (but I just started writing this book, I get more clever as the day wears on) but in certain segments of the African-American population, the "N" word is acceptable as long as African Americans say it to each other, but if a someone else says it, all hell breaks loose. This is true of derogatory nicknames within many minorities and ethnic groups. But to even have referred to the problem, some of you are offended already.

If I were God, I would simply get rid of these derogatory words altogether. Wipe all words that are indeed offensive because of bigotry from all languages as if they had never existed. As a matter of fact, if I were God, I would get rid of bigotry. But we have bigotry, and simply the need to call people whose skin is dark African Americans, and call those who inhabited the territory that became the United States originally Native Americans, is a sign that bigotry abounds. But what about the rest of us? You know, the white folks. If we were all created equal, then we would all be referred to in the same way. White, black, brown, yellow, red, or whatever. Society has totally screwed this up. I would get rid of bigotry and racism and all the derogatory words they bred.

I'm just getting started.

PA BROOK

By the way, I think I am going to refer to white folks as European Americans, since Chris was from Spain and John was from England. As in Christopher Columbus, who we all know discovered America. And John Smith, captain of the *Mayflower*, or at least I thought he was the captain of the *Mayflower*. But he was not. It was another guy named Chris. As in Christopher Jones. OK, so John Smith wasn't the captain of the *Mayflower*, but he was the leader of the Pilgrims in Plymouth Colony, right? Oops, not so. He was part of the Jamestown, Virginia settlement, which was the first permanent settlement in America. He arrived in Jamestown in 1607 and was almost immediately killed for attempting a mutiny against another Chris, Captain Christopher Newport. I guess Chris was a popular name back then. He was spared by unsealed orders from back home and ultimately became the primary leader of the Plymouth Colony.

Does anyone really give a shit? How this is relevant will remain a secret between the two of us.

The Pilgrims actually came much later, in 1620, and were actually trying to settle much farther south than Massachusetts...duh. They ended up landing at Provincetown, which is now a vacation destination for gays and lesbians. Not what the settlers had in mind at the time, I am sure.

But this is not a history book, nor should anything that seems stated as a fact in this book be given such high moral standing. Especially since I thought John Smith was a Pilgrim. But if I really were God, the first thing I would do is make us all born with all this knowledge of history so we didn't have to go to fucking school for twelve years only to forget all the shit we learned by the time we are 60.

The topics in this book are controversial—duh. Conflict facilitates change, so without a little controversy, how will anything change for the better? My opinions are strong but not to be taken too seriously. The point of the book is to have some fun by enjoying someone else's point of view.

IF I WERE GOD

Mine. If you take offense easily at controversial topics and strong opinions that might not agree with yours, don't read further. If not, go have some fun!

My primary goal is to entertain. My secondary goal is to entertain change. If my rants create a reaction that causes positive change, that is a good thing. If not, fuck 'em. I'll have to take over the world.

You think I'm nuts?

Are you sure?

LIFE

काव्य

CHAPTER 1
AUTOMATED CUSTOMER SERVICE
(Press 7 to Kill Myself)

IN THE GOOD OLD DAYS, we used to call a company, let the phone ring several times, and get to speak to a nice woman who would help us. She could access a directory if we were not sure who we wanted to speak to or what their extension was. She stayed on the phone with us until someone picked up the transfer. She was always polite and would often bring a smile to our face. We were able to talk to the right person about the right topic and get what we called for resolved.

Then all hell broke loose. It started innocuously, with a simple automated phone system that had an automated answer but was relatively easy to navigate to get to the right person. See, back then when we called a company, we had to have a name or extension or there was no reason to even call. We were OK with this system because that was what we knew.

"Hello, this is X company. If you know your party's extension, please press it at any time during this message. If you need to speak to an operator, please press 0. Have a nice day."

So we ask the robot to transfer us to Mr. So-and-so or extension whatever. Or the operator. The operator was sure to connect you to person you needed to speak to. That was simple and nice. A little automation, but all was still relatively well.

Companies were loving this as they were able to save money on people. Of course, they passed the savings along to us customers. Ahem.

Ahh, but those nice ladies who used to answer the phone were now on unemployment. The companies soon realized that they could make the system even more efficient with a menu of items to choose from. Most people would call a bank to find out what their account balance was, so why not automate that first?

"Press 1 if you want to know your account balance. If you know your party's extension, please press it at any time during this message. If you need to speak to an operator, please press 0. Have a nice day."

Not too much of an inconvenience, because if you knew what your account balance was already or didn't care, you could easily and quickly continue on to a live person. But that still meant paying a live person. Maybe she was part-time or maybe she did multiple jobs, but there was a lot of unemployment insurance still being paid. So companies hunkered down and came up with additional automated options.

"Press 1 if you want to know your account balance. Press 2 if you want to pay your bill. Press 3 to update your personal information. Press 4 if you have a question on your bill. If you know your party's extension, please press it at any time during this message. If you need to speak to an operator, please press 0. Have a nice day."

Of course, we soon got used to these and to bypass listening to all the options, we would just press 0 at the beginning of

IF I WERE GOD

the message. But some really, really narcissistic asshole got wind of that and just had to fuck with us.

"If you need to speak to an operator, please press 8."

Seriously, there is simply no other reason in the world to change the 0 to an 8 except to fuck with us. We know none of the options give us a live operator, and we know that we need a person to speak to, so we save a few seconds by pressing 0. Simple, strategic, and we can almost accept the automated system as we sip our coffee and expect a real person to shortly pick up.

"I'm sorry, but that is an unacceptable selection. Press 1 if you want to know your account balance..."

Ayyyyyyyyyyyyyy!

So we now have to listen to all the options to find out the operator is a fucking 8.

WHERE WERE WE?

Every once in a while, an automated option actually is relevant.

Ahh, 4, yes that's the one I need. I have an issue with an item on my credit card bill. I need to talk to someone, so I press the 4 key on my dialpad.

"Please enter your account number."

Hmm, pretty easy request. Just where did I put my credit card? I like to talk to voice response systems, so I respond, "Just a minute, honey."

"I'm sorry, but I did not understand that. Please enter your account number."

Ugh. No fun. So I enter it.

"Please enter the last four digits of your social security number."

At least this one I have memorized. OK, whatever is necessary in the name of security. But now I will get to speak to someone.

"Good afternoon, Mr. Brook, could I have your account number please?"

Fuuuuuuck!

REAL TIME

I tried calling several real businesses to experience their automated response systems. Some were actually OK, but most were annoying. I liked the one that had two numbers. It was labeled "24-hour WOW! service." One number was for "Automated," the other was for "Real People." Little did I know that Real People just meant a live person was used for the automated response.

It starts with the usual Spanish option (that is a rant for another day), then she nicely asks if I have my account information handy.

"If you do not know your account number or do not have your account number handy, please press 1."

"1"

"Press 1 for our store hours.

"Press 2 if you want to order checks or deposit tickets.

"Press 3 if you are applying for a new account.

"Press 4 if you have questions about your existing card.

"Press 5 if you have questions about your bank account."

"4"

IF I WERE GOD

"Please enter the first four numbers of your credit card."

"I'm sorry, honey, but I already told you I do not have the number handy."

"I'm sorry, but I did not understand your response. Please enter the first four numbers of your credit card."

Uh, this is where I become a psychopath. I start yelling at her, thinking it will make a difference.

"I'm sorry, but I did not understand your response. Please enter the first four numbers of your credit card."

"Representative" followed by pounding the zero button 750 times.

"All customer service representatives are assisting other customers at this time. Asshole. We value your business. There will an approximately fifteen-minute wait time. Please listen to our lovely selection of really shitty music and advertisements so we can be sure to make this a tortuous wait."

By the way, this was an actual company with the actual responses above noted verbatim. OK, up to "Asshole."

NOUVEAU AUTOMATION

So, when I start a company, I am going to install a state-of-the-art computerized, automated response system. It will sound something like this. See if you like it.

"Good morning. Welcome to blah blah blah. Please pay close attention to the following choices as our menu has changed so we can fuck with you better than ever. So we may better be able to assist you, please provide the 64 digit account number we assigned to you to make sure no thief could remember your account number. 64 digits ensures that we have enough account numbers for the population to reach 1 vigintillion."

Digits properly input.

"Thank you for your entry of your account number. I will repeat all 64 digits so you can verify you entered the proper account number. One, seven, three…

Please press 9682732667663673646428746377948463 (which, if you look at your phone, stands for "you are a moron for doing business with me") if that is your account number."

Damn, I feel like a moron.

"Now since there is still a chance you are not you, please answer the following 17 security questions. As you know, our security questions are designed to ensure no one could ever guess the answers. What was the name of your grandfather's uncle-in-law's pet ferret that died in Ireland?"

A mumbled response is in order.

"I'm sorry, sir, I did not get that. What was the name of your grandfather's uncle-in-law's pet ferret that died in Ireland?"

Louder mumbling, this time perhaps understood.

"I'm sorry, sir, but 'Go fuck yourself' is not the right answer. Let's try a different security question…"

GOD 2.0

While automation and technology are good things almost without exception, automated phone systems have gone too far and make for bad customer service. If I had a company, a Godlike one, of course, I would streamline the entire process.

"Hello, please press 3 and we will read your mind and connect you automatically to the correct party."

God can do shit like this.

CHAPTER 2
JUNK MAIL
(Making Beavers Happy)

" A PIECE OF PAPER FROM SOMEONE you don't know, selling you something you don't need. And you have to recycle."

God, circa 2019

Is there anyone out there who is happy to receive junk mail? OK, maybe a coupon clipper or maybe someone really bored. I am not one of those people. We have "do not call" lists. Why can't we have "do not send me shit in the mail" lists? Was it always like this?

HOW IT ALL STARTED

It is not an accurate statement to say there was no mail before the Pony Express, but certainly it prompted a new wave of creativity in delivering mail. I always thought of the Pony Express as a really cool, long-lasting way of delivering mail—you know, Lone Ranger and Tonto shit—but it only lasted nineteen months. Then came the telegraph, and there went delivery of mail by ponies. But for that brief period of time, it was revolutionary. It took mail ten days to go from Missouri to California, about 1,900 miles. Perhaps its greatest feat was bringing word of Abraham Lincoln's election to the West Coast. It took less than eight days and was deemed miraculous at the time, making the Pony Express part of that momentus story.

Riders of the ponies were mostly teenage boys and rather small in stature. The Pony Express likely spawned an entire profession—jockeys. Or vice versa. They had to be small since the idea was to deliver as much mail as possible at once. More mail weight, less rider weight. The horse could only carry so much. And you think Secretariat was put to the test? These horses would run at full speed for 10 miles, which was the distance between resting stations. The rider would then change horses and continue for another 10 miles. This continued (with appropriate rest for the rider as needed) until the mail got to the West Coast. How much did this cost? In today's dollars, the cost to send a letter was $130. I guess there wasn't much junk mail being delivered in those days, but then it got cheaper to deliver the mail. Shit.

IF YOU PRINT, THEY WILL DELIVER

Yes, junk mail. We all get it. Most of us throw it out unexamined. I get my share of junk mail. From magazines and other publications I never subscribed to (or in some cases never heard of) to offers from banks and other financial institutions I never did business with, and everything in between. I get plenty of it, mostly on a weekly basis. The one I hate the most is from the local grocery store. It is pages long, in color, and falls apart. The worst part is that you can't just throw it out because real mail can get stuck in the middle of it. So you have to go through it page by page or shake it to make sure other junk mail I need to read is not buried inside. I would guess that 80% of the mail I get goes right into the garbage. That's the 80/20 rule: 80% I don't want. 20% replaces Twinkies.

IF I WERE GOD

One type of junk mail I have embraced is from charitable organizations looking for donations. They are very proactive. Pictures of the afflicted and related stories are very moving and emotional. This mail often includes things like pens, notepads, greeting cards, and my favorite, address labels. For a $10 donation, I can get a lifetime's worth of address labels. They come in different shapes and sizes, some for the holidays, others just pretty. But the best part is they include my address. No more having to write the address on the back of the envelope. Not so bad when you live at 1 Oak Lane, NY, NY, but pretty annoying when you live at 1505 Northeast Kentucky Industrial Parkway, Greenup, KY. Or my favorite, 107 Lower Cuchillo Creed Road, Truth or Consequences, NM. These are real streets. I looked them up.

Why is it a lifetime supply? We don't need address labels as much as we used to, with the internet available to pay bills. Even so, the charity sends just enough to last a year so they can get another donation next year. But they screw up their annuity by selling your address. It becomes a lifetime supply as every other charitable organization finds out that you donated $10. And sends you address labels. And then sells your address so you get more labels. Again. I think they get more money from selling the address of the poor schmucks who donated $10 than the sum of the $10 donations. You become swamped with donation requests. Complete with more address labels. I have so many address labels that I can never move.

The first one with the address labels actually became the one and only response to junk mail I have ever made. And what did I get for my nice gesture? Greed from all the rest. They should have gotten there first themselves, and they would have gotten my $10.

Am I a hypocrite to be ragging on junk mail when I, in fact, responded to a junk mail request? I say "no," because I had a perfectly good alternative in the address stamp. It worked perfectly well and cost less than $10 before I found the address labels. It would run out of ink at annoying times and then I would be stuck in manual mode, but I could gauge the stock of address labels I had left and make contingency plans if needed. Like donating another $10 to replenish my supply. But now I would gladly replace the address labels with an address stamp if I could get rid of all the other junk mail.

ALCOHOL CREATES USELESS CALORIES, BUT AT LEAST IT'S FUN

Outside of address labels, junk mail is useless. More than useless, it is a pain in the ass. I accumulated all my junk mail for six months and kept it just to see how much it would come to in weight. I was very meticulous, to be fair. I did not consider it junk mail if I was a current customer and the company was offering additional services or products or if I was a former customer. Just the stuff that gets you to go "Ugh!" when you grab it from the mailbox. It came to 30 pounds. That may not seem like a lot, but a piece of paper does not weigh much so it takes a lot of paper to add up to 30 pounds. It's like having a medium-sized dog delivered to you.

Hair by hair.

Some of it was recurring. Every week I got a one-page brochure from a company I never heard of, providing a service I would never need. Every week I got a menagerie of coupons all rolled up into a package, like you find in the Sunday paper. Every week.

I decided to look at the menagerie in more detail. Who are these people, and what are they trying to sell? The companies were retail in nature and were pretty much household names. It was interesting when I dove deeper. OK, I need a life.

IF I WERE GOD

Walmart, which must offer in excess of 100,000 products, had an eight-page ad. Four pages were devoted to clothing and two were devoted to gardening. Not unreasonable, even though it was the end of the summer, and most gardeners were hibernating. Then I found that one page was devoted strictly to Ninja Turtle shit. All sorts of stuff that had the Ninja Turtles on it. I can't imagine that more than one-tenth of one shelf in a store of 1,000 shelves would carry Ninja Turtle shit. I would bet anyone looking for that shelf would get lost in Walmart, give up, and buy some superhero shit instead. But the last page was my favorite, even worse than Ninja shit. An entire page was devoted to birdseed. Birdseed. One full page. To make sure Woody Woodpecker doesn't starve. Get me the name of the marketing genius at Walmart who thought of this so I know never to hire him.

Then there was Lowes, marketing Stainmaster carpet at $1.39 per square foot. The ad noted that it was better for pets because it made pet hair removal easy, and it was waterproof so stains did not soak in and were easily removed. There was a picture of a dog sitting on the carpet. The obvious inference was that if you have a dog and he pees on the carpet, this is the product for you. There is no question a carpet that allows easy removal of stains from child spills to everyday accidents might make for a good purchase, but to imply that it is a good product if your dog pees on your carpet is insane. Only an idiot would allow a dog to pee on the carpet. And only an idiot would admit that getting a carpet that allows easy stain removal would help make their peeing dog more tolerable. If you have a dog that pees on the carpet and have done nothing about it but buy a carpet that allows easy stain removal, you are an idiot. Lowe's was marketing to idiots.

Get the cheap carpet and get rid of Fido.

Grocery store inserts included Acme, Pathmark, and

ShopRite. ShopRite was my favorite. I thought about providing a comparison of prices, but quickly reconsidered since almost anything would be a better use of my time and hopefully readers of this book didn't give a shit that they could save $.30/pound on chopped meat at Pathmark. But ShopRite did something that at first glance seemed stupid, but upon further reflection was ingenious.

It would not be an unnatural thought to deem seniors as a target market for grocery store flyers. In ShopRite's 14-page insert, it repeated the same product at least five times. On page one, ShopRite tuna was 99 cents a can. On page five, the same can costs the same 99 cents. Just one example. Contrary to what you might think, this is smart marketing. If your primary target audience is aging and perhaps losing its memory, then repeating products makes a lot of sense. Mmm, if they forget it from page one, maybe page five will remind them. But what happens on page nine? This could be the never-ending flyer. OK, maybe not so smart. Maybe the marketing director designed this piece before he left for Walmart.

Then there are simply the items advertised. Extra-virgin olive oil has always intrigued me. Somehow, I thought being a virgin was like being pregnant. There were no adjectives that could be attached. You cannot be a little pregnant. How can you be an extra virgin? Is that the innocent chick who is a background actress in a porn flick?

There is Smart Source, which seems to be a Best Buy wannabee. It advertised a Free Home Security System, savings of $850. If you are saving $850, how much does the fucking thing cost? Ah, but they promised "NO COST to you for parts and activation with only a $99 Customer Installation Charge and the purchase of monthly alarm monitoring services. See terms and conditions below." The terms and conditions included a 36-month commitment in

IF I WERE GOD

print so small that, literally, you needed a magnifying glass to read it. If there is truly no cost, how can you be saving $850? But you are saving the $850, which makes it no cost.

Just take me out and shoot me.

Finally, mums. Yes, I have bought flowers at the grocery store. Usually not for someone special unless desperate. And my sister raised mums and made a business of selling great mums. So when I saw an advertisement for mums, I consulted the family expert. She told me what I already knew. If you want to buy mums, go to a flower shop.

Just stop sending this shit to me.

HAPPINESS IS PAPER

But there are people junk mail benefits. We will start with them.

Postal workers. Admittedly, sorting this type of mail is easy, since it is going to every person in the neighborhood, but it does add to the need for postal workers.

Mail carriers. If they sort it, it will be delivered. There is talk about eliminating postal deliveries on Saturday. If they get rid of junk mail, we might be able to eliminate Friday also. And Thursday.... Mail carriers love junk mail.

Paper manufacturers. Let's cut down some more trees.

Ink sellers. If it is written, ink is needed. And that color ink is soooo profitable. I think Dell gives away printers because the cost of ink is $3 per cartridge but a cartridge is sold for $129.99.

Printers. Inkjet, laser, dot matrix, thermal. You can't print what you have not cut down.

Designers. Just what do you advertise and where do you

put those pretty pictures of the extra-virgin olive oil bottle? And just where do they get the pictures of succulent meat that looks like it is from Smith & Wolensky? Do you really think the meat you buy from the grocery store at $4.99 a pound is going to look like that? They have to come up with something since career options are obviously slim if they are designing junk mail ads.

Marketing. You go to college and major in marketing. Your visions include creating the next Go Daddy ad for the Super Bowl or the marketing campaign for the iPhone 33. But it's slim pickings out there. You end up hired by the local pharmacy to create coupons for their mailing to all residents of Gravette, Arkansas. Not what you had in mind, but if it weren't for junk mail, you'd be in line waiting for nonexistent mailman gigs.

Recyclers. Chop down those trees, print those ads, and make sure you put it in the recycle bin. I have no idea how this industry works. How do they take those newspapers and make them into printer paper I can then print my crazy book on? How do they take the dirty, empty plastic water bottle and turn it into a sparkling, brand new water bottle? Ever see shit people put in empty water bottles or coffee cups? How about Pepsi cans? I once had to use a Pepsi can when I was stuck in my car in the middle of Manhattan in a snowstorm and nature called. The Pepsi can was a last resort. Not cutting myself and aiming were obstacles enough. Worse was the can was finished before I was (think about it). At least I learned something about my bladder. And the value of supersizing.

Viva tap water.

Sponsor of coupons. It is obvious that the process of sending coupons and special deals on products or services available for purchase to random people works. Otherwise, they would no longer do it.

Sellers of mailing lists. One of those businesses that became a predator of other businesses. What a great way to make money. Companies take their customers' contact information and sell it to someone else. I buy something from you, and to show your appreciation, you guarantee that I will be pissed off because you sold my address to someone who has a product that I could never possibly be interested in.

Scissor manufacturers. Finally, what good would a coupon be if you could not cut it out to take to the store? In this digital age, one could take a photo of the coupon with their cell phone. But if they are savvy enough to know how to use their cell phone camera, they are not reading junk mail coupons.

This is far from a complete list, but a solid glimpse into how society benefits from the dissemination of junk mail.

SPAMATOSIS

So who gets hurt from junk mail?

Garbage collectors. Well, it depends. If they get paid by the pound collected, they will benefit. If not, they just have more shit to collect.

People not interested. I haven't taken a survey, but I suspect the folks most interested in checking out junk mail and coupons are people with limited income and retired folks. Both may get a benefit from price shopping paper towels. Or something to read. And I am totally in favor of getting them on the bandwagon to benefit from those deals. Just leave me off of it.

Environmentalists/tree huggers. These guys love the internet. No flyers in the mail, no catalogs left at your door. Buying things online saves trees as long as you don't print out the purchase confirmation.

Beavers. Environmentalists love trees; beavers need trees. You cut them down to make junk mail and there are fewer for beavers to chomp on. If you are not familiar with beavers, they do not just sit back and watch reruns of *Duck Dynasty* when trees are not in the area; they need to chomp. Their teeth require chomping. No trees, no chomping. No beavers. No *Caddyshack III*. Another internet advertising champion.

GOD 2.0

Sometimes proclamations are not easy. To junk or not to junk? Both courses of action have benefits. It seems that society benefits most from keeping junk mail. More jobs, more products to sell. Sorry, beavers. So my ultimate decree will be to create a "Do Not Mail" list so those who are annoyed at having to throw out sixty pounds of junk a year will be placated (including me). Compromise breeds society. I do what I have to do.

CHAPTER 3
TITS ON A BULL
(Like Studying Quail Sex-Useless)

A LOT OF MONEY IS SPENT on a lot of shit in this world. Sometimes we do not have a choice, as we must pay taxes. We are not always sure what the government does with our money. We care about that. Other times nonprofits and other organizations spend money that came from our donations or products purchased, and we don't seem to care what they do with that money. We should.

Research studies fall into this category. Especially the ones that are useless and a waste of money. I refer to them as Bullshit Studies. The government spends our money funding these studies, and other organizations spend their money that they indirectly got from us funding these studies. Researchers laugh their way to the bank and pretend they are doing something good for mankind. You can't even understand what they are talking about. I would repurpose that money for better use and those careers to replace the suffering quails. If I were God.

NOT THAT THERE IS ANYTHING WRONG WITH IT
The US government funded a study to find out why Argentinian gay men go to bars to meet other men to have sex. Gee. Really. A bar. What a novel way to meet someone.

The study cost $400,000. I could have answered the question for a cool quarter mil. And bought all of those gay guys a lifetime supply of condoms. I am not sure whether Argentina is the gay capital of the world, but it does not appear that mattered. The participants were solicited and apparently given monetary incentives to participate. Is there little wonder that 29% of the participants had *no* income? Well, other than from being in the survey. The results noted that a lot of gay men were having anal sex, the majority without condoms.

Another revelation.

The population was broken down into the following categories based on surveys filled out by the participants: gay, bisexual, heterosexual, and other. Other included "hombre," "macho," and "activo." Dare I note the educational level of the average participant? I could not discern that any conclusions were reached other than the population requires "further study." I smell another $400,000 grant.

Not to be outdone, the National Institutes of Health spent more than $400,000 to study the behavior of male prostitutes in Vietnam. It concluded that more research was needed. What the fuck was the first $400,000 spent on?

If we are concerned about the gay population, the prevalence of AIDS, and the need for education, we should focus on the behavior of American men.

SINCE WE ARE ON THE SUBJECT

"US Government Spent $181,406 to Study How Cocaine Enhances Sex Drive of Japanese Quail" read the internet headline describing this event. One has to conclude that the headline is sensationalized and that there must be some substance to the story. Wait. "Controlled preclinical studies that utilize animal models have demonstrated that prior repeated exposure to cocaine enhances sexual motivation and behavior" notes the article. You need a quail for that conclusion? Just ask millions of college kids and save $181,400 of your cost.

"The goal of the proposed experiments is to utilize an animal model whose sexual behavior system has been well-studied, Japanese quail." Sounds reasonable until you ask yourself, "Why is the sexual behavior of Japanese quail well studied?"

The study notes that its results tie in with the observations that cocaine is linked to increased sexual motivation in humans (what! a study that is relevant) and thereby increasing the likelihood of occurrence of high-risk sexual behavior.

Someone needs to talk to some Argentinian dudes.

ESTRUS

I had to look that one up. It is the point in time during the "cycle" when women are most ready for procreation. It's called "heat" in the animal species.

One of the things I love/hate about researching research is the technical terms used for things that should be Mom-and-Pop easy to understand. But no, decadunolfragislistic words need to be used. No, that's not a word.

Anyway, this study was about estrus or, more specifically, how men react to women in the different stages of their menstrual cycle. Why? Does anyone really care? What benefit to society will there be if we conclude that women are "hotter" when their period is not imminent? But alas, I was not God when this study was commissioned.

Someone thought that tracking the amount of money women made from lap dancing and correlating it to when they were in "heat" might help cure cancer.

Seriously.

The survey encompassed some estimated 5,300 lap dances with women in various stages of their menstrual cycles and included both those on and off contraceptive devices. Women earned almost double when in heat versus not. The study notes: "These results have clear implications for human evolution, sexuality, and economics." And should definitely clear the way for similar studies in quail.

FISHULENCE

Many men are proud of their farting abilities. When in the woods with fellow he-men, they take pride in how loud and toxic they can make them. There is no embarrassment like there might be on a date. Often, with an announcement like, "I feel a good one coming," or with a sly snicker that only fellow woodsmen understand, a staccato-like entourage of noise emanates, accompanied by uproarious laughter. More normal people pretend it's the guy next to him on the subway who let one fly. "Ooooh, God, what is that?"

That works.

But the only communication goal men make when they fart is to either brag about it or deny it. Not so with fish. According to one study, it appears that herring make unusual farting sounds at night. No he-men here, but the conclusion was that they use farts to communicate. About what we don't know. And why we don't know. We just know they break wind when it's dark and there are lots of fish around. That's called communication. It was the first study of fish farting—and hopefully the last.

In a related story, $700,000 was given to a group of researchers to study methane gas emissions from cows. More fart facts.

IF I WERE GOD

A MAN AFTER MY OWN HEART (OR OTHER ORGAN)

Finding out that fish fart was not enough for our beloved researchers, we just had to find out about barnacle penises. A study concluded that barnacles have the longest penis relative to their size of any animal. It can grow up to eight times their body length. It allows them to mate with distant sister barnacles. I guess their personalities won't get them anywhere. Lady barnacles deem them "nice." Not only can it grow to such lengths, but it really does have a mind of its own. I know there are times when I can't control mine, but these guys take it to another level. They can control the stoutness of their member to allow a thinner projectile to efficiently weave through heavy waves to reach their target, but create a shorter, thicker version in calm waters to be more maneuverable in their search.

I can't even doggy-paddle.

My scuffling with barnacles was significant as a kid. My dad had a boat that had a ton of them to scrape off each spring. I had no idea I was cutting off the manhood of hundreds of barnacles every year. Maybe I did, and that is why I am so fucked up.

I have no idea what I would do with a 48-foot dick.

WHAT I COULD DO WITH A PAIR OF "Fs"

I hitchhiked cross-country when I was in my twenties. Unfortunately, I had no aids to my hitchhiking success. Big thumb, big nose, no tits. Others are more fortunate. It reminded me of a fake news report (with thanks to Howard Stern) that once reported that in order to incent girls to obtain better grades, a high school offered a prize. The slogan was "Double D's for A's and B's." Very clever.

Fast-forwarding to finding a practical approach for utilizing big boobs appropriately, a research study endeavored to correlate chest size with frequency of hitchhiking success. Women with various sized breasts stuck their finger out awaiting accommodating drivers. Unfortunately, this time the A's and B's failed. In a conclusion that amazes only in the fact that evidence was needed to make it, women with big breasts got more offers of rides than women with small ones. Praise the Lord, we have a revelation. For me, the only criteria to provide a ride would be a letter.

Any letter.

BUSTER

I was bullied as a kid. I knew I was a nerd and so did everyone else. But at least I looked normal. When I got to high school it was a fresh start, since I interacted with some who were ignorant of my reputation. I survived. But what about fat kids? If they are fat in grammar school and don't thin out by high school, they can't get a fresh beginning, because, unlike nerd hood, which is not worn on your forehead, fat is worn on your entire body. And fat kids are the butt (sorry) of jokes. Really. I swear. I know it is hard to believe that anyone would make fun of someone who is fat, but my experience in life supports that. And if you don't believe me, there was a study to prove it. So there. It concluded that fat kids are at a higher risk of being bullied than average-sized kids. See, I knew it was unbelievable until a much needed and very expensive study was commissioned to prove that fat kids get bullied more than skinny ones. Wow.

Thank God I wasn't fat *and* nerdy. Even a 48-foot dick wouldn't have helped me.

RATS ON COCAINE

There is a concept called positive reinforcement. Its premise is that if you want someone to repeat a behavior, make the results of the behavior pleasurable. Simple enough and universally accepted. In addition, it is held in many circles that music can be used as an effective treatment for a variety of disorders and be part of positive reinforcement. So, to combine the concepts, say every time someone plays Bach at a restaurant, a plate of delicious veal parmesan is placed in front of me. Mmm, nice. At the same restaurant, every time someone plays the Beatles, the waiter brings me a plate of overcooked, disgusting, smelly liver. Now I am not a fan of classical music, and since I am part of the human race, I am a big fan of the Beatles. But if music foretold my dinner, which performer would I be selecting to listen to? Yeah, doesn't take a scientist to figure that out. As a matter of fact, if I were dumb as a rat, simply playing Bach could eventually make my mouth water and hearing "She Loves You" make me vomit. Again, no rocket science here.

Oops. Rocket science needed. The above logic was not sufficient for a group of researchers who decided they wanted to determine whether rats could be conditioned to react differently to music based on stimuli associated with the music. Like veal Parmesan vs. liver. But since the researchers were unable to determine the eating habits of rats (I bet even rats like veal Parmesan and hate liver), they had to come up with a different reward. They could have come up with lots of stimuli that represented a positive experience versus a negative one. Too hot or comfortable. Food or no food. Hell, sex or celibacy. I could think of 50 more that could be part of a rat's mainstream existence (well, maybe not). But what did these "scientists" choose as the stimuli?

"Cocaine."

"Really?" asked the skeptic.

"Yes."

"Why not alcohol or weed?"

"The researchers exhausted the supply of liquor and weed while coming up with this one."

So, they injected rats with cocaine and put on music while they were under the influence. Then they put on different music when they were straight. When the rats were later given a choice of which music to listen to, guess which music they preferred? I am sorry, but this sounds like an incredible waste of time.

And good cocaine.

IT'S BETTER THAN THE BLUE PILL

OK, maybe not as exciting as cocaine, but another stimulus study tried to ascertain whether smells could cause an erection in monkeys. I am not talking about that lotion your girlfriend uses that can create instant readiness. I am talking about lemons.

"No shit! Why not something pleasant like flowers?"

"That's the point!"

"Sounds like overkill—they're monkeys."

The study set out to prove that a scent can create arousal. It was successful. Part of the study was to count erections. As in proudly stating that erections were observed 79.2% of the time. There are certain reasons we all want to pursue a career in a particular field of study.

I never thought counting monkey hard-ons would ever be one.

MONKEY SEE, MONKEY DO

Cocaine, lemon, and now what? Cooing. Apparently, certain monkeys squeal during mating season. This study aimed to clarify whether female monkeys invited sex verbally and whether that verbal invitation affected the male's ability to bang the shit out of her.

"I don't get this."

"It's like the hot new girlfriend."

"What do you mean?"

"You know, when she screams, 'Fuck me, Baby!'"

"That's what these lady monkeys are doing?"

"Bingo."

The researchers concluded that these broads were promiscuous, desiring to have sex with multiple partners. Damn, I was born to the wrong mother. Their theory is sperm competition and paternity confusion. Basically that means "let's fuck a lot of guys, they won't know for sure who the dad is, but they will all want to protect me just in case." Monkey dudes are dumber than humans.

There is more. They had to determine if a male orgasm was achieved (not going any further there), the thrust rate of the male (I can just picture the cheerleading squad of researchers: "Whoo-hoo.") and how long the event took (I threw my stopwatch out).

And I thought counting hard-ons was bad.

HOW TO LOSE FRIENDS AND INFLUENCE MONKEYS

We have all experienced being with someone who yawns, and we find ourselves instinctively yawning ourselves. Well, we think its instinct. Sometimes it's beneficial because I can't say anything stupid in the middle of a yawn. I like having boring friends. Or is it yawning friends? There is some scientific reason for yawning begetting yawning that I am sure is well-known to anyone who cares. I don't. I just know that an ex could always tell when I was stifling a yawn (maybe that is why she is an ex). But she was not boring, I was just running my own experiment. She didn't get it.

I could be a scientist.

Of course, this is the subject of a study. The premise is that if you see someone you know yawn, you are more inclined to yawn than if you see someone yawn that you don't know. Familiarity breeds boredom. Actually, this research study noted that previously there had been several studies that had studied the same thing. Including one with dogs.

"Yawn, Spot. I am conducting an experiment." Just how do you get a dog to yawn anyway? Imagine being boring to a dog?

For some reason, some researchers wanted to test the theory again with chimpanzees. So they had a group of chimps watch a video of other chimps yawning (must have been watching the dog video). One group watched chimps they knew, and the other group watched chimps they did not know. The results were that the chimps who watched their brethren yawned more. Maybe they just need better friends.

If they are still not convinced about contagious yawning I know some out-of-work stoned rats.

SO THAT'S WHY I SCRATCH MY NUTS SO MUCH

I never gave any thought to how often I wash my genitals. During showers, of course; after sex, usually, but it's not a requirement. Other than that, when? Before sex? Only in the context of the shower, and the overriding notion was her joining me. I really couldn't come up with anything else. But inquiring minds want to know. So a study that cost $800,000 was commissioned to study the hygiene habits of men. In?

IF I WERE GOD

Nairobi.

"No!"

"Yea, really."

"Why not in the United States or a developed country?"

"Guys were too busy with rats and chimps."

The object was to determine how often and why guys wash their balls. Why Kenya? Maybe there is prevalence of hygiene-related disease. The hope was that the study might help future studies to evaluate the effect of intervention on reducing transmission of such diseases. Oooh, another brilliant conclusion. And why is it that this study can only help future studies? Why not develop a study that can conclude itself instead of setting the stage for more waste of money?

Ah, but the study. Men were asked if they washed their genitals at times other than bathing. Like before sex or after sex. Most men did not. But the reasons were not because of laziness or a purposeful lack of hygiene. No, in Nairobi, bathrooms are often shared. Sometimes, at the same time, running water is not always available, and sometimes one has to buy water. So, yes, we conclude that lack of hygiene can lead to disease, but didn't we know that already? And why dissect the behavior of a society that has no choice? Why not observe those that choose not to cleanse themselves as opposed to those that *cannot* cleanse themselves? Oh, maybe because if you can shower, you will. Novel.

It was interesting that several participants noted that they did not wash before sex because it might ruin the mood (do I hear shrinkage?), or because their partner might suspect infidelity if he took a shower right before sex. Mmm, wonder why he would think that?

Instead of commissioning a study to determine whether an intervention of medicine might assist a society that has no choice but to endure bad hygiene, perhaps just bringing the medicine would be a better idea.

TOOTSIE

My favorite soap opera is not really a soap opera, but a movie about a soap opera—*Tootsie.* Actually it is my second favorite movie of all time (you have to read the rest of this to find my favorite—like you fucking care). I could never watch real soap operas, but apparently there was a study in which the scientists were paid to watch soap operas. Not a bad gig. You can do your crossword puzzle, read a couple of books, and still not miss anything.

"What were they paid to watch?"

"Comas."

"What?"

"Comas—you know, like the movie."

"So they watched soap operas to study comas?"

"Right."

"Nice gig."

"I just said that."

The question that was begging a scientific answer was whether TV soap operas portrayed comas too optimistically. That has kept me up many a night. The fear was that soaps were contributing to unrealistic expectations of recovery. But most people that watch soap operas are comatose to begin with, so who gives a fuck? These guys did, and went to great lengths to study the coma phenomenon in soap operas. Through a painstaking and incredibly thorough review of 9 soap operas over 10 years, 73 comas were identified. The recovery or lack thereof of the patients were compared to real-life statistics with the astonishing result that people on soaps survived more than in real life. We can't be killing off too many of the stars at once.

Well, this prolific finding led the researchers to admonish the soap opera community for telecasting results of comas that were more positive than real life. Oh, my God, soaps are not real life?

Really?

Fuck!!

The report actually concluded that viewers of soaps may be more likely to believe the more favorable prognosis of a coma noted in soaps compared to real-world statistics. OK. Who cares? First, they must think only stupid people watch soaps. I know lots of very smart comatose people. Secondly, they criticize mass media for portraying too optimistic a view of comas. Come on, it's fiction for a reason.

These researchers should go comatose. Or not return from *Apollo 13*.

COULD YOU REPEAT THAT IN ENGLISH, PLEASE?

A hallmark of any research study is to use as many technical terms as possible. While I am sure it is the correct way to present a completely detailed and accurate account of the study, many normal people have no clue what is being said. That does raise the question as to why they created the terms used to sound so complex. And even some they use seem to be used for the sake of making them seem smarter than the reader. Maybe the goal is to make sure only their colleagues can understand it so they can be commissioned to do more studies to study the effect of not being able to understand their studies.

Exactly.

Some words/phrases I came across that seemed to be for show only:

- *Taxa*-plural of taxi? No. It means "group," an interchangeable term; the only reason not to use "group" is to force me to look up the definition of the term they did use.
- *Cohort*—son of taxa.
- "*Dyadic*" interaction—means two individuals interacting. Well, in the actual case, two monkeys.
- *Attenuate*—maybe most of you know the meaning of this one. I was not that smart. It means diminish, which would have fit the context perfectly without forcing me to resort to the internet.
- *Nucleus accumbens*—a part of the brain.
- *Intromission*—in the context of the study, it meant fucking. I know you can't use "fucking" in a formal study, but if you were studying the effects of using the word "fuck" rather than "make love," you would have to use it. In any event, "sex" or any one of several other real words would have been just fine.
- *Enteric methane emissions*—I believe this means farting.

If words are not bad enough, how about some of the complete sentences that are used. I use the term "complete sentences" loosely because sometimes you can't tell if there was a verb included. Here are some examples, with my very uneducated guesses at what they were really saying.

DISCUSSING THE LAP DANCE STUDY:

"For these reasons, we suspect that human estrous cues are likely to be very flexible and stealthy-subtle behavioral signals that fly below the radar of conscious intention or perception, adaptively hugging the cost-benefit contours of opportunistic infidelity."

IF I WERE GOD
THE WORLD ACCORDING TO PA (TWAPA):
"She's not sure why, but her boobs in his face spell bigger tips."

DISCUSSING MONKEY SEX:
"Neither the nature of the salient acoustic parameters nor the detailed temporal relationship of female and male behaviors was investigated."

TWAPA:
"We didn't try to figure out whether she could sing or liked one-night stands. We just watched."

MORE MONKEY SEX:
"Male rank was assessed by transcribing submissive and aggressive behaviors as well as the outcome of dyadic interactions into an agnostic interaction matrix."

TWAPA:
"We wrote shit down."

THE LAST OF MONKEY SEX:
"We used a general linear mixed model (GLMM) to analyze the effect of categorical variables (e.g., cycle phase, male rank) and continuous variables (copulation intensity, intromission time, copulation length) on a dependent continuous variable (e.g., call latency, acoustic structure)."

TWAPA:
"We masturbated to monkey sex."

I LIED - MORE MONKEY SEX:
"In this study we demonstrate that male marmosets can be conditioned to a novel, arbitrary odor (lemon) with the

observation of erections, and increased exploration of the location where they previously experienced a receptive female, and increased scratching in postconditioning test without a female present."

TWAPA:

"Lemons gave them erections and made their balls itch. Let's try grapefruits next."

MALE SEXUAL HYGIENE IN NAIROBI

"We performed all quantitative data analyses with the SPSS 11.5 statistical software package (SPSS Inc, Chicago, IL, USA). We used all hygiene behavior outcomes as dependent variables and the demographic factors as independent variables in a series of bivariate and multivariate logistic regression models. After evaluating bivariate associations, we entered all demographic variables into multivariate logistic regression models. We then performed backward stepwise elimination, removing variables from the model one at a time until reaching a final model containing all variables associated (at the p (0.1 level)) with the outcome of interest."

TWAPA:

"Dr. Wong won the Twister contest."

COW FARTING:

"It is believed that supplemental lipid can change the Fatty Acid (FA) composition in the milk, and decrease methane production."

TWAPA:

"If you don't feed 'em beans, they won't fart as much."

IF I WERE GOD

MORE COW FARTING:
"However, the molar proportion of propionate increased linearly with the feeding of incremental dietary levels of ground flaxseed."

TWAPA:
"I think he got brain freeze."

RATS ON COCAINE:
"This study showed increases in both locomotor behavior and extracellular dopamine in the nucleus accumbens after music was paired with MDMA during operant self-administration."

MDMD is short for methamphetamine, which is nowhere defined in the study. I had to look it up. Perhaps this is second nature to all researchers.

TWAPA:
"The rats moon-walked to 'Thriller' after getting high."

This was only a sample of evidence that my comprehension of the English language is execrable (shitty).

GOD 2.0
Stop the presses! No more money! You're fired! If it doesn't benefit humans, it doesn't happen. If its only prupose is to spawn another study, it doesn't happen.

If it doesn't make sense to a bunch of third graders, it doesn't happen.

Finally, some fun in third grade.

If I were God, I would have the monkeys run the experiments and the researchers yawn.

And then eat the liver.

PA BROOK

I would put the researchers out of business and the money to work for a study that could unquestionably benefit man. Like finding out if big-breasted monkeys hitchhiking on cocaine get picked up more frequently than farting rats with giant penises listening to Bach on their iPhones.

CHAPTER 4
POCKET CHANGE
(Rolling a Joint Is a Lot More Fun than Rolling Pennies)

We jingle change in our pockets. Well, men do. Women's pants typically don't have pockets. Why is that? Oh, so they have to buy a handbag. And carry our shit. Genius!

We men fumble with coins when we pay for something in cash. But does anyone really do that anymore? It is more than annoying when someone uses a debit card for a stick of gum and has to sign for it, or puts in the wrong pin, or is just pissing me off on purpose. But there may be a middle ground. Should we get rid of change? Or at least the penny? Nickel...?

The penny is the smallest coin denomination in US currency, but it is not the smallest coin. That distinction, as we all know, belongs to the dime. But since the penny is the smallest in terms of value, is there a point in keeping it? How much is a penny worth? Is it worth enough to bend over and pick one up?

I ran an experiment.

I randomly threw a penny ahead of me on the ground to see how much time I would spend picking it up. Of course, I knew there was one there, so I had to put on my Dr. Seuss hat and pretend that I didn't know. I imagined thinking nice thoughts about being rich and then suddenly eying a tiny shimmering thing on the ground.

Start the clock, please.

My mind works very fast. I went from fantasizing about having a trillion pennies (that's $10 billion. What? You don't fantasize big? That kind of thinking spawned threesomes.) to thinking about stooping to collect my first one. I won't accord any time to this thought process. But here I go. Stop. Stoop. Pick up and pause to look around for others. Unbend knees. Check the year in case it's a really old one worth something more. Put in pocket. Lift leg and continue walking. Reengage fantasy, this time about a threesome.

In the interest of scientific accuracy, I repeated this three times. The average amount of time I spent was 8.32 seconds. I also tried it without checking the year, saving about 2 seconds. That is, assuming there is good light. Mine was a 2015 penny, so can't quit the day job.

Assuming no one can resist checking the year, it takes an average of 8.32 seconds to pick up a penny from start to finish. An added benefit is the one deep knee bend that you can add to your exercise log. Earning a penny every 8.32 seconds means your hourly wage for picking up pennies is $4.33. The federal minimum wage is $7.25 an hour.

That doesn't make a lot of sense.

But that assumes each penny pick up is a discrete event. Say there was a trail of pennies, each one requiring a deep knee bend, but the cognitive time was not necessary to repeat, and you stuffed them all in your pocket at the same time. You just got a raise.

But is all of this worth it? What if it were nickels instead? Dimes? Kennedy half-dollars?

By the way, why are dimes so small? In case you give a shit, coins were all made with silver in the amount of their denomination. So a dime was made with ten cents worth of silver, quarters with twenty-five cents, etc. Since a dime had less silver, it was smaller, but the five-cent pieces ended up too small and were made bigger with different ingredients so the total value of those ingredients was still five cents.

Too Much Information.

MORE TMI

Somebody estimated that the average person loses $38.92 in pennies in her/his lifetime. How one figures this out is beyond me. That is some study. Someone else estimated that $1.2 million worth of pennies are simply thrown away every year. This is at least a more concentrated time period, so more realistically measurable. You would need generations of really bored scientists to estimate the amount of pennies lost in a lifetime. At least with the annual survey, researchers could move on to something new after a year.

Like counting ant farts.

It was always my belief that if you threw a penny off the top of the Empire State Building, it could kill someone it hit on the street. Perhaps this was just my parent's anti-deterrent, anti-litter campaign for junior, but a 1997 study by two researchers started with the hypothesis that, indeed, a penny thrown from the Empire State Building would kill someone it hit on the street. The results of the study, complete with effective cross-sectional areas measured and drag coefficients calculated, debunked all that school age teaching by concluding that a penny tossed from the top of the Empire State Building will *not* kill a passerby it hits on the ground. Two researchers spent six years studying this question, originally believing as I did. Unfortunately, they ended up doing research studies on throwing shit off buildings.

I know some constipated ants.

If you carry a penny in the coin tray in your car, how long would it take for that penny to cost you more than a cent in extra gas? The weight of the penny adds weight to the car. The heavier weight causes the car to work harder and, therefore, additional gas to be used to transport that penny around. At what point does that extra weight cause a penny in gas to be spent? Who thinks of this shit?

Better yet, who tries to figure it out? Someone did. It's 140,000 miles.

A LITTLE HISTORY (YOU CAN SKIP THIS IF YOU DON'T GIVE A SHIT)

In the 1770s, colonists could buy a "penny knife," a 5.5-inch folding utility knife, for a penny. Of course, this wasn't an American penny of today. Each state minted its own pennies, which were pegged to the English penny.

The Coinage Act established the US Mint in 1792 and printed the first American pennies and half-pennies. The first cents were about the size of a modern quarter and made of 100% copper.

The first "penny press" debuted in Boston in 1830. At the time, most newspapers cost six cents and were targeted toward the rich. Three years later, penny papers took off in New York, bringing newspapers to the masses. Of course, at $2.00, the Sunday *New York Post* is still a bargain today.

The halfpenny was discontinued in 1857 as too penny-ante,

IF I WERE GOD

even though its buying power in today's money is estimated at 10 cents.

In 1870, a penny could buy a loaf of bread.

The first pre-stamped penny postcards were introduced in 1873. Today, it costs 34 cents to send a postcard.

In 1900, street vendors sold "penny licks" of ice cream. The ice cream was in a serving glass and sold by the taste. For a penny, you could take a lick. Of course, sanitation was a major problem.

I used to play poker with a bunch of guys who lit up a joint every time the tournament started and passed it around. While I am no lightweight when it comes to getting high, the thought of swapping spit with ten 70-year-old dudes was not my thing. I had several vodkas before I got there.

The modern Lincoln-head penny was introduced in 1909.

During the Depression, "penny candy" helped kids get through the day. Not sure how that helped with dental bills. Apples were a penny, as were many arcade games.

A penny in 1972 was worth what a nickel is worth today.

Today, there is nothing you can buy for a penny.

See, aren't you glad you didn't skip it.

HUFFING AND PUFFING

Another cost/benefit to picking up a penny is calories burned. A 70-kilogram person who lowers their center of mass by half a meter will burn about half a calorie of energy standing back up. This study must have been done by some British researchers. I guess there are no ants in England.

Well, I conducted my own useless study. Crouching to pick up a penny is equivalent to 2-3 seconds on an exercise machine. Fifteen minutes of moderate exercise per day can add three years to your life expectancy. Sounds reasonable. But wait. That is only the time spent actually huffing. What about travel time to get there? Change? Shower? Wash the smelly clothes? Make amends to the spouse for all the time spent at the gym and not helping with Junior? Buy new clothes? That comes to a lot of huffing and puffing.

Ouch, now we need a formula. You can trust me or do your own math, but I came up with spending an overall extra 2.5 years of your life in pain and suffering to add an extra three years to your life. You decide.

You really want to challenge the math?

Talk about a fucking digression.

So, do you pick up the penny or not? You would have to pick up 360 pennies in discreet events to equate to 15 minutes of exercise. I'm walking on.

What about tossing pennies in a fountain? More exercise. It's not exactly throwing a Nolan Ryan fast ball, but just the throwing motion of the arm is going to use up some calories. My exhaustive research came up with no studies covering the calories burnt by throwing a penny in a fountain. Let's just say it's additive to the process.

PENNY SAYINGS

There are lots of sayings that refer to the penny, and it would be a shame to get rid of them if we got rid of the penny. Of course, they would stick around for a while, but then at some point, they would be forgotten. Does anyone remember any halfpenny sayings?

The word "penny" is the singular word for the British monetary unit the "pence." The pence is a unit of the pound, which is also a unit of weight in the United States. The

IF I WERE GOD

penny is a unit of the dollar, which has nothing to do with British currency or weight, which, by the way, is based on kilograms and not pounds. This could get ugly.

To "spend a penny" in British idiom means to urinate. As in pee. The etymology (look it up) of the phrase is literal. Some public toilets used to be coin-operated, with a penny being the charge levied. This could lead to confusion.

"Honey, I need to spend a penny. Be right back."

"OK, dear. Can you bring me back some nachos?"

"Ugh!"

"Penny-ante" as in "spend a penny" playing poker. Hopefully not peeing while playing poker. Or losing your ante in the john. Stick to gin rummy. Penny-ante means small time or petty, but that's no fun.

"Penny loafers" have been around since the 1930s. "Loafer" came from the lazy cows who used to loaf around before being used for more noble purposes. That little strap on the front of the penny loafer with the slot was designed for pennies so that the wearer always had money to make a phone call. Half the people eligible to read this have no idea what I am talking about. When was the last time you saw a working phone booth?

But even back then, I'm not sure what was wrong with pockets. With phone booths a thing of the past, you would think they would be redesigned with a slot for the iPhone 8.

Just saying.

We all know what "pinch a penny" means. Saving money.

"I pinched my pennies so I could go to college."

PA BROOK

For others, "I pinched my pennies so I could buy some weed in college."

But how can you really pinch pennies? Why not squeeze a dime? Or fondle a nickel?

"A penny saved is a penny earned." Wait, does that makes sense? How can you save a penny before it is earned? Maybe that is not what it means. How about it is just as useful to save money you already have as it is to earn more money? Bullshit! It may not be as fun to earn more money, but it sure as shit is more useful to have more money than it is to save what you already have. If you are not getting any more, you are fucked! I think. I told you this was confusing.

"Pennies from heaven" doesn't exactly sound like a prayer answered to me. Who did you piss off?

Then there are "99 cent stores." I guess if we got rid of pennies, these would have to become 95 cent stores. Although some bad marketers have come up with the idea of dollar stores: Dollar Tree, Dollar Rent-a-Car, Dollar General. What's wrong with these people?

"Penny slots." Is that a cheap hooker?

"Not worth a red cent." How about a blue one? My exhaustive research came upon many reasons for the use of the term "red." I embrace none of them. Do your own research. I am not your mother.

"Penny with heads up is good luck." That implies if it's tails, walk away. As long as you don't walk under a ladder. Or cross a black cat. OK, but if it's a twenty, I don't care if I'm staring at "In God We Trust" or Andrew Jackson's blue eyes, I'm picking that bad boy up. How do I know they are blue? I am not your mother.

"A penny for your thoughts" is a nice way of asking someone

IF I WERE GOD

how they are feeling or asking for their opinion. I guess they are not worth much. But not so for others. Former presidents get paid millions of pennies for their thoughts, topped by Bill Clinton, who was reportedly paid 75 million of them for one speech he gave.

Maybe when the penny goes away, the saying could be an "app for your thoughts."

"My two cents." That's an ego trip. Your thoughts are only worth a penny, but me, I'm worth two. Or 75 million.

"Penny arcade." Of course someone would have to take my tilt-ridden childhood afternoon fun and turn it into some web-based millennial-generation mind fuck.

"Penny wise, pound foolish" is a reference to saving a lot of pennies and then wasting them on big items, referencing the British pound. A literal view could raise the question: Does this relate to money or weight? If you are wise with your pennies, maybe you have the next new diet. Or maybe it's the other way around. Or I have no clue.

"Take care of the pennies and the pounds will take care of themselves." Another weight reference. Maybe. Imagine the sayings if we used US currency. "Penny wise, c-note foolish." That has a certain ring to it. Or "take care of the pennies and the quarters will give you a blow job." Now we're talking.

"Take a penny, leave a penny." What the fuck is the point of that?

"It cost a pretty penny." Means what you bought is expensive. Means ugly is cheap. What about "cost an ugly penny." Fucking bargain. Whoo-hoo! Can we say that? Oprah?

"Turn up like a bad penny." I guess that meant there were counterfeit pennies back in the day because who would forge a penny today? With inflation, it's been replaced with "turning up like a bad trust fund."

"A penny waiting for change." Mmm, that makes little sense, but what would a good saying be if it did not require interpretation? That's what you have me for.

"Excuse me, spelling bee master, can I get that in a sentence?"

"Certainly. I felt like a penny waiting for change."

"Ah, yes. Worthless."

Like this fucking exercise.

"Be ten a penny." It means something is very common, like you can get ten of them for a penny. Fuck, it's only a penny. Just go with the flow.

If you say "the penny drops," you mean that you have finally understood something. Let's take fighting with your spouse as an example.

"I get it, honey. You are always right. The penny just dropped."

But fights don't usually go that way. More often than not, it's, "You are a fucking penny waiting for change. You want my two cents? I can get a blow job from a quarter!"

At this point, she is fully pissed off, and you will profit from the final penny references. "A friend in court [your lawyer] is better than a penny in your purse." As she will be suing your ass. If she has her way, you will soon not have "two pennies to rub together."

NICKEL-ODIOUS?

We cannot disrespect the worthy penny brethren, the nickel. While not as prevalent, the nickel has some standing in the vernacular of currency.

IF I WERE GOD

We start with a Yogi-ism. "A nickel ain't worth a dime anymore." There is no need to explain Yogi-isms—just enjoy them.

"I wish I had a nickel for" every penny joke made. Or whatever it is that you think is in abundance, and you got shafted by not profiting from.

"Not worth a plugged nickel." It appears that nickels were subject to counterfeiting as well. Surprise, surprise. Some smart dude decided to knock the expensive shit out of the middle of the nickel and replace it with some inexpensive shit. He hoped the dudes in Wyoming wouldn't notice. Those even farther west, or just dumber, could fall prey to the totally counterfeit wooden nickel.

"Nickelback" in football. Finally! Sports! There are four defensive backs in most football team defensive lineups. When they want another compatriot (fuck Bill Belichick), they refer to him as the fifth defensive back.

Or...nickelback.

Love it! But get this, when they want even another defensive back, because the first five really suck, or the other team is really good, they call the sixth guy...

"Dimeback." Huh? I think sextet, five-0, five plus, sixth guy (the choices are almost infinite) would all work. But dimeback?

How did Wrigley's gum make money charging a nickel for a stick of gum? Just wondering.

DIMES

Ah, the ten-cent piece. Smaller than its siblings, but worth more than some. Hopefully, no Napoleon complex. Cute, shiny, and housing my favorite president, FDR. I wrote a paper on him in 8th grade. I actually like the dime sayings better than the nickel ones. But that could be because of my ever-faulty research methods.

"Dime a dozen." Ordinary, unexciting, like the horse you want to bet on because of its name. Despite my manic zeal for analyzing numbers I actually bet on a long shot once simply because it was named after my wife. Well, no, the horse was not actually named after my wife. It just had the same name as my wife. Since she is now my ex-wife, nag has a double meaning. By the way, the long shot came in for a healthy payday. Maybe I need some more ex-wives.

"Five-and-dime stores" were aptly named (sort of) in the day because many things sold there cost five cents or a dime. Why not a "nickel-and-ten store?" Many things sold there cost a nickel or ten cents. But wait. Why not call it the "five-and-ten store," or the "nickel-and-dime store?" Don't ask me. Some marketing genius from back then must have come up with that idea. What he was thinking (or smoking) remains a mystery.

"On my own dime" means using my time to facilitate whatever. Maybe this was a typo? Time, dime, get it? Think about it. Why a dime? Lots of other coins to choose from. No chance of a typo with nickel. On my own pickle. Don't think so.

"Don't nickel and dime me." Don't sweat the small stuff. Leave me the fuck alone!

"Stop on a dime." "Turn on a dime." Maneuver within very small spaces. The dime is the smallest coin, but not the smallest thing you could stop or turn on. I do like the visual, though. How about making it more challenging? Stop on a grain of salt. Turn on an amoeba. Now there's a visual.

IF I WERE GOD

THE CANDY MAN CAN

Or the US Mint can. And does. Make coins. All of them. And it is a business. Not a very smart business, however. It is the government.

According to the US Mint 2016 Annual Report, the unit cost for both pennies (1.50 cents) and nickels (6.32 cents) remained above the face value of those coins for the eleventh consecutive year. In 2016, the nickel lost $21 million, and the penny lost $46 million. In other words, combined, it cost the US Mint $67 million more to make pennies and nickels than they are worth.

By comparison, the dime cost 3.1 cents to make, and the quarter cost 7.6 cents to make in 2016. The dime made $217 million in 2016. The quarter made $431 million. Now we are talking.

Overall in 2016, the US Mint made $579 million. The profit of the US Mint is contributed directly to the US Treasury to support the overall budget. So this is big business. But it is also government business. I guess we should be happy with an overall profit. A rarity in government.

SHOULD WE GET RID OF THE PENNY?

The penny has some sentimental value, and Abe Lincoln is a revered president by many, but has it overstayed its welcome?

The United States eliminated a small denomination coin in the past with relatively little trouble. If you read the history section, you know that in 1857, the US Mint stopped making the halfpenny. The cost had exceeded its value, and it was considered a denomination too small to be worthwhile. Back in 1857, the halfpenny had the purchasing power today of more than 10 cents. This could lead us to consider eliminating even the dime. Heavens!

Despite the lowest denominated coin being struck from the coinage markets, commerce in the United States continued without any major issues. In addition, Canada, New Zealand, and Mexico have all eliminated their smallest denominations with virtually no impact.

History has shown us that updating the monetary supply in countries where currency is very stable has had little if any negative effect on the economy or on people's acceptance of the coinage. No riots in the street. No crazy tweeting by the president.

LEAVE A PENNY

Those who think we should keep the US penny cite the following arguments to support their position.

Prices will increase. If we eliminate the penny, we have to round to the nickel. Up. You didn't think down, did you? There are actually studies on this with nothing conclusive resulting. Except that more studies are necessary. It's a cottage industry.

The poor pay the most, relatively speaking. They are most likely to make more frequent, smaller purchases, thus suffering from the rounding up more often.

Charities need pennies. There are thousands of small charities that depend on penny drives to bring in donations. People think nothing of pouring out their old penny jars to support these drives, but they won't part with nickels so easily. Pity the poor volunteer who has to wrap them. Just where did all those coin machines go?

Nickels cost even more to make than pennies and lose more money than the penny. If we eliminate the penny, we will need to make more nickels. That is some fucked-up logic. Lose more money to prevent losing even more money. Or the other way around. I'm not sure what that would be.

IF I WERE GOD

Pennies are sentimental. Americans love their pennies and hate to change things. We've always had pennies and therefore always should have pennies. Americans are traditionalists, and the Lincoln cent is the epitome of modern-day circulating coin tradition.

Recent polls have noted that more people prefer to keep the penny around than get rid of it. The poll had a margin of error of +/- three cents.

TAKE A PENNY

The folks who want to retire the penny also have some compelling arguments, including those below.

Pennies are worthless. They don't buy anything, many people just throw them away, and nobody wants to use them, so let's just get rid of them! Or throw them in the fountain for exercise.

If you try paying for something in a store with a fistful of pennies, you can expect dirty looks from both the clerk and other customers. Even your dog hates you.

Once pennies drop out of circulation, the nickel will become the lowest-value coin cluttering up people's pockets. So instead of penny drives, charities could start holding nickel drives, putting out bottles or wishing fountains to collect the new "useless" coins. And since each nickel is worth five times as much as a penny, charities would gather five times as much money with each spare coin tossed into the jar.

Until your dog gives you the evil eye again.

Making pennies wastes taxpayer money. The US Mint readily admits that. What business admits it's losing money in a product but continues to produce it? The United States government.

It takes time to handle pennies. Various people have decided to quantify this. And you thought you needed a hobby. Results include that 48 million hours are wasted each year dealing with pennies. Another 48 million were wasted figuring this out. The cost of this wasted time has been estimated in the $1 billion range.

Maybe not compelling.

Consider this. Would retailers round down as an incentive for cash transactions to eliminate credit card transaction fees? Retailers could actually make out better, and so would customers. You think they are smart enough to get this?

Limited utility—pennies are not accepted by all vending machines or many tollbooths (for those fools who still don't have EZPass), and pennies are generally not accepted in bulk. Or by humans. Or Fido.

LOBBYING

There are lobbying efforts and organizations on both sides of this argument. Really. For the fucking penny. Talk about hobby-challenged. Well, it is big business, and the company that manufactures the penny puts out many of the pro-penny arguments. That makes sense. But why are all these other people spending money and effort to get rid of the penny? There is no company that profits if pennies are no longer manufactured. Don't these people have something more important to do?

Maybe they are out-of-work researchers.

PLUG A NICKEL

While we are at it, let's create a lobbying effort for the nickel. Either side is fine. I just want to have some fun. Reasons to keep the nickel:

IF I WERE GOD

- Whoever is on it is really important to my life. It's Thomas Jefferson. He was on the $2 bill and got dissed. Can we really do that to him again?
- Getting rid of the nickel makes five-cent denominations a bit more challenging to deal with. If something costs $1.15, there can be no exact change. OK, three quarters and four dimes will do it, but who's going to do that?
- They are easier to wrap than those stupid dimes.
- The people who are fighting to keep the penny in circulation would have a backup crusade to save the nickel.

Reasons to get rid of the nickel:

- They cost more than they are worth.
- The United States government would save $21 million.
- The United States government would save $21 million.
- The United...

GOD 2.0

As you can see, both sides have some good points. And just as I have spent way too much time debating this, others have spent way too much time defending one side or the other.

Fuck 'em both. Get rid of the penny *and* the nickel. I believe businesses should make money, even the government. Then there would be less change to jingle. And I wouldn't get pissed at the guy using a debit card for a stick of gum. Can you even buy a stick of gum anymore? How much does it cost? I should know this. Fuck it, get rid of gum too.

CHAPTER 5
TAKING A SEAT
(It's Not Gay)

THE FIRST TIME I MENTIONED this to my best friend, he immediately said "You're gay!" Now, there may be a lot of things I am unsure of in life, but my sexual orientation is not one of them. I am not gay. I have to admit, I did see how he could think that it was less than manly, but when you think it through, it is so totally logical that the only person who would think I am gay must be homophobic. Or jealous.

But my friend is not homophobic. Of course, he is just breaking my balls. It is unfortunate that others think like him too, because the men are all missing the point. And getting themselves into trouble and causing more work for themselves and, quite frankly, giving all of us guys a bad name when one simple act could go a long way for all maledom.

If I were God, no one would ever think it was gay for a man to sit while he pees.

I always got up to pee in the middle of the night when I was younger and the night was full of drinking. More liquids in, more liquids out. Logical and deserved. At least the night was fun. So I would wake up with that feeling, the one that

IF I WERE GOD

says, oh, shit, I have to pee, but the last thing I wanted to do was get out of bed. It's warm, I'm sleepy, and the wife is probably going to grunt her annoyance at my disturbing her. And it may be several grunts if I got particularly drunk that night. Actually, she was probably hoping I was getting up to throw up. Logical and deserved.

So I finally gave in to the urge and slouched my way to the bathroom, half asleep and probably still drunk. Standing there and letting it all out was a relief, and I looked forward to climbing back into bed. Maybe the wife would want one of those middle-of-the-night quickies. Hey, this 3 AM peeing may not be so bad after all. But then I got older. And there were no more 3 AM fantasies. And it wasn't getting out of bed once, or only on drinking nights. It was getting up two and three times every night. If it was a drinking night, ouch. Oh, and if I forgot to put the seat down after, I was in trouble. And if I leaked on the toilet rim and didn't clean it up, I was in trouble. And if by some chance I sprayed all over the bathroom floor and didn't clean it up...well, you get the picture. We guys struggle not to screw those things up while in our primes. Now I've got to do it right two or three times every night?

By the way, women don't believe we can spray. Our dicks are like a hose with options, so it can be dialed to stream, spray, drip, and more. But we can't control the dial. It may stream, spray, or drip without our knowledge or approval. I would love to walk into the bathroom and bark instructions, "OK, dick, stream." No, the bastard has a mind of its own. It's sometimes a surprise, and sometimes you just get a feeling it's going to be one of *those* options. I have even peed sideways. Well, not totally sideways, but I completely missed the toilet right in front of me. Not sure how the physics work there, just that it was a major pain in the ass at 3 AM, cleaning up after one of those.

So that leads me to one night when I got up to pee for the one too manyth time. I said, "Not again." Dick said, "Sorry, dude." The wife grunted. Now, if I know when I go to pee that it will *not* be the last pee of the night, then I don't have to clean up after myself until that last pee of the night. But who knows when it will be the last one? I am always hoping that this will be the last one. It actually may have happened once in 2007, so I retain hope. In the interim, I have to clean up after every pee. And lest I forget, I also need to put the seat back down. This is way too much to think about at 3 AM. So on this particular night, I decided to sit. Like put my ass on the toilet seat. Yes, like a woman.

Fortunately, I remembered I had underwear on.

A new habit was formed. It turned out to be a very good new habit. But no one gets it. I wonder how real gay men handle this. Hire a maid?

IT'S MY LOGIC—YOU CAN STAND

Compare the effort it takes to pull down your underwear (sleep naked if that is too much work) to the effort it takes to (1) clean up after you pee and (2) put the seat back down. Add on the disturbance it causes with the wife if you forget (1) or (2). Are you with me here? Pull down underwear and sit vs. whip it out, aim, go "oh, shit" when it's a spray, rip off some toilet paper (say "fuck" ten times if there is none), fold the toilet paper, turn on the light, hear the wife groan that the light is on, wipe down the toilet, check the floor for evidence, wipe the floor, throw the toilet paper in the toilet, curse at yourself.

Or sit.

After all of this incredible logic, my friend still did not get it.

The worst part may be that even if you put the seat back down and clean up after yourself, you may not get any credit from the wife for leaving the toilet exactly the way you found it. It is expected. There is no sympathy for the wayward penis.

But I do have limits and rules. I started only at night and continued to pee standing when I had clothes on. If I am fully clothed, the effort to drop two pairs of pants is much greater, though the benefits of not having all that work after the pee became quite attractive. It was supposedly gay, so I was loath to give in early on. Then I rationalized. Hell, no one had to know, and I knew I wasn't, so I began to sit while peeing regardless of clothes. But I kept it to only at home. Standing in other places still seemed appropriate. Until I was at Mom's. She wouldn't care and would certainly still love me if this indeed meant I was gay. So I began peeing while sitting at the home of all relatives and in-laws.

Well, only the in-laws that liked me. I have had multiple in-laws, which I am not proud of. Not sure my wayward penis had anything to do with accumulating ex-in-laws. Probably being an asshole prompted my "ex-" status more than anything else. At least she would think so.

VISITING THE JEFFERSONS
At the risk of showing my age...

What about a friend's home? That took a little longer. I still remember the first time. A typical weekend summer party, and nature soon called. It was a really nice bathroom and looked like it had just been cleaned. Ironically, it was at my anti-sitting friend's house. Perhaps subconsciously I thought this was fitting. He would never know. Maybe I should tell him just to fuck with him. I didn't. At least not that day.

But it stopped at friends, and not all friends. No need to discuss further. No public restrooms, of course, especially if they had urinals. Ever been to a New York Jets game? No sitting even if you have to sit. 'Nuff said.

So my transformation was complete. Except now I was empowered by this amazing time-saving, trouble-saving concept I had created. Thinking it would be universally embraced, I began telling people I was close to about what I had discovered. The women loved the idea. The men thought I was gay. Not really, but they thought the idea was gay. One even admitted to not having to clean up after himself. He either has a pea shooter for a dick or the most tolerant wife in the world.

I have yet to convince any male to do this or to even admit it is a good idea. But no one knows what they do behind closed bathroom doors. Closet pee-sitters? Mmm.

This would have made a great *Seinfeld* episode.

GOD 2.0

No way to get me to recant here. At some point, flailing your dick for all the voyeurs to see will become taboo, and I will be vindicated. Ever try to text while flailing?

Just my luck, women will start leaving the toilet seat up.

CHAPTER 6
RUDE PEOPLE
(Do Unto Others as You Would Have Them Do Unto Your Bitchy Ex-Wife)

HUMAN BEINGS ARE NOT MUCH different than animals. Our females produce youngsters who are eventually let loose on the rest of the species. The youngsters are armed with whatever ammunition their parents gave them. That ammunition is predicated on the ammunition the parents got from their parents. And so on. It only takes one shitty "and so on" to fuck up the whole family tree. So if your parents were given blanks by their parents, you could be in deep shit.

This leads to several other topics discussed elsewhere, but we will keep this one to human decency. I like to think of it as a commandment. Do unto others as you would have them do unto you. I am not sure that this is a commandment, but it is pretty catchy. I actually live by this, almost to my detriment. If I would not treat someone a certain way, I get angry if I am treated that way. The issue is, it may not be a big deal but because I wouldn't do it, don't dare do it to me. And a lot of it is "sweating the small stuff."

Imagine living with me.

Tailgating is an example. Not the 'get drunk before a football game' tailgating. The other one. I hate tailgaters, so I never do it. Not because I am a driving saint, but because I was in an accident in my early driving days and had to take a remedial driving course. I learned that you should never follow someone closer than two seconds. In English that means, there should be two seconds between you and the car in front of you at all times. As in, see the tree the car in front of you is passing? One-one thousand, two-one thousand. If you have passed the tree, you were following too closely.

Why? Because it takes two seconds to come to a complete stop if you brake as hard as you can. So if the car in front of you loses its transmission, you can stop before you run into it. Perhaps a more realistic example is if a truck is carrying cargo and that cargo becomes disengaged and ends up in the road right in front of you. You need two seconds to stop before you become it.

So much for the science lesson.

This created my obsession with tailgaters. I would get pissed if someone tailgated me even though it would not cause me harm. I was not anticipating losing my transmission and did not have any other cargo that could disentangle and create hardship to my pursuer, so why was I pissed when someone tailgated me? Because they were doing something I thought was improper. And since I would never do something that I considered improper, they were getting away with shit I couldn't get away with. Ergo, pissed-offness.

Is there a connection somewhere? Yes. Maybe.

We use what our parents gave us to figure out how to act in life. My parents did not provide me with a tailgating response roadmap. Actually, it was a matter of self-esteem. I took it personally when someone tailgated me. It was totally my issue, but it was spawned by how I was raised.

IF I WERE GOD

So are most things that we do. If someone treats you poorly, the behavior is likely a result of how that person was raised. But you can't take it out on the parents, so you take it out on the perpetrator of the activity. Or just hate 'em.

One of my favorites is cutting in line. Whenever I get into a queue, I am always anxious that someone may cut in front of me. There are two issues here. One is my self-esteem that someone is taking advantage of me. Their behavior might cost me twenty-five seconds of my life, and I get pissed off enough to account for twenty-five days of my life. My issue. The second one is the reason the person who cut me off did so. He/she felt compelled to fuck with me because they have issues. Cutting me off gave them a sense of self-worth not available elsewhere. And I fell for it. If I show no pissed-offness, then they will likely not have quite the same feeling of victory than if I give them the finger.

This is embodying the entire topic of rudeness and its causes. When someone is rude to someone else, there is an issue going on that has nothing to do with the subject of the rudeness. So don't take it personally. I do. Working on it. But lest this fall into total psychobabble, let's just kill all the motherfucking rude people.

But that might include me, so we will show some compassion and take it case by case.

IT'S RAINING MEN
The Weather Girls had a number one disco song that created the need for new and better rain protection. What they had in mind might be different from what I am thinking.

Those of you who do not live in big cities can just go to the next section because this will likely not resonate. Not because you don't get it, but because you probably have not experienced it. But feel free to stay tuned.

PA BROOK

It's a rainy day in New York City. I have experienced hundreds of them. Vendors appear out of nowhere on almost all street corners, selling umbrellas. They cost $2.50 but because it's raining, they can get $15 for them. God bless entrepreneurship.

I am one of those who never has an umbrella, so the $15 is well worth it. Others who are more fortunate or more able to be foretelling brought their own. And since it is raining, they have opened theirs to protect them from the rain. Not that the rain will cause any harm. It was raining well before umbrellas were invented, and man seemed to survive, so at best, the umbrella is a luxury. But here we are in the middle of midtown Manhattan at rush hour, and it is raining. Some of us are tall and some of us are short. Streets are crowded, and many folks must move to get out of another's way. To frame this for those who live in smaller towns, in New York City during rush hour, it is impossible to walk in a straight line because there are so many people in the way. They have the same issue, so everyone must compromise and move a little this way or that so passage can be achieved.

Seems simple enough. You sashay this way, and I will sashay that way. But when it's raining, the sashaying must include the umbrella too. We all know the harder it rains, the closer the umbrella must be to our head. Sometimes to the point of not being able to see in front of us. And certainly not being able to see above us. If one is short, this has no consequences. If one is tall, look out.

It's pouring rain. You need to keep the umbrella at as close quarters as possible. Does your need to keep dry give you the right to ignore the passage of others who have the same goal? Your selfish focus puts the eyes of tall humans at risk. Think for a moment of the height of your hunkered-down umbrella that extends 18 inches over your head. Its pointed ends are at eye level of tall people who are also trying to keep dry.

Ignoring other people's rights when not controlling your umbrella will incur My wrath. And the Weather Girls actually will make it rain men on you. Very, very large men.

DON'T LET THE DOOR HIT YOU IN THE ASS

No, actually I prefer that it knock you down. The "you" being those who don't say "thanks" when you hold the door for them. I'm usually in a good mood, saying hello to everyone. I am the courteous sort, so I go out of my way to perform those little niceties in everyday life. Like holding the door open for someone. Most people acknowledge a kind gesture with a "thanks" or a nod or a smile. Others walk past you while you hold the door open and say nothing. Almost like they think you are a doorman, or just inferior to them.

I like to follow that behavior up with a loud "you're welcome" as they pass through, but that won't make a rude person miss a step. Once an asshole, always an asshole.

Perhaps an appropriate punishment would be for this rude person to get stuck in an elevator for hours with a bunch of migrant farm workers fresh off a 12-hour shift in the sweltering sun.

I JUST GOTTA TAKE THIS CALL

We all love someone answering their phone on public transportation. Or at a sporting event, or in any public area where the natural attention is not oneself. A corollary is when someone acts like you're disturbing his very loud public cell phone conversation.

"So how is little Judy doing today, dear?"

Dirty look from commuter sitting next to Judy's dad.

"Oh, cool, she had some string beans for lunch. So glad to hear she likes her vegetables."

Stares from other commuters.

"Maybe we can get her to try broccoli next week."

Tap on shoulder from someone trying to read.

"Excuse me, hon. I've got rude commuters to deal with."

A pleading look from the reader with a "Shhh."

"Dude, I'm talking to my wife. Deal with it."

Somehow, mysteriously, he drops his phone into the public transportation vehicle's toilet. The one that has not been flushed for days. I wonder how that happened...

YOU ARE NOT THE ONLY ONE IN A HURRY

We all have sat in bumper-to-bumper traffic and then seen in the mirror or heard someone gaining on us fast. How can that be? Shoulder shit. Someone thinks they can ride on the shoulder and pass everyone. Why? Guess they feel special.

This one bothers me because I want to do the same thing and get to where I am going more quickly, so part of me is jealous that I don't do the same thing. But it's wrong and illegal, and I am a rules person. I do take a deep breath and imagine that the person has an emergency so that allowing the driver to get away with this is acceptable. Execution of this thought usually depends on whether I am having a good day or not. Usually not.

Regardless, I would just make sure someone partially pulls onto the shoulder to block the perpetrator from advancing. And then I would summon a state trooper who will find that roach from 1979 in their back seat.

IF I WERE GOD

DINING ETIQUETTE

I always wait until everyone is served before starting my meal. If I am the one who has not been served, I always tell the rest of the table to start eating. You wait unless given permission. And if others are waiting on you, you give that permission. When either of those do not happen, I get pissed.

Maybe the appetizer just sucked.

In any event, punishment should be that the first bite of the vegan dish you ordered includes some wayward buffalo.

LIFE IN THE FAST LANE

As in the express lane at the grocery store. I'm sorry, but anyone capable of shopping can count to 12. I know, you look at the basket full of shit and quickly surmise there can't possibly be 12 things there. That's probably because you can't see below the top floor of all the shit you threw in the basket. Or maybe you think you are above the rules. Probably you just don't care because you are in a hurry and think you are the most important person in the world.

I like to call people out when they have 27 items in the 12-item lane. I can handle 13, or the lemon that got stuck at the bottom of the basket and you missed it. But 27? And when you do call them out, their reaction is usually to look up at the lane number and go, "Oooooh, so sorry," and stay right where they are as if the mistake is already made and cannot be corrected. I say put them at the back of the longest line twice. Once for doing it to begin with, and when it's their turn, send them back a second time for acting like it was an honest mistake and not correcting it themselves.

What is equally bad is that the checkout person NEVER says, "Sorry, ma'am, you are in the wrong line." Just once

I'd like to see some balls from her. Figuratively speaking, of course.

Or I will just give her some.

STAND DOWN

Just being a member of the human race should be enough credentials to stand up for an elderly person or pregnant woman on public transportation. I am a senior myself but will always offer my seat to someone less fortunate than I. Even if it is just someone struggling with groceries or kids, or it looks like they could use some element of compassion. It makes me feel good to help those less fortunate.

What can you be thinking seeing someone struggle and doing nothing when something is so easy to do? Ah, maybe I have found a use for that stick of gum. Pants, meet seat.

DOUBLE-DIPPING

I don't know about you, but I'd never heard about double-dipping until *Seinfeld*. I cannot swear that I never double-dipped before that, but ever since, I turn the celery stalk upside down for the second crack at the pepper ranch dressing. Let's think about this. We often kiss friends, sometimes on the lips. We often share food with a friend who perhaps has fingered it first. We have no clue what goes on in the restaurant kitchen. And we really have no idea what our host was doing in the preparation phase of the celebrated pepper ranch dressing.

I have had sex in the kitchen. Before company arrived. Can I swear that everything was sterilized before guests arrived? Depends on how many cosmos preceded the anointed act. Although the cosmos could have had their own sterilization effect.

Bottom line is that double-dipping has a negative connotation, but in reality, close talking (more *Seinfeld*) is more likely to spread germs than double-dipping. It's just that the optics suck. So let the double-dipping naysayers use someone else's toothbrush. Perhaps their dog's.

GRAFFITI THAT MOTHERFUCKER

What about the guy (girls would not do this) who takes up two spaces in the parking lot? Is his car that special, or did he just fail the parking portion of the driving test? It's not even parallel parking. He is acting like he is the last person on the planet. Wish he was.

On Mars.

The ones who have their shitty car covered by some tarp make me laugh. I bet it's a dilapidated 1962 Mercury Montego. Under the tarp, passersby might think it's a Lamborghini.

I am going to marry the homeless man with a weak bladder to an open gas tank, and he hasn't learned the sitting lesson yet. That'll be fun.

"THOSE" DOG OWNERS

I love dogs. I had three growing up. I walked them all the time. And stepped in a lot of shit along the way. And never once picked up theirs.

I still love dogs, but will never have another one because I will never want to pick up dog shit. You've got to put on that plastic glove like you are about to check someone's prostate, bend over, and pick up warm squishy stuff. Oh, and they make it easy, so you can roll the glove off your hand and the squishy stuff is on the inside. Clever!

Fuck that! I don't care. So I will never have a dog.

If you do not want to pick up dog shit, then don't have a dog.

Or I will see to it that you find another owner's contribution to fertilization on your flip-flops.

MR. MAGOO ON A 10-SPEED

I like to ride bikes and had never ridden on main streets for more than a block or so. There were usually sidewalks. I would hear how bikes needed to heed the same traffic rules as cars. Stop at red lights, give pedestrians the right of way, and ride with the flow of traffic. This latter one never made sense to me. The thinking is that if you ride with the flow of traffic and get hit by a car, the impact will be less than if it were head-on. I get this logic and do not dispute it. I am riding at 15 mph and get hit by a car behind me doing 25 mph. It's like getting hit standing still at 10 mph. Problem is, I am on a bike and will go flying no matter how slowly the car is going, so my risk of injury is significant. The bottom line is that it will likely also be a surprise as I cannot see the car coming and have no ability to get out of its way.

On the other hand, if you ride against the traffic, you have much more control over whether you get into an accident. You see some idiot texting and he begins to swerve, you have a chance to get out of his way. Not so if he is behind you. I acknowledge that if he hits you anyway, you are a lot more fucked than if it was from behind, because now it is like getting hit standing still at 40 mph. But you will, without question, get hit less often.

So where is the trade-off?

I had a bad experience with the red light thing. When I was living in New York City for a while, I began to take a bike to my office. Riding a bike in New York is a very daunting endeavor. The city has created bike lanes on almost every main street, so it is less dangerous than it used to be, but you still need to exercise a lot of caution and attention.

IF I WERE GOD

Biking has become very popular in New York. Most use the bike lanes and travel in the same direction as the cars. I got with that program. But few observe the red lights. Some may slow at an intersection that could be hostile, but they plow through as if nothing is lurking despite the red light. I know it is illegal, but I also do it. It's kind of like jaywalking. That may be illegal, but no one gets a ticket for it.

Except me.

I was riding up First Avenue in Manhattan one morning and went through a red light where it was clear there was no harm lurking. Lucky me, I was the victim of probably the only red light bicycle sting operation ever. I got a ticket and then found out the news. Getting a ticket for riding a bike comes with the same penalty as driving a car. I had gotten a ticket a year previously for coasting through a red light in Manhattan. This was now my second moving violation. The fact that it was a bike was of no concern to the legislature of New York. I had to pay a fine as though I had driven through a red light in a car for the second time. I actually fought this in court, and the judge totally commiserated with my plight of having to pay $350 for my bike faux pas. Commiseration was all she could muster as it was what the law said. She didn't charge me the court costs.

So now, I am the only person on a bike that stops at red lights in New York City, and it pisses me off. To all those guys that run red lights or go the wrong way or ride a bike recklessly, you win. I'm calling Uber. Better hope I'm not *driving* an Uber next time you run a red light.

TEXTING ABOUT SERIOUS STUFF

This is a complete taboo no matter how important you think the text is. You are just going to get into trouble. You will likely include a typo that will send someone off the deep end. Or be sarcastic and they don't get it. Or just be an asshole and wait for the return fire.

Some people insist on fighting by text. Don't do it.

If you don't heed my advice, the next time you send a text to the love of your life trying to make up for a fight that you know was your fault, "I need to go fix myself" will autocorrect to "U need to go fuck yourself."

GOD 2.0

I have only scratched the surface, and only with my personal pet peeves. Admittedly, many of mine are minor. Hopefully that means I am tolerant of worse. Or I just have a boring life.

Just do unto others. You know, the Bible thing. If they don't completely comply, have some compassion for the small stuff and don't sweat it so much. If it really bothers you, hire a homeless man.

CHAPTER 7
ADDICTIONS
(When Fun Turns into FUBAR)

WE ARE A SOCIETY OBSESSED with addictions. Because something is labeled an addiction, it is almost as if it becomes acceptable, mainstream. It's an addiction and, therefore, responsibility can be abdicated. Suddenly it's cool to have a sex addiction. Better than being called a cheater or sexual harasser.

What is an addiction? What causes it? I'm no scientist or psychologist, although the shrink bills I have accumulated should have garnered me a PhD in something. But from what I have read, behavior becomes an addiction when it negatively impacts your ability to lead a healthy, productive life.

If you spend 40 hours a week playing video games, are you addicted simply by the math? Not necessarily. Perhaps you have no life or are stranded on Mars. Life's choices may not be robust, so video games may be a viable alternative. But if you work 40 hours a week and have a wife and a child but ignore them, it is a problem.

There are clinical definitions of what kinds of behavior constitute an addiction. Things like an overriding preoccupation with the behavior, conflict with other necessary activities, withdrawal when unable to engage, increasing need, feeling out of control, or spending way too much time in the garage by yourself. Simply, does it interfere with your ability to carry out a normal and responsible life? Does it affect your work, your necessary relationships, your ability to function as a law-abiding citizen? If it does, some people will call it an addiction.

I think labeling bad behavior as an "addiction" gives someone an excuse. It breeds sympathy. "Poor guy's addicted. He needs help. We'll give him a pass on being an asshole."

Fuck sympathy. I call it a Problem. You are an adult. You can't function normally? Fix it. I am not dismissing addiction. Addiction is just a subset of what I label a Problem.

In my world, there are two types of addictions. Physical and mental. To reiterate, I am not a doctor or shrink. I speak out of logic and could be challenged by those without a sense of humor, or those who just know more than me. But I don't care. Logic trumps. Plus, I'm God.

There are physical addictions in which a substance is ingested that causes a chemical reaction that leads to a physical need to have more. I don't dispute the science here. Drugs are the most obvious example in their very many forms. Tobacco or nicotine is as well. I am a former smoker, and personally have felt that pang inside me, yearning for a puff. Some even label caffeine as addictive.

But what if you don't ingest something? Can it be an addiction? Examples that some have labeled as addictions include gambling, internet use (including video games and pornography), exercise, work, anger, and shopping. These are all activities that can be done to excess. Why? There is no chemical substance that is causing an uncontrollable desire. There is a psychological imbalance causing the behavior. I'm not going to get clinical because I don't have

IF I WERE GOD

the clinical background for it. I am just going to posit to those that do, that behavioral activities are not addictions. They are Problems. I can understand the behavior of an addict whose body cannot stop him from satisfying his craving. It is physical. It can't be overcome without help. But the mind is different. A craving for shopping, gambling, or exercise is a substitute for something else that is missing from someone's life. But it's not physical. Ergo, I cite a difference. There are physical addictions that require withdrawal, substitutes, and a lot of support. Aberrant behavior caused by the mind requires psychological help. I am not diminishing the craving, I am just not calling them addictions.

THE GOOD STUFF

Let's start with alcohol. I believe that people drink to escape. The high allows them to think about something other than what is bothering them. It anesthetizes the hurt. You can go through the 12 steps, AA, and/or abstinence, and the mindset is that those are the only ways out. But that is treating the symptom, not the cause. You drink to escape feelings. The best way to stop drinking is to eliminate the need to escape those feelings. AA is not going to help that. Good old-fashioned therapy will.

What are the 12 steps anyway? I had no idea. I figured it was a step-by-step way to reduce and then eliminate alcohol dependency. Figured it required a lot of soul-searching to figure out why one sought alcohol along with a heavy dose of therapy, but my exhaustive research staff has unraveled the mystery.

And shame on Me, when, what to my wondering eyes should appear but visions of God coming out from too many beers. The fricking thing is all about religion. Guess I slept through that one. I seem to be doing a lot of cutting off My nose to spite My face. But here they are, with some very un-Godlike embellishments.

THE 12 STEPS

1. We admitted we were powerless over alcohol—that our lives had become unmanageable.

   This is a good start. Step 1 is baptized.

2. Came to believe that a Power greater than ourselves could restore us to sanity.

   That's asking for a big favor. This first assumes that alcoholism is insanity. That's quite untrue. Then it permits abdicating responsibility.

3. Made a decision to turn our will and our lives over to the care of God *as we understood Him.*

   Now it's getting personal. So in order to stop drinking, one must give oneself to God. So atheists are fucked. And what gives you the idea that I want to care for a bunch of drunks?

4. Made a searching and fearless moral inventory of ourselves.

   Don't need Me for this.

5. Admitted to God, to ourselves, and to another human being the exact nature of our wrongs.

   I don't take confession. That's been delegated to the Robes.

6. Were entirely ready to have God remove all these defects of character.

   There goes responsibility down the drain again. Let God fix you. And if He doesn't, you can blame Him as you take your 12th drink, one for each step.

7. Humbly asked Him to remove our shortcomings.

IF I WERE GOD

I ain't removing shit. I got enough to do with all these drunks begging for my help.

8. Made a list of all persons we had harmed and became willing to make amends to them all.

   That's a good one. We'll keep this.

9. Made direct amends to such people wherever possible, except when to do so would injure them or others.

   Finally, taking some real steps to make life better.

10. Continued to take personal inventory, and when we were wrong promptly admitted it.

    Do not need to be a drunk to do this one. This should be Step #1 to life.

11. Sought through prayer and meditation to improve our conscious contact with God *as we understood Him*, praying only for knowledge of His will for us and the power to carry that out.

    I don't know about you, but mediation did not work out too well for me when I got divorced.

    Oops, medication. Needed a lot of that after the divorce.

    Oh, meditation. Even His eyes need glasses.

12. Having had a spiritual awakening as the result of these steps, we tried to carry this message to alcoholics, and to practice these principles in all our affairs.

    Where is therapy in all of this? Where is attacking the problem? Is this 12 steps to bring more money to organized Christianity? I am ashamed.

Before I get stoned, I do not argue that the 12 Steps can and do work. For all of those who found that as a way to sobriety, it was a miracle. I just don't like using religion as a crutch to get better. I do not have to invoke the power of God to improve my life. We are all adults. There are no excuses.

My Three Steps:

1. Ask yourself what is truly important in your life. Write these things down.
2. Focus on that and have that by your side to help you get through the day. Hopefully it is not a Heineken.
3. Find out why you need alcohol (or another drug) as an escape. Address the why, and the need to escape can evaporate. Use therapy in heavy doses as needed.

EVEN BETTER STUFF

Sex addiction is bullshit. If I have sex with my girlfriend five times a day, I am merely the stud of the neighborhood. But if I have sex with five of my neighbors' wives every day, I can claim to be a sex addict and the world will feel sorry for me. There is rehab for that. Wonder what goes on there. Hopefully, it's like methadone where they wean you off heroin gradually. My kind of rehab. Sex four times a day for the first week, then three times a day the second week. Shit, I'm still way ahead of most guys my age. Most guys any age. But at what level is sex no longer an addiction? Do you have to give it up completely, like other addictive behaviors? Yikes. That is not natural. So what becomes normal sexual behavior?

Ah, this is all bullshit! It makes someone a lot of money to treat and give a ton of assholes a reason to be perverts. But my girlfriend loves it!

Let's consider if there was a 12-step program for sex addiction.

1. We admitted we were powerless over sex—that our lives had become unmanageable, full of hard-ons and horniness. Penis really does rule.
2. Came to believe that Viagra was the Devil himself. And it's fucking expensive.

IF I WERE GOD

3. Made a decision to turn our desires and our lives over to a good chardonnay.
4. Made a searching and fearless moral inventory of ourselves. Concluded that our penis was fearless.
5. Admitted to God, to ourselves, and to another human being the exact nature of our wrongs. Hopefully, she doesn't sue you.
6. Were entirely ready to have God castrate me. Then the chardonnay took over.
7. Humbly asked Him to remove our shortcomings. Bought a penis pump.
8. Made a list of all persons we had sex with. Went through two ink cartridges.
9. Made direct amends to such people wherever possible, except when to do so would injure them or others. Kissing is such a nice way to apologize.
10. Continued to take personal inventory, and when we were wrong, promptly admitted it. Another inventory. Hopefully we can count.
11. To improve our conscious contact with the opposite sex, we sought medication and Tinder.
12. Having had a spiritual awakening as the result of these steps, we tried to carry this message to sex addicts, and to practice these principles in all our affairs. Especially those with married women.

GOD 2.0

We are adults. And we all have Problems to deal with. If those Problems prevent us from dealing with everyday life and responsibilities, we need to get help. Problems are caused by voluntary actions (absent a child born with a drug addiction) and need to be dealt with accordingly. No sympathy for the smoker who cannot quit. Keep your

PA BROOK

fucking smoke away from me. For the kid who misses school because he is "addicted" to video games, there is no tutoring at home. He gets an F and goes to summer school. Take responsibility for your actions and inactions.

Of course sex and alcohol can be combined effectively. Offsetting addictions. Like football. Do over. Or do again.

Check with your pharmacist.

I don't think I have ever read about a female sex addict. What a shame.

CHAPTER 8
THE SELF-INFLICTED
(Hey, Have Another Cookie)

Now, I understand that there are all types of sizes and shapes in the world and that to some extent, we don't have much control over it. We don't have any control over how tall we are, although we can enhance our height with high-heeled shoes or lifts, or just walk on our toes. Extremely tall people have to deal with ducking in doorways, knees in their face on airplanes, and always craning their necks downward. All with no choice.

Society has not created higher doorways for the extremely tall. Why should they create accommodations for extremely wide?

Before being labeled an ogre (or much worse), I am excluding those that do not have a choice. I expect they are not the obnoxious and aggressive ones claiming they have been wronged by society. They garner my sympathy. I am speaking of the self-inflicting segment when I express my disdain. And I will refer to them accordingly. Self-inflicted. Perhaps an attempt at some form of political correctness. Hopefully my only attempt.

Some people are naturally large and some are naturally slim. Some metabolisms are fast, some are slow. I was lucky enough to be born with a fast metabolism, so I have always been skinny. Until I got older. While I cannot fully empathize with heavy people, I have opened my mind to the possibility that they do not always have control over their weight. There are many non-diet related reasons for weight gain. Stress, lack of sleep, medication, physical ailments that lead to weight gain. All of these are legitimate reasons for gaining weight. Except in rare occasions, none of them are legitimate reasons for getting obese. Plus, many of the self-inflicted are that way simply because they eat too many Twinkies.

And then they sit next to me.

My dad was obese. As in 300-plus pounds. He was also very aggressive verbally, with a temper that showed up frequently. This led to many fights with my mother and a rather smothered upbringing of me. But at one point when I was a young adult, he decided to lose weight. A lot. He never got skinny, but he lost at least 100 pounds. He looked good, had more energy, and was generally a nicer person. Ahh, but that was the rub. He was no longer aggressive; rather, he became docile. And then an interesting thing happened. Over time, he began to put the weight back on and with it, the hostility resumed. His personality was such that the weight gave him the confidence to be aggressive. That aggression made him successful in business even though it was detrimental in his personal relationships. Fat meant success to him. So he was fat. That didn't help the guy sitting next to him in the plane feel any better. Obviously, his unsuspecting flying companion could not have known the reason. And would not have given a shit if he did.

Dad had psychological issues that made him *want* to be fat. Fat equaled power to him, but that did not give him the right to make his physical presence debilitating to others.

IF I WERE GOD

Obesity can often be a psychological issue like it was with my father. And everyone has a choice about how they deal with their issues. Gaining weight is the scientific process of eating more calories than spending. Go to any health website, and behavior is the number one cause of obesity. As in eating too much. Not exercising can contribute, but only if you eat more than you spend. You can watch TV all day as long as reruns of *Bonanza* use as many calories as you ingest. Other factors come into play, such as environment, genetics, and disease. Genetics cannot be helped and certain diseases not prevented, but environments can be changed.

Overweight people have stigmas attached to them and are often ridiculed, sometimes publicly. One would think this might spur them to change. Look what happened with smoking. First, you had to go outside; then, even public places became taboo. A lot of ex-smokers (including me) stopped smoking, in part, because it became so socially exclusive to do. One way to stop the ridicule is to lose weight.

Some people consider obesity a handicap. How would you feel if you had a true handicap and your parking spot is taken by a self-inflictor, just the party in need of a nice walk across the parking lot?

But the self-inflicted have their apologists. I have heard arguments such as lack of awareness causes obesity. As in an onslaught of advertisements with conflicting messages about the healthiness of foods got in the way of one figuring out that food dripping with grease is unhealthy. But is not that person aware that he now weighs 350 pounds and eats a variety of "healthy" donuts every day?

Or the excuse that my wife hates me or my mother only took me to Wendy's. Or my father's excuse. Legitimate psychological concerns. But instead of suing McDonald's as a contributor to one's self-infliction or asking for a first-class seat as an expected accommodation, go see a shrink. The French fry made me do it. Or better yet, since the weight of a passenger is directly proportional to the cost of jet fuel, charge for oversize self-inflictors just like you do for baggage. Put a couple of donuts in your carry-on instead of your belly and *voila!* Cheaper travel.

If not, there is plenty of room in the baggage compartment.

You don't see tall people suing for a first-class accommodation. And *none* of them have a choice. They just duck.

MIGHT AS WELL FACE IT, I'M ADDICTED TO JUICY FRUIT

There are those who believe obesity is an addiction and should be treated as such, but that merely explains the reason for it. It does not come up with societal solutions to deal with it. Nicotine is an addiction, but smokers are not given any accommodations. Smoking makes it uncomfortable, and some say medically harmful, for those nearby. Society has isolated smokers so they do not burden others.

Alcohol can be an addiction. Drunk people can be disorderly, or worse, people in their path can be disadvantaged, sometimes severely.

There are many other behaviors in society, whether caused by addiction or simply aberrant behavior, where the perpetrator causes harm, inconvenience, or discomfort to others. Society, either through laws or simply through negative reactions, does not tolerate the results of those addictions/behaviors. Eating should be no different. Smoking leads to smoke that bothers others. Smokers need to be the one inconvenienced. Drunk drivers can kill people. They are inconvenienced by not being permitted to drive. The self-inflicted become fat and take up more room than they have a right to take up. They too should be the ones inconvenienced.

IF I WERE GOD

Overeaters Anonymous could have a one-step approach.

Don't eat.

GOD 2.0

It kind of sucks that if you have no control over a situation (e.g., tall), then you get no relief from society. Genes made you tall, not behavior. But if you choose a behavior that creates an inconvenience for yourself (e.g., not enough room because you are fat), then there is a chance someone might call this a disorder or a disease or an addiction. And suddenly, society has to accommodate you.

Bullshit!

I don't need a study to conclude on this topic. All I need to do is see how profitable McDonald's is. Eating at McDonald's is a choice. One that makes the seat next to me in an airplane suddenly too small for its occupant.

Sorry, squeeze into that seat and keep your arms folded and your mouth shut about there not being enough room. Be happy we are not charging you extra because you take up more room. Maybe you can avoid the $7,000^{th}$ potato chip next time and accept responsibility for your actions.

Otherwise you walk. Plenty of elbow room on the street. It will benefit both of us.

CHAPTER 9

END-OF-LIFE SUICIDE
(They Don't Hang Dead Men)

A VERY BIG INFLUENCE IN MY life contracted lung cancer in his 50s. He was a smoker, quit, and then took it up as a hobby. I can't say that is what brought on his illness, but it likely did. He fought a very long, brave fight. I remember getting a communication from his family that he had been transferred to hospice and had three to six months to live. He died within a week.

He gave up.

My mother contracted cancer but did not find out until it was too late to do anything about it. She was one to fight illness with nutrition and lifestyle. Her illness was too strong to be defeated with food and yoga. She was given three to four weeks to live when she was transferred to hospice. She died that night.

She gave up.

In both of the above instances, the afflicted was able to decide on their terms that it was time to go. Do I know this for a fact? No, but I can understand how it can happen. At some point in your life, sleeping is better than being awake. As I have gotten older and become afflicted with my own

IF I WERE GOD

minor aches and pains, I have begun to understand that today is the best I am ever going to feel physically for the rest of my life. It is all downhill from here. Very slowly, but downhill. I am very far away from it being anything other than minor at this point, but I now understand how I could get to the point of preferring permanent sleep.

Should we be allowed to choose permanent sleep?

When answering this question, we must distinguish between physical and mental ailments. If we are mentally incapacitated, we no longer have cognitive ability to make a choice. Choosing permanent sleep would not even be in one's thoughts. We can't let crazy people choose to die because we don't know if their desire is caused by the pain or the 17 voices in their head.

But if it's physical, then one is aware of the pain, and worse, aware it will only worsen. And if it truly is downhill, and the slope is steep, one may wish to ski the ultimate mogul.

FACTS

History has provided differing levels of acceptance of suicide. The ancient Scythians believed that suicide was a great honor when one became too old or too much of a burden on one's family.

Who the fuck are Scythians?

They were some nomadic Iranian dudes who migrated from central Asia to southern Russia circa several hundred BC and became pretty good at conquering. And committing suicide. Until some bigger, stronger nomad types took them out a few hundred years later. The Scythians weren't the only ones that sanctioned suicide as an honorable way to go, just apparently one of the coolest.

Today, we have physician-assisted suicide, or PAS. It is

when a doctor prescribes medication in lethal doses at a patient's request. The patient administers the medication; therefore, the doctor does not participate in the suicide and may actually be unaware of whether the patient bites the ultimate bullet.

Physician-assisted suicide is illegal in forty-five states at the time of this writing.

Voluntary euthanasia is where the doctor actually administers the medication with the patient's full knowledge and consent.

Involuntary euthanasia is murder.

In a perfect society, people would die painlessly in their sleep when they are really, really old, having been no burden on anyone and leaving the family fortune to a wonderful, charitable set of offspring who desire nothing more than to make everyone else's life in the world better.

In reality, people suffer, are a burden, leave nothing to nobody or too much to schmucks.

Should one be allowed to have more say than God in his own demise?

As with many controversial subjects, there are compelling and passionate arguments for both sides.

VOICES IN FAVOR OF PAS
Patients have every right to refuse medical treatment, which would directly lead to their death. That isn't considered suicide, but what is the difference? Why is dying by refusing medication any different than dying by taking too much medication? Yet suicide is illegal, though that is, and has always been, irrelevant. You are not going to arrest a dead guy.

IF I WERE GOD

Is there a societal difference between allowing one to die and killing them?

Apparently there is.

Those in favor of PAS argue that since assisted suicide is legal in only a few states/countries, it leads those wishing to utilize PAS to possibly travel abroad to voluntarily die. Perhaps to avoid discovery of their intentions, or it may actually be cheaper or more logistically favorable than traveling to a legal state. Or a last hurrah. Once away from home, they may experience a lack of proper healthcare where PAS is legal.

Or the plane may crash.

Another benefit to traveling abroad may be that the afflicted gets away from the rabid relatives and finds a nice nunnery in the Netherlands to donate his fortune to.

In a similar vein, when abortion was illegal in one state, a pregnant woman wishing to terminate her pregnancy would travel to a different state where abortion was legal. Or would turn to an illegal method in her home state. Either way, she executed her desire, but in less than desirable circumstances. PAS would eliminate the less than desirable circumstance option.

What happened to life, liberty, and the pursuit of happiness? If happiness means dying because living is unbearable, does it not mean that dying is the pursuit of happiness? And that pursuit is an inalienable right of every American.

That is inalienable logic.

How does PAS differ from pulling the plug? I understand brain dead is clinical and widely accepted, yet many believe that pulling the plug is involuntary killing. Isn't it really PAS with a bag over its head?

PA BROOK

We can put pets to sleep. We don't even know if they are really suffering and how often these decisions are made based on economics and hardships on those responsible for keeping the patient alive. Veterinarian medical advances allow pet owners to keep their pets alive much longer than ever before. There is even pet medical insurance, and it includes wellness visits.

Oh, the visuals. I can just see the vet:

"Bend over and bark," as he grabs your dog's balls.

And the prostate exam. That could be illegal in most states. They may even have colonoscopies. Oooooh! Ultrasound to determine the sex of the litter and flu shots could be next. Is there a doggy speculum? Do cats pee into cups?

Let's not forget dental care. It is actually recommended that you brush your pet's teeth. That sounds like lots of fun for Fido. Why could that possibly be necessary? Cats and dogs have lived for centuries without the need for dental floss. Nature has given them their own way to either clean their teeth or eat stuff that doesn't make plaque.

Oh. They are now eating stuff that causes the need to brush. Whose fault is that?

I read that one of the afflictions of older cats is obesity. Another food-related issue. Left to their own devices, cats eat what is natural prey for them and eat enough to nourish themselves. There is no need to overeat or ingest a Big Mac. I do not think obesity in cats was an issue before...

Human intervention.

We can kill pets *without* their consent, but we can't kill ourselves *with* consent.

IF I WERE GOD

VOICES AGAINST PAS

One fear is that legalizing PAS would prompt some unscrupulous relatives to talk a weakened, maybe not dying relative into taking some drugs to commit suicide so the shitty relatives can start spending not-so-sick relative's money prematurely. That is a legitimate fear, though said unscrupulous shitheads have been turning to that all along, legal or illegal. Who's going to know if they talked Dad into taking too many pills, or even forced him to? They can just claim Dad did it on his own (sob! sob!), and they are too grief-stricken to remember any details. Evil daughter may actually keep Dad alive longer so she can pilfer his assets without her even more evil siblings finding out.

Legalizing assisted death can create opportunities for abuse. A death that is non-voluntary becomes legal under the pretense of being voluntary. If you don't legalize it, it can't be abused. But that is saying that a law is inappropriate because it will lead to abuse. Kind of like saying that requiring background checks before the purchase of a gun will lead to repeal of the Second Amendment and the militia storming our front doors. (I hear another rant.)

Legalizing physician-assisted suicide would bring subtle and perhaps not-so-subtle pressure to bear on terminally ill patients who fear their illness is physically, emotionally, or financially burdensome to families or caretakers. The legal option to commit suicide with a physician's help could be perceived as an obligation by many terminally ill patients concerned about being such a burden. How do I get adopted into that family?

End-of-life care has made significant strides in allowing patients to devote attention to unfinished business of their lives. Advances in pain management now make it possible to control pain more effectively in dying patients and only rarely is it necessary to induce sleep to relieve pain or distress in the final stages of dying. You can be high all the time. Not much of a silver lining.

People who request death are vulnerable. They need care and protection. To offer lethal drugs to assist in dying can be a form of abandonment. There could be psychological issues causing one to think he wants to end his life. Depression has led many to that decision. There are drugs and counseling available to lessen those feelings, potentially leading someone from the brink of PAS back to valuing his life. No need for adoption with this family.

In some instances, the extent of palliative care may not be known, leading to an uninformed decision to end one's life when there are alternatives. What the hell does "palliative" mean? Must come from a study.

Legalizing assisted suicide and voluntary euthanasia will gradually lead to involuntary euthanasia.

Murder. I smell a TV series.

Officially sanctioning PAS could lead to less of an effort to treat severely and terminally ill patients, as PAS would be deemed an appropriate alternative. Back to adoption.

These all lead to the conclusion that PAS is bad for society, especially for those most vulnerable whom society is charged with protecting.

I was always amazed that our justice system will work so hard to keep a dying death row patient alive so he can be executed. There is a lot of money wasted trying to cure cancer in someone we are going to whack tomorrow. Some things require no further comment than a shake of the head.

GOD 2.0

There are so many overdoses from medically prescribed drugs that are improperly administered or taken. There are fatal overdoses in the illegal drug industry (I smell *another* rant) due to differing hidden and unknown strengths/additives of drugs purchased. There is also indiscriminate dosage use owing to lack of knowledge and oversight of the process. Both lead to unexpectedly lethal results. These are true tragedies with people dying who *didn't* want to die.

Let's concentrate our legislative efforts to help those who do not wish to die rather than spending so much effort trying to keep alive those who prefer ultimate sleep. In an argument similar to abortion, leave the government out of it. PAS should be a personal decision, a private act, with society able to be called in for judgment when and if the *motive* comes into question. That makes it civil in nature, not criminal. This is where it should be. No crime.

CHAPTER 10
HANDICAP PARKING
(Limp at Your Own Risk)

Handicapped parking spaces are specially marked spaces designated only for those who have a handicap sticker and display it. And hopefully need it. Good for society. Let's give those who are unfortunate a small opportunity to improve life by just a bit. I agree that there are too many parking spaces designated as handicapped, but I would rather walk a few extra feet than force someone less able to do so.

Obtaining a handicap sticker is not difficult if you need one. Society will err on the side of giving it to someone who may not need it to avoid mistakenly not providing one to someone in need. It is like our justice system, which is designed to prefer 99 guilty people go free rather than one innocent go to jail. I don't agree with that, but when doling out handicap stickers, I have no issue.

Handicap parking permits cannot be left in wills like New York Giants tickets are. Well, they can be, but they won't be worth much. If you are going to raid Mom's stuff before the estate sale, take the seven sets of table linens instead. Even the permanent permits need to be renewed from time to time. The person to whom the permit is issued is theoretically the only one legally allowed to use it.

IF I WERE GOD

Common conditions that permit issuance of a handicap parking permit include:

- Anything that makes it hard to breathe, like lung disease;
- Impaired stamina, like heart disease;
- Limitations on mobility or the ability to walk; needing a wheelchair or other assistance to walk;
- Vision problems, although I hope you are not the driver;
- Loss or substantially limited use of your legs or hands.

Common causes of these conditions that some would like to result in the issuance of a permit include:

- Shortness of breath from too much sex;
- Conversely, impaired stamina because your ED medication ran out;
- Limitations on mobility or the ability to walk because that Mexican Gold you smoked had too much bullion in it;
- Vision problems causing your wife to look fat, requiring the need for Mexican Gold to fix the problem (your vision or her weight?);
- Loss or substantially limited use of arms or legs because you are in handcuffs from getting caught with Mexican Gold.

Fortunately they do not.

There are other abuses of the system. One company sold fake permits, but since the fine print disclosed it was a fake, they were not deemed illegal. Of course, if you buy a handicap parking permit based on an internet website and get caught, don't come crying to me. Similarly, if you buy drugs from some internet ad, I don't want to hear you complain about growing a second nose.

Finally, on a personal note, I knew someone who had both knees replaced. He quite appropriately was given a handicap sticker, which he quite appropriately used. Then he actually offered it to me one day, so I could park near the front of something (I forget where I was going). Not OK with someone else using a handicap sticker who was not handicapped, I declined.

Is offering your parking permit to someone who is not in need as bad as using someone else's when you are not in need?

It is worse. As someone who needs a handicap permit, one should understand and cherish its value. Was there not even a thought that if I used his permit and parked in the last handicap spot, his equivalent might show up and have to walk farther because of his indiscretion?

To somewhat balance the scales of justice, his daughter got a ticket for unauthorized parking in a handicap spot. Where is that damn sticker when you need it? Must run in the family.

So, I sometimes wonder about the able-bodied wrestler type who emerges from the very large pickup truck parked squarely in a handicap spot. Carrying large quantities of very heavy shit. I feel bad that he has to carry heavy shit a long way, but that is what they made hand trucks for.

Or Mexicans.

GOD 2.0

Someone who abuses handicapped parking spaces should become temporarily disabled and have to park at the opposite end of the parking lot. No frills, no fine, no time. Just limp, motherfucker.

LIBERTY

CHAPTER 11
PUNITIVE DAMAGES
(When Really Good Lawyers Meet Really Dumb Judges)

AMERICAN DEMOCRACY IS WIDELY HELD as the best system of justice in the world, but it isn't perfect. There will be many who defend it to their death, and many have, literally. I would like to see a few things changed. I will start with the concept of punitive damages, which will then lead to related issues.

Punitive damages represent money awarded to an injured party in addition to that which is necessary to compensate them for physical, emotional, or other losses. Punitive damages were designed to serve the dual purposes of punishing the defendant and deterring similar conduct in the future. They often are awarded when the bad guys act bad on purpose and don't care about the outcome. This is an established practice in our legal system. But all of those damages (including the punitive ones) go to the plaintiff (and her attorney). So the plaintiff gets more than she "deserves" simply because the bad guy was really bad.

They were not designed to unjustly enrich the plaintiff and her counsel, but they do.

Punitive damages are awarded by a jury or judge, with the jury awards typically getting all the press. There is often a tremendous amount of latitude given to juries in deliberating punitive damages. A famous punitive damages case took this to an extreme. It involved a man who sued a car company because he bought a "new" car that had been damaged and repainted during shipment. That made it no longer "new." The purchaser was unaware of the damage and when he subsequently found out, he sued the car company, claiming he was sold a damaged/repaired car not a new, undamaged car. He claimed that his actual damages were $4,000 based on testimony that a repainted "new" car was worth about 10% less than a real "new" car.

He'd found an expert in "not new" cars. I guess this happens a lot.

Figuring he wasn't the only victim of this insidious plot, the purchaser asked for $4 million in punitive damages. The seemingly random but rather ample sum did have some logic. He figured maybe this had happened to another thousand "new" car buyers, got out his calculator, and came to the anointed $4 million. His attorneys cheered. Where did 1,000 other buyers come from? If there were records of this, there would have been more lawsuits. Perhaps an "expert's" opinion? I smell my next profession.

The jury bought it and awarded him his $4 million. No experts on the jury. Actually, no IQ on the jury. Not one nickel to the poor, imaginary other buyers. Why was it that I did not go to law school?

So a seemingly fair result might have been to compensate the plaintiff for his actual damages ($4,000) and perhaps a bit more for his "suffering." In addition, it would not be unfair to punish the car company for being really bad guys, so perhaps some punitive damages should come into play. We need to deter other car companies from similar bad behavior. Let this go and the next thing you know, car salesmen might stop being so honest. But the plaintiff's suffering wasn't worth $4 million. In theory, he was being compensated for damages incurred by others through the calculation premise of the punitive damage award.

How does a jury determine that this one purchaser should be compensated for damages incurred by others?

That's why jury consultants make the big bucks.

The Supreme Court eventually struck down the punitive damage award, but this is a classic example of what can, and does, happen.

Proponents of punitive damages believe that this type of award serves as retribution against the bad guys, deterrence for future bad guys, and compensation for the good guys. The latter provides incentives to the good guys to sue the bad guys; otherwise, it would not be worth their effort to sue for only pain and suffering. Whose effort? The lawyers, of course.

Critics of punitive damages believe that large monetary awards are unfair, unreasonable, and not productive for society. They provide the good guys with an undeserved financial windfall. They also note that deterrence can be undercut when defendants are insured against punitive damage awards. In addition, when a government employee is found liable for misconduct and punitive damages are awarded, the taxpayers must pay the award.

That sucks.

The measurement of punitive damages when left in the hands of a jury can spin out of control, as we saw above. To determine the amount, the jury or court must consider the nature of the bad guy's behavior, the extent of the good guy's loss or injury, and the degree to which the bad guy's conduct is repugnant to a societal sense of justice and decency. In other words, how bad of a motherfucker was he?

Punitive damages come into play in many civil cases. Not all lawsuits are created equal. There are many, many cases where the lawsuit is warranted and the damages are deserved. Many believe since a jury (a supposedly impartial panel of peers) awarded the damages, then by definition, they are just. We will discuss a jury of peers later, but let me say that there are many lawsuits where the jury does not get it right.

Courts have the power to reduce or throw out punitive damages. Not enough do.

GOD 2.0
The obvious solution is to give the punitive damages to society. I would prefer a well-run nonprofit, but if it must go to the government, then so be it. Punitive damages smell like a fine. Companies are fined by the government all the time. Let's just make this another one. I will deal with government waste later.

CHAPTER 12
FRIVOLOUS LAWSUITS
(Suing God Because You Got Sunburned)

A FRIVOLOUS LAWSUIT, ON ITS FACE, is one that the plaintiff has very little chance of winning, knows this, but sues anyway just in case he can find a sympathetic jury or a defendant willing to settle. Or one where the goal of the plaintiff is to harass the defendant, knowing there is little chance of ultimately winning the lawsuit but needing to satisfy his revenge tendencies.

The poster child for frivolous lawsuits is the famous McDonald's "coffee is too hot" lawsuit. I have read varying accounts on this, depending on whether the author is yea or nay when it comes to frivolous suits. I am sure there is exaggeration on both sides, so the truth lies somewhere in the middle. One account talks about how the woman opened hot coffee while driving and spilled it on herself, then sued McDonald's because the coffee was hot. The jury awarded the woman $2.7 million in punitive damages.

While the jury awarded an unseemly amount, there is a back story that is often not reported when someone has an agenda. It appears her burns were significant and required a hospital stay, skin grafts, and a commensurate amount of pain and suffering. The jury did find her 20% at fault, so her settlement was 20% lower. Also, she apparently had originally asked McDonald's to pay a rather paltry sum of $20,000 to cover her costs, but they played hardball. Oops. The punitive damages were eventually reduced, with the entire settlement coming in around $600,000. Even my math makes that a big fucking error for not settling for 20 grand. I guess the lawyer responsible for those negotiations didn't get much when bonus time came around. Maybe he now designs Walmart ads.

Or eats them.

So how frivolous are some of these suits? As with many things, it's in the eye of the beholder. There are obviously many lawsuits that are clearly full of frivolity and adjudged so by the courts, either by simply throwing the case out or, more harshly, bringing sanctions against the egregious plaintiff (and his attorney). But sometimes the judge is just as dumb as the jury and doesn't throw out the case, which then wastes a whole lot of time and a whole lot of somebody's money, mostly to the benefit of lawyers. And gee, who makes the laws in this country?

So this is an exposé on some of the more interesting lawsuits that appear to be trolling around on the internet. I do not profess to endorse the stories I read, nor do I believe that all of them are written without bias or agenda. And the spin I put on them is because I have an agenda. I am, as you know, God, so I can do this.

If nothing else, they are a fun read.

DEAD SPACE WALKING

Several companies were sued because there was too much empty space inside the package, giving the appearance that there was more in the package than there was. This despite clear labeling of the amount of product included. What if a package contains the same number of pills as another, but since the pills are bigger, the package is bigger? Dead space sounds like good marketing, since there is a presumption from the suit that companies made profits from the dead space. Sounds like a good use of resources (air) to me. It's free and abundant—good way to leverage.

What about when they use peanuts in packaging? Not the crunchy kind. You know, those little Styrofoam thingies that protect packages. There are always way too many of them, and they jump to your clothes like lice and don't want to leave. They certainly made the package much bigger and are a large pain in the ass to clean up. Where's that lawsuit?

Call 1-800-PEANUTS.

MY BOYFRIEND MADE ME DO IT
A woman sued her ex-boyfriend because she failed a college class, claiming his breakup with her caused lots of issues for her. Presumably for pain and suffering. I wonder what kind of pain and suffering he endured dating someone like her. I never caused someone to flunk a class when I was in college.

Guess I wasn't F-in' worthy.

THE SNEAKERS MADE ME DO IT
A man convicted of stomping another man in the face repeatedly sued the sneaker company because the sneakers he was wearing did not contain a warning that the sneakers could be used as a dangerous weapon.

"Warning: If you get mad, wearing this sneaker can cause harm. If you are really pissed, replace with work boot."

In a related suit, a man used the sneaker laces to strangle his college girlfriend, who sued him for flunking a class.

Talk about your next Nike commercial.

AT LEAST SHE DIDN'T HAVE A BOYFRIEND

A nursing student failed a required course and claimed a disability arose, resulting from the depression of flunking. Let me see if I can understand this. She requested special accommodations from the school for her disability and then sued the school, claiming the accommodations were not provided.

I hope she's not in charge of my meds.

ANOTHER LOUSY SCHOOL

This school got sued for almost six figures because a graduate could not find a job after graduation, claiming lack of cooperation by the college career counseling service. Good luck being her employer.

HIS BITE IS BIGGER THAN HIS BARK

A man sued because a neighbor's dog barked too much, or too loudly. Or maybe sang off key. The dog's owners thought the suit was a joke and didn't show up for a hearing, which led to a large settlement against them.

They bought sneakers.

DIETARY WRONGS

A restaurant is being sued for charging more for gluten-free food than other food, with the person suing claiming discrimination under the Americans with Disabilities Act. Whether it costs more to prepare a gluten-free meal than a regular meal is a fact that would be of relevance to the claim. Perhaps $1 more would make sense. The claim came to about $4,000 per meal served.

Lawyers always add zeros.

NEIGHBORS
A woman (she was an attorney, no surprise) sued a neighbor for making noises in the middle of the night. She claims it was done on purpose, alleging that the neighbor's sole purpose in life was to annoy her. I had a neighbor who liked to have loud sex at night. She was smoking hot.

Can you sue for sexual favors instead of money?

Now is when I want a good lawyer.

SPRECHEN SIE DEUTSCH?
A brewery was sued because its drinkers thought they were drinking a beer brewed in Germany, while in reality it was brewed in the United States. The packaging clearly noted a United States address, but a suit ensued nonetheless. The class action suit resulted in a $50 rebate to all class participants and $3.5 million in legal fees to the attorneys.

The lawyers bought the brewery.

BAD SERVICE
A woman whose husband broke a date with her for a Valentine's Day dinner because he was full from lunch went to a restaurant by herself. I don't think this is what florists had in mind. The couple had made a reservation for two but she sat down at the table by herself. The restaurant, upon realizing she was only one, asked her to sit at the bar for dinner. Apparently this upset her so that not only did she not pay for two glasses of wine, but she is also suing the restaurant for six figures and demanding an apology.

I am not sure what kind of relationship she has with her

husband, but apparently she would rather dine by herself at a restaurant than eat at home with her husband, even if he doesn't eat. And the husband would rather stay home than go to the restaurant and sit with a drink while his wife eats.

Sounds like some of my exes. No wonder I am divorced.

GENIE IN A BEER
More beer shit. Upon watching a commercial where normal guys suddenly had beautiful women chasing after them as they drank a beer, this guy tried the same thing. Only the results were not as good. As a matter of fact, no hot women appeared. So he tried another beer. And another. Still no hot women. So he sued the beer company for emotional distress and a bunch of other things.

He is clearly not The Most Interesting Man in the World.

TAKEN TO THE CLEANERS
Ever lost your luggage when flying? Did you sue the airlines? Nah, they probably just paid for new luggage, clothing, and your time, and maybe threw in a free ticket for a little emotional distress. Sounds reasonable. Ever lose your dry cleaning? Did you sue the dry cleaner? Well, some lawyer did. Actually, he was a judge. He lost his pants and wanted to make the dry cleaner lose his shirt. To the tune of $54 million. That's a lot of pants. Well, in this case only one. But there were millions for emotional distress and an amount attributed to the cost of renting a car to travel to another dry cleaner.

Apparently in Mongolia. He lost.

NO SUGAR DADDY HERE
Apparently, a rather famous playboy tried to have sex with a teenager. When she refused, he sued her. For age

discrimination. Now I like the creativity. The case was dismissed. If she had refused because she was lesbian, he could have sued for sex discrimination. Maybe a better chance? If he was Jewish, for religious discrimination. Now we are talking. If he was mentally disabled, he could have sued her for disability discrimination.

He was.

WE GOTTA GET OUT OF THIS PLACE
A thief burglarized a house and ended up trapped inside the house. I am not sure how that can happen. How the fuck did he get in? According to the story, he was stuck inside for eight days and lived on soda and dog food. Where was the dog? He sued the homeowner and won half a million.

In a related story, a dog sued his owners for allowing a burglar into the house who ate all his dog food. The suit was filed posthumously as the dog starved to death. The SPCA is picking up the cause.

I'M SORRY, HONEY
A woman sued herself, claiming that she caused the death of her husband. This appeared to be a ploy to be judged guilty and then get an insurance company to pay the death benefit to her husband's heir.

Her.

NOW THAT'S A MASSAGE
A class-action lawsuit was filed because a spa did not honor prepaid massages even though it disclosed that any prepaid massages are forfeited if you cancel your membership or stop paying if you are on a payment plan. What is the point of all that fine print if it still causes lawsuits? As with most class-action suits, if successful, the lawyers would get millions

while the class participants will get one free massage for each one forfeited. Maybe.

Not exactly a "happy ending."

NOW THAT IS A NUMBER

A man is suing virtually the entire world for all the money in the world. Well, he is suing a bunch of people for various alleged indiscretions. For two undecillion dollars. In case anyone wants to know, undecillion shows up as a misspelled word on my computer. It happens often, but I usually can correct it with the correct spelling. Not here. It apparently means $2,000,000,000,000,000,000,000,000,000,000,000,000. That's thirty-six zeros.

I don't think he's going to win.

SHE TOLD ME BASEBALL IS BORING

A man sued a television station for making disrespectful remarks because he was caught on camera sleeping at a baseball game. For $10,000,000. That's a lot of *zzzzz*s. He needs to hire a good lawyer. Maybe he will get a free hot dog at his next ballgame.

The lawyers will own the team.

WHO EATS BEAN SPROUTS ANYWAY?

A customer who ordered a sandwich with bean sprouts sued the restaurant when her sandwich arrived with, alas, no bean sprouts. Apparently, this was traumatic enough to cause a lawsuit. Under what premise, I haven't a clue. But a class-action suit emerged with class participants getting a voucher worth $1.40 and the attorneys a paycheck for over a quarter million.

They started a tofu farm. That is where tofu comes from, right? Like pasta trees?

IF I WERE GOD

COME AND GET ME

A man who was fleeing the police sued the police department after he was subdued with force he deemed too strong. The police department settled the case for $460,000. He got one of them, the lawyers got the other 459.

Must have been wearing work boots.

THIS NEEDS SOME SALT

An inmate sued the prison he was in for lousy food. For an amount equal to only one third of the zeros of the man suing the world. Or about $10 trillion. That's a lot of salt.

Good luck at your next parole hearing.

COMMUTER ANXIETY

A woman who was stressed by her commute to work asked if she could change her work hours to avoid the commute. In this day and age of flex hours, many companies are adjusting work hours so their employees can avoid bad commutes. Even work at home is becoming more prevalent. All in the name of employee relations. So, on balance, this was not that bad a request. Come in early and leave before the evening commute. Or come in after the morning commute and leave late. Same hours. Many companies would at least consider this request, but this woman wanted to come in *after* the morning commute and go home *before* the evening commute.

The company actually accommodated her, but because she was working fewer hours and not in the office full time (presumably), they changed her job to be more in line with a part-time employee. She objected and was eventually fired. Her lawsuit claimed her commuting anxiety was a disability protected by laws.

If only stupidity was a disability.

GUI
A man sued a casino for its contribution to his GUI (Gambling Under the Influence) and subsequent gambling losses. He claims that he was visibly drunk and the casino should not have loaned him more money to gamble. It is a casino's inalienable right to get its gamblers as intoxicated as possible.

This would be like suing a hooker for premature ejaculation.

TWO (MILLION) POINT CONVERSION
A football fan signed up for a service whereby his favorite team would text him a maximum of five text messages a week, presumably informing him of what was going on with the team. He received three more than the maximum over a two-week period. And sued.

This was apparently a statutory violation. That is one messed-up statute. The result was a settlement of more than $2 million, but no one fan got more than $75, except for the biggest fan who got $5,000, and the lawyers got more than half a million. For too much texting.

Teenagers would be bankrupt.

FAST FOOD EQUALS FAST MONEY
A man is suing a fast food restaurant because it gave him only one napkin with its apparently too large meal.

Too bad he didn't request them to supersize his napkin. Or his IQ.

TEQUILA MADE ME DO IT
A man sued several bars and liquor stores for contributing to injuries he sustained while inebriated. He climbed up an electrical tower, for what reason we do not know. We do know that he had no easy access and, even if sober, should

have avoided this. But he got hurt in his intoxicated, devil-may-care stupor.

He also wanted to sue God for giving him feet with no warning about ladders. OK, sometimes I make shit up.

THE DEVIL MADE ME DO IT
An inmate sued himself, claiming his civil rights and religious beliefs were violated when he got himself drunk, which of course led to his life of crime. Citing his own deleterious behavior as causing his own deleterious behavior, he sued himself for $5 million. But having nothing, he demanded the state pay him the damages since he could not. Imagine being this guy's attorney.

The American Bar Association is still confused.

THE BODACIOUS TA-TAS MADE ME DO IT
I have heard people claiming whiplash from a car accident but not from breast implants. Until now. A man sued a local strip joint because he suffered physical injuries and emotional distress when the girl giving him a lap dance had rock-hard breasts.

Nipple malpractice.

DEATH BY VODKA
A woman (or rather her family) sued a car manufacturer for a faulty seat belt because the very drunken woman was unable to undo her belt when she drove her car into a bay and drowned. A jury actually awarded the family $65 million.

It was thrown into the bay on appeal.

DEATH BY VODKA, PART II
A man broke into, or rather tried to break into, a rather well-

protected establishment. There were ample warning signs noting that an attempted break-in could prove hazardous to one's health, but this gentleman attempted anyway. He, of course, was drunk and under other influences, and lost the battle to electricity. He did not survive, and his family sued the establishment. A jury awarded an ample sum, but it was decided the perp contributed to his own demise, and the award was halved.

Somehow dead seems like more than 50%.

DAMN SUBWAYS ARE ALWAYS LATE

Talk about sour grapes. A woman tried to commit suicide by lying down on the subway tracks and awaiting an oncoming train. When the train did not do a good enough job of killing her, she sued the city and won an award of $14 million. The award was later cut to under $10 million because it was deemed she contributed to the issue. The $10 million should have been awarded to her family to compensate them for having to continue to put up with her.

Or to hire a hit man.

LAWSUITS SOON TO BE FILED IN A TOWN NEAR YOU

A 7-year-old will sue Mom and Dad because the Tooth Fairy did not leave enough money under her pillow. When informed that the Tooth Fairy does not exist, she will instead sue for the emotional distress caused by being lied to.

A man will sue a large-breasted woman and the doctor who inserted her implants because it distracted him from driving, causing him to plow into a storefront during rush hour. He loses his penis in the accident, so will sue for lost services to his wife who has small tits.

A dog owner will sue his dog for emotional distress because the owner was jealous that the dog could lick his balls and

IF I WERE GOD

he couldn't. So he did. Sue? Lick? But he can't. Dog? Owner? I'm just gonna sit here and give it a try.

I'm not a dog. Damn.

GOD 2.0

Here are some things to be decreed that will create incentives against filing frivolous lawsuits:

Giving judges a brain bigger than a scarecrow's would be a start.

Or more balls than a cowardly lion.

Or a bigger heart than the tin man.

If all else fails, just shove one of those flying monkeys up his ass.

CHAPTER 13

PUNISHMENT THAT FITS THE CRIME
(One Way to Stop Sodomy...or Maybe Not)

THE 8TH AMENDMENT TO THE Constitution prohibits cruel and unusual punishment. It basically requires that the punishment fit the crime, but that standard has morphed over the years. Our society has created a regimen of punishment where the variable is primarily measured by time. This has mitigated the concept of punishment fitting the crime. The severity of the crime is now measured in years of incarceration, not a prudently imposed standard of comparability. Is it really fair to say that the punishment for stealing a car can be deemed appropriate by X number of months or years in jail?

There seems to be a disconnect there. One would think that the punishment for a crime against an individual should be measured by the harm it has exacted on the victim and the punishment for a crime against society should be measured by the harm it has exacted on the general population. Admittedly harder to adjudicate, but there are a lot of creative people with law degrees (oops, maybe that is my crime of overindulgence). We can come up with something. Basically, I am suggesting a quasi-literal application of "an eye for an eye."

IF I WERE GOD

"If there is serious injury, you are to take life for life, eye for eye, tooth for tooth, hand for hand, foot for foot, burn for burn, wound for wound, bruise for bruise." (Exodus 21:23–25).

I have to be "crying icicles instead of tears" to be quoting the Bible. Thank you, Meatloaf.

But is an eye for an eye enough of a deterrent? Criminal punishment serves two purposes. Societal retribution and deterrence. One eye for another will provide the retribution, but will it be a deterrent? This discussion is enhanced with the open-mindedness of considering even two eyes for an eye.

We need also to keep in mind that the execution of the punishment will not always be easy. If we wish to replicate the crime on the criminal (assault an assaulter, shoot a shooter), someone needs to stand in the stead of the punishing "criminal" and perpetrate that same hardship on the actual criminal. Sometimes it will be easy, in the case of personal infringements that friends or relatives of the victim will happily mimic. Other times when the crime is against society or inhuman objects, it will be more difficult to find an equivalent eye. We will try.

Do unto others is a commandment from Moses. Oh, shit, maybe not. So much for research. However, it is a widely held belief. Treat people nice because you want them to treat you nice. If they treat you like shit, you have carte blanche to reciprocate.

Let's do it in our justice system. We will start with easier ones to enforce.

Rape. This is obvious. If a man rapes a woman (or a man), his punishment should be to be raped by a man. It takes the concept of the Hangman to another level. We need to think outside the box here. I am sure there will not be a shortage of Bangmen to deliver the punishment. Who does this hurt? No one. The question is, is it a better deterrent than jail. I smell a government study.

Torture. Now we are talking. Again, there is the issue of deterrence. Will a psycho be deterred by torture as his punishment if caught rather than jail time? He is a psycho for a reason, so maybe not. Does society then get any pleasure out of torturing someone? At first, no. But we are talking about punishment regime change here, and it will all be unfamiliar territory. A very real question is emerging regarding deterrence. If no punishment will deter, one is left with a decision as to whether an eye for an eye should be used. Hard to take at first, since we are used to jail being the appropriate punishment. I still say, do unto him what he did unto others. We will get used to it.

This could make waterboarding a poolside recreation.

Lots of murders. One murder is easy—just execute the bastard. And he should be executed in the same manner that he killed his victim. Fuck this pussy injection shit. And all those activists who think the poor murderer is suffering. Fuck them too! You shoot a guy in the head, you get it too, execution style. Knife someone, get ready to bleed. But how do you compensate for multiple murders? Stab *and* shoot the dude? Maybe you can kill his pet goldfish, but surely there will be an animal activist who will protest (are there fish activists?).

Arson. They say that drowning and burning to death are the two worst ways to die. Witches used to be burned at the stake. Horrible. But if you purposely douse someone with gasoline and light a match, there should be no sympathy. Light my fire.

IF I WERE GOD

Assault and Battery. People often mistake assault for battery. Assault is a threat, battery is illegal touching. So if you threaten someone, it is assault. If you hit them, it is battery. Battery is pretty easy. You touch someone illegally, he (or a designee) gets to touch you in the same illegal manner. Beat the shit out of someone, and you end up with the same number of stitches, broken bones, etc. as your victim.

Assault is a little different. It's not as severe a crime since it only involves a threat. You convict someone of assault because he scared the shit out of someone, but how can you really mimic that fear when the convict knows it's only a threat? There is no beating forthcoming. You can't tell him the threat is real. His liberal lawyer already told him about the eye analogy thing. So we have to be a bit creative here. Tell him the judge is mulling over his sentence. And then hole him up overnight with Moose from Cell Block C and give Moose carte blanche to fuck with him any way he wants.

Without touching him. That could work.

Terrorism. Just torture these motherfuckers to death.

Public mischief. This could be anything from drunkenness to vandalism to a host of other unseemly acts. How about sex in public? Is this even illegal? It shouldn't be. Just close your eyes or walk away. Let them have some fun. Are they bothering anybody? But to put this back in context, how do you exchange an eye for an eye when the eye is spelled "vagina?" Or "penis?" If I have my own argument straight, if one got arrested for having sex in public, then the punishment would be…

My kind of rap sheet.

Fraud. You ripped off grandma's life savings. Maybe you

should be forced to have public sex with her. Better yet grandpa. Better still if he's dead.

Now there's a deterrent.

I think.

Smuggling. This is the illegal transport of goods over borders. Oftentimes it pertains to drug smuggling. Drugs can be illegally brought into a country in many fashions. One of the more interesting is through the stomach or rectum. Drugs can be inserted into plastic bags and swallowed or stuffed up the rectum to avoid detection through many manual or electronic techniques. This is not a comfortable method of transportation and is fraught with breakage risk. An overdose can easily occur (perhaps death) if the bag breaks. A quick trip is preferred. Lengthy airport delays or really bad baked beans can make this very tricky to consummate.

What should the punishment be? If convicted, the perp should have something of equivalent size and risk shoved up his rectum with a really cheap plastic bag guaranteeing eventual breakage and commensurate discomfort. The bag should be strong enough to last a reasonably torturous time, and then, once broken, the contents should wander around the innards of the perp for a period of another reasonably torturous time. Medical intervention should only occur if the situation deteriorates to life threatening. Otherwise, let nature take its course.

Of course, if you are smuggling animals, we might have to come up with a different solution.

Or not.

Child abuse. Some things just can't be replicated. Quarantine them with the terrorists.

IF I WERE GOD

Drugs. In a different reality, this could have fun possibilities. But it needs to be a punishment. How about forcing addiction and then withdrawal with no help? But will this be a deterrent or incentive?

Disorderly conduct. This could be anywhere from vulgar language to loitering to peeing in public, depending on the jurisdiction. Replicating this as punishment might be difficult. For vulgar language, you could try having someone confined to a room and have George Carlin's seven dirty words piped in over and over again like Chinese water torture. Shit, piss, fuck, cunt, motherfucker, cocksucker, tits. How many times does that have to be repeated before it becomes punishment? For peeing in public, there is the obvious, but you may have to find one of "those" websites to find someone to enforce the penalty.

I hear it won't be hard.

White-collar crime. These dudes usually get to spend their time in the country clubs of prisons. It's almost better than being at home with your third, money-grabbing wife. They do their time and come out ready to continue spending the millions they were left with or hid. Honestly, there is quite a divergence in punishment meted out to white-collar criminals, with some state laws and judges handing out seemingly very harsh penalties. It would be better to use math in these cases.

Joe stole $500 million from his company, or customers, or the Mafia. What should his punishment be? If he has $500 million and only has to pay it back, then there is no incentive not to do it. Clearly, two or three or seven eyes are needed for this eye.

If Joe has more than $500 million, he gives the $500 million back, the excess goes to the government, he declares bankruptcy, goes on food stamps, and can never board a yacht again, his or anyone's.

Or he is dead if he fucked with Tony Soprano.

If he has less than $500 million, he becomes the indentured servant to those he swindled until all is recovered through the value of the servant's services. If it is a class-action suit, a company, or the government, he can work it off serving in the military. In harm's way.

Still dead with Tony.

Theft. You lose something of equal value. But there are two issues that come to mind. First, does the thief *have* something of equal value? If he does, why is he stealing? It's supposed to be worth the risk of jail. Maybe he flunked math. Perhaps the punishment needs to be a multiple of the value stolen. Now we really have a problem. This may require some inventive thinking.

Where's the scarecrow?

Sodomy. Animal lovers will squirm at this one. Well, anyone will squirm at this one. The issue, of course, is getting the aggrieved animal to cooperate with the punishment. We may need to look elsewhere for a punishment that fits this crime.

But let's not completely underestimate Mr. Ed.

Attempted stuff. This is a prickly little mother. You attempted to do something but failed. Attempted murder. Either you missed or conspired but never actually accomplished. Attempted sodomy. The horse stared you down, or the rat vagina was just too small. There is no offset eye here. What is an appropriate punishment for a failed attempt to do something illegal? Maybe Moose is still available.

IF I WERE GOD

GOD 2.0

These were just a few examples of crimes for which I would make the punishment really fit the crime. Society cannot be shy about applying a new regimen for criminal punishment. At best, it will be a better deterrent. At worst, society will be getting a more equitable retribution.

And some really good material for *Judge Judy*.

CHAPTER 14
JURY OF YOUR PEERS
(Or If You Are Lucky, Jury Consultant Groupies)

WHILE IT ISN'T SPECIFICALLY STATED anywhere in the Constitution, criminal defendants generally have the right to be tried by a jury of their peers. This has been interpreted by courts to mean that the available jurors include a broad spectrum of the population. Not just your peeps. Contrary to popular belief, defendants are not entitled to a jury containing members of just their own race, gender, age, sexual orientation, academic background, drinking habits, or first cousin marriages.

What if it were?

Absent any guidance, what is a jury of your peers? Peers means equals, but just what does equal mean? Equal means being the same in quantity, size, degree, or value. So a jury of your peers means a bunch of people of the same size and value as you (the defendant). Sounds pretty reasonable to me. If I am an average person, I should be tried by a group of average people. And if I am an average criminal, I should be judged by a group of average criminals.

Oops. Not sure that is what the courts meant.

But wait, if I am a criminal, what is my peer group? Oh,

IF I WERE GOD

maybe I am a black criminal, so I should be judged by a group of black people. But why does black define my peer group more than criminal? Oh, but wait again, one is innocent until proven guilty. So I am not a criminal yet. But if I am a carpenter and committed murder, should I be judged by a bunch of carpenters? Are they any more qualified to determine whether I am guilty than say, marine biologists? But marine biologists don't sound like my peers, and we can't use murderers because, as appropriately noted, we don't know if I am a murderer yet until after my peers say so. So we are back to carpenters. But what if there are not enough carpenters where I live to seed the entire jury? Can electricians be effective peer substitutes?

Who's on first?

And what about civil cases? A schoolteacher sues a doctor for prescribing the wrong medication for her. Is a jury of schoolteachers (assuming it's the summer, of course) in the *best* position to determine what the drug choices were for her affliction and whether the doctor chose the best one? Or perhaps there were other treatments available besides drugs. Mental or physical therapy, acupuncture, spiritual readings, tickling. Schoolteachers have a lot of experience there.

But what about the doctor? He is the one on trial. So why shouldn't there be a jury of doctors presiding over his contribution to this person's issues? Ah, but maybe he doesn't want doctors. In case he did something wrong, the docs will be able to flush him out, and he will be screwed. So depending on his guilt or innocence, he wants a jury of either idiots or doctors. Same with the schoolteacher. Depending on whether she got sick because of improperly prescribed medication or too much tequila will determine whether she wants a jury of doctors or idiots. No, she will always want the idiot jury.

PA BROOK

What happened to the teachers?

I'm confused. And I'm writing this shit.

What is on second.

While a jury of "peers" is not required to include members of a defendant's race (or occupation, or social status, or...) to create "a jury of peers," a juror cannot be excluded based on race during jury selection. So any race is my peer. Doesn't sound kosher.

But that's it. Everyone else is a peer, it seems.

So if a nuclear plant is being sued by a group of West Virginia hillbillies for pollution, how does one select a jury of peers? Whose peers should it be? Plaintiffs'? The Clampetts et al. v. Nuclear Scientists. The peer jury should include only those who are married to first cousins. But what about the defendants? Rocket scientists with all their teeth should dominate the jury. There has to be a compromise. Dentures?

I Don't Know is on third.

And he's got cavities.

So the basic premise of a jury by one's peers is almost impossible since one side's peers are very different than the other side's peers. So I guess the idea is to have a bunch of average people be the peers of everyone. Regardless of what they know. Or don't know. Perhaps that is the point. If average Joe knows nothing about a topic, he is eminently qualified to determine whether lawyer A or lawyer B is full of shit. Makes sense. Average Joes are also shrinks.

But let's be serious here. Maybe not entirely. If we are going to embrace the centuries-old tried-and-true concept of the fairest of all jurisprudence techniques, a trial by one's peers, let's really do it right. And because we need to look at it from centerfield with eyes to both sides, let's explore

IF I WERE GOD

how the following criminal or civil proceedings would truly include a jury of peers:

Marijuana possession. Does the jury have to be high during the trial?

Peeing in public. Would this exclude women since they don't pee in public except under the most dire of circumstances?

An attorney embezzling trust fund money. Do we need corrupt attorneys on the jury? Or will any attorney do? Maybe it's the same thing. Imagine a jury of all lawyers.

Espionage. Shaken not stirred. Will we be serving martinis during the trial?

Necrophilia (is it really a crime?) Won't we need dead people on the jury? Oh, they are the aggrieved party. Not quite the peer. But if it's a civil suit, now we are talking. What if it's necrophiliac sodomy? Going to have to be creative here.

Perjury. We won't be able to believe the verdict.

Libel/slander. As long as they went to perjury class.

Imagine the jury for an insanity defense. I don't want to be the bailiff in that jury room.

Buggery is anal intercourse between a man and another man, woman, or animal, better known as butt-fucking. Can animals be on juries? Might make better decisions.

Male prostitution. Excellent chance for a hung jury.

To give all of this a real-life spin, my one jury experience was for a civil case about a chiropractor being sued by his patient. Medical malpractice, very common. Without going into too much detail, the patient sued the doctor because his back hurt, even though the patient had ignored the doctor's orders. Seems a tad frivolous, but we have seen worse. In selecting the jury, the judge asked if anyone might be biased. This could mean hating doctors or chiropractors in particular, having had back issues, having had a bad experience with insurance companies, or knowing someone of any of those ilks. I honestly answered that I'd had a significant back issue in my twenties, but it was of my own doing and I certainly could be impartial. All jury members were asked the same, and we went on our merry he said/she said way into the guts of the trial.

It was clear to me that the doc had done nothing wrong except have an asshole for a patient. The asshole did nothing the doctor recommended and all the things the doc said the patient should not do. No wonder the guy didn't get better. When we went to the jury room, we started like they do on TV and went around the room asking for initial judgments. Maybe this is a quickie. It was, but as we circled the room, one of the jurors stated quite emphatically, "I'm not giving that man a dime. My sister had an issue with her doctor, and she never got a cent. Why should he?"

OMG, just the kind of person you don't want on a jury. And she was asked specifically if she had any experiences that could make her less than impartial. She said no, effectively committing perjury. Fortunately, we all agreed the bum (patient) didn't deserve a nickel, but my point is that this woman did not excuse herself when she should have. How many other jurors are there that either consciously or subconsciously judge based on personal prejudice rather than impartiality? I bet a lot.

GOD 2.0

So my solution is an easy one. A trial by a panel of judges. Appointed by other judges. No campaigns here. Or politicians needing a favor. Three, five, some odd number. You might have to hire more judges, but I guarantee you there would be fewer cases and they would be resolved more quickly. The advantages should be obvious.

IF I WERE GOD

Judges know the law and what should or should not be considered. No objections muddling the testimony and confusing the jury. No more hearsay, relevancy, or other confusions.

Judges can parse through lawyer bullshit. There are a lot of slick lawyers out there who are good at swaying juries. Look at all the jury consultants that have created an entire profession over trying to pick jurors who can be convinced of anything. Witness Jason Bull. Judges will not allow that to happen.

Will there be flaws in the machine? Of course. If it were perfect, what the hell would I do? Some judges will have an axe to grind against a lawyer, will make their own judgment before the evidence is presented, or will just be prejudiced. Guess what, so are most of the regular jury members. At least judges can see through the bullshit and will not be swayed by it. At least not swayed as much. This will put the cottage industry of jury consultants out of business, but we will need more judges under my system, so there will be employment opportunities.

Because of the above, there will be fewer trials. How often have we heard a lawyer say, "Once I get this case in front of a jury, I will have them eating out of my hand." There will be a lot more civil suit settlements and criminal plea bargains freeing up the courts for the real cases.

The naysayers would claim it is not a jury of your peers as is our right. I say, it is better than a jury of peers. If it is a civil case, it will be adjudicated without prejudice or partiality. If it is a criminal case, there will be no sympathy engendered for the defendant by some slick-talking defense counsel.

With all due deference to *Bull*, there will be no more bull.

Next case!

CHAPTER 15
THE FOURTH AMENDMENT
(What Many Internet Dates Need)

O K, IF YOU ARE A *Law & Order* junkie like me, you don't need this spelled out for you, but just in case some of you aren't...

The Fourth Amendment to the US Constitution guarantees freedom from unreasonable search and seizure.

I know several women who have sought such freedom in their internet dating exploits.

This also means that law enforcement agents need probable cause, and a warrant in most cases, to search your person or belongings. If there is no probable cause and you are searched illegally, any evidence collected from the search will be excluded from evidence at trial. Probable cause means there must be enough evidence that a reasonable person would believe a crime was committed. This evidence is presented to a judge who must agree before authorizing the search by granting a warrant.

So, Joe who serially raped and murdered 17 women is arrested and taken into custody. Under questioning, he confesses to all 17. Oops, the arresting officer forgot to read him his Miranda rights. You know, "you have the right to

IF I WERE GOD

remain silent" and all that. Guess what, the confession is not admissible in court. And anything the confessor said that leads to hard evidence that he in fact is guilty is not admissible. That completely sucks.

Anybody know who the fuck Miranda is?

I will use another example of how the Fourth Amendment can work against law enforcement. An off-duty officer is going house to house to sell tickets to the PBA ball. His knock results in someone opening the door and, in the background, the officer sees a pile of white stuff on the table. It could be rice, it could be sugar, it could be dog food—he has no reasonable clue as to what it is. He barges in anyway and finds out it is cocaine and arrests the homeowner. There was no warrant, and there is a question as to whether there was probable cause. Let's forget Miranda for now, but the homeowner's lawyer claims violation of the Fourth Amendment, and the case is thrown out of court and the perp gets off scot-free.

And the cop didn't even get high.

In reality, the result of something like this could go either way depending on the facts, as the good of society may trump the rights of privacy in certain instances, all at the discretion of the judge. My issue is that obvious crimes are going unpunished because of bad due process. The issue with loosening the interpretations of the Fourth Amendment is that police may take advantage of this and become more aggressive in their searching and seizing, perhaps because of laziness (why go through the trouble of getting a warrant when I don't really have to), overzealousness, or a power trip.

GOD 2.0

We as a society have erred on the side of crimes going unpunished, and many agree with this. However, I think there is a middle ground that can work. We first must agree that regardless of errors in due process, if there is 100% certainty that someone is guilty, the case will not be thrown out because of those errors. Now, how do we minimize the occurrence of those errors? This is where training and education of law enforcement becomes critical. If the punishment for not following due process (e.g., getting a warrant) is sufficiently severe in instances where the officer is wrong, then that will provide a sufficient deterrent to officers considering breaching due process.

While I am on the subject of cops, I believe the two highest paid professions in our country should be authors and God-impersonators. You think it's easy being me? The next two highest paid should be police officers and teachers. Those who protect us and those who are the guardians of our future. Yes, doctors save lives, attorneys defend us, accountants do stuff no one else wants to.

But I would not just change the pay scale, I would make the job much tougher. I hate tenure for teachers when the job security is given simply for time on the job and not any measure of competence. Teachers, save for parents (and not always so), are the most important influence on young people. They are charged with giving our youth the knowledge to become productive adults. We as a society should make sure we only hire the most competent teachers and then track their success. Then we pay them a lot to do the job right. Many doctors are in it for the money. Same with other professions. We should make teaching one of them. I will not accept that it's a government job and therefore can't pay well. That's just an excuse. Get it done!

And only a chosen few who have shown the ability to react

IF I WERE GOD

properly under stress would be eligible to be police officers. Training should be much more intensive, psychological screening much more of a factor. Someone who has the potential to be shot at any time, and therefore the ability to shoot at someone else any time, needs to be able to *properly* react to any stressful event that occurs. That does not happen simply because Uncle Joe was a cop. It should be an elite profession with elite pay.

And the unions will have to get with the program or go away. There are no unions for doctors.

Or authors or God-impersonators.

CHAPTER 16
CONSTITUTIONAL AMENDMENTS ACCORDING TO SOCIAL MEDIA
(#MyKindofInalienableRight)

THE FOUNDING FATHERS OF AMERICA were the most prominent statesmen of their time. Brilliant minds, forward thinkers, wonderful orators. Rich men, poor men. Common men, powerful men. Thirty-nine of them signed the United States Constitution in September of 1787. There were many more who contributed to the democratic concept, and it was historical from several perspectives.

They kicked the ass of the most powerful military and economic power at the time.

They established the first large scale republic.

They created separation of church and state without a war.

But I think they failed English. The Constitution is a difficult read. The Bill of Rights, the first 10 amendments to the Constitution, at times is downright incomprehensible. At least for me. However, the good news is that it seems like the Bill of Rights was written for Twitter. They were alarmingly short on character usage in an era where it did not matter.

So if the Bill of Rights were written in today's social media conscious society, would it have sounded differently? Let's look at the Bill of Rights and reconstitute it for Twitter. Maximum characters, hash tags, and the like. We may need more than 10.

The First Amendment has 272 characters in it, with spaces counted, of course. It states:

"Congress shall make no law respecting an establishment of religion, or prohibiting the free exercise thereof; or abridging the freedom of speech, or of the press; or the right of the people peaceably to assemble, and to petition the Government for a redress of grievances."

A little long for Twitter, even with their extended new character minimum. It was challenging when it was only 140 characters. Made you think. Now its too easy to tweet. I'm keeping with the old tradition. Our Founding Fathers were smart. They would have dealt with it.

So, maybe we need two amendments here. There are two concepts. Free speech. Freedom of religion. Why one amendment? Today, it would clearly have been two.

Breaking down the First Amendment, we will start with the first part:

"Congress shall make no law *with respect to* the establishment of religion, or prohibiting the free exercise thereof."

Nice, only 117 characters. Room for some hashtags. See, and I'm not smoking anything. Yet.

FIRST AMENDMENT FOR TWITTER
Congress shall make no law with respect to the establishment of religion, or prohibiting the free exercise thereof. #fuckthechurch

Perfect.

PA BROOK

SECOND AMENDMENT FOR TWITTER

The second part of the First Amendment will become my Second Amendment.

"Congress shall make no law abridging the freedom of speech, or of the press; or the right of the people peaceably to assemble, and to petition the Government for a redress of grievances."

A little long at 180-plus characters. Some fancy words too. I guess these guys *were* educated. They could have made it so a reference to a dictionary wasn't necessary with every other word. But let's use simpler words as we streamline to Twitter territory.

Congress will let you say anything (except the N word), hang out wherever you want, and seek damages. #suetheshitoutofeveryone

This is fun.

Let's do the rest of them. Since we bifurcated the First Amendment into two, we now have an 11-amendment Bill of Rights. So far. This may get a little confusing. Let's see where this takes us.

THIRD AMENDMENT FOR TWITTER

The Second Amendment states:

"A well regulated Militia, being necessary to the security of a free State, the right of the people to keep and bear Arms, shall not be infringed."

Oh, shit, the gun one. This is one fucking hot topic. I feel some good hashtags. There is a whole chapter on this (see Chapter 17), so I will keep this to the basics. Of course, this is another amendment that was not in English. A word is missing. This is only a little over the Twitter max, but we

IF I WERE GOD

need some room for hashtags. So let's have it make sense and add in some tweeting reference. Remember this is our Third Amendment, so it could go like this:

An Army is needed and everyone can own a gun. #Ifyoufuck withmeIllblowthisshotgunupyourass

Nice and short. And there can be no mistaking it.

FOURTH AMENDMENT FOR TWITTER
The Third Amendment (this will drive me to drink) states:

"No Soldier shall, in time of peace be quartered in any house, without the consent of the Owner, nor in time of war, but in a manner to be prescribed by law."

Appears to mean that a soldier needs permission to stay over at a non-soldier's house during peace, but during war, Congress could legislate sleepovers. Who gets the couch?

I'm not even sure why this is a Constitutional right. Whose right is it? Mine or the soldiers? It is my Constitutional right to tell a soldier he has to sleep in the yard. Not sure I need that. Shit, I have a gun. I'll shoot the motherfucker if he tries to break in.

Assuming I do need this right and my interpretation is correct, this needs some Twittering adjustments.

Congress regulates slumber parties during times of war. #youcanhavethebedroom #buttakethebitchywifewhenyouleave

FIFTH AMENDMENT FOR TWITTER
The Fourth Amendment, as we now know, is the search and seizure right. *Law and Order* fans have this one memorized.

"The right of the people to be secure in their persons, houses, papers, and effects, against unreasonable searches and seizures, shall not be violated, and no Warrants shall issue, but upon probable cause, supported by Oath or affirmation, and particularly describing the place to be searched, and the persons or things to be seized."

OK, maybe not memorized. The founding fathers decided to get wordy. It's almost good English except for the run-on sentence and missing verb. I think I understand this one. Some kind of due process is needed before you can take my stuff or check out my chachkas. But it's not clear who gets to Oath or affirm or deem it probable cause.

How about if I think I have *probable cause* that my neighbor is banging my wife, and I *affirm* to blow his balls off with my Second Amendment bazooka?

Is that how it works?

Whatever. We need to Twitterize it.

No one can take your stuff without some Big Shot legally deeming it OK to do so #leavemyshitaloneasshole

Much easier for *L&O* fans to memorize.

AMENDMENTS SIX THROUGH NINE FOR TWITTER

The Fifth Amendment is typically referred to as the right to *not* self-incriminate. In other words, if you fuck up and are asked, you don't have to lie. That would be perjury. You can tell them you aren't going to answer. Like a five-year-old.

"OK, Johnny, did you let the cat out?"

"I'm sorry, Mom, but on advice of counsel, I plead the fifth."

Like pleading the fifth is not an admission of guilt. I say force everyone to tell the truth. It would not be self-incriminating if you didn't fuck up. So don't fuck up, and you won't have to plead the fifth. This clause also is why a defendant does

IF I WERE GOD

not need to take the stand. Because he would be lying his ass off and therefore his ass is protected by this amendment.

The Fifth Amendment is also the double jeopardy amendment. You can't be tried for the same crime twice. The whole amendment reads as follows.

"No person shall be held to answer for a capital, or otherwise infamous crime, unless on a presentment or indictment of a Grand Jury, except in cases arising in the land or naval forces, or in the Militia, when in actual service in time of War or public danger; nor shall any person be subject for the same offence to be twice put in jeopardy of life or limb; nor shall be compelled in any criminal case to be a witness against himself, nor be deprived of life, liberty, or property, without due process of law; nor shall private property be taken for public use, without just compensation."

That's a mouthful. That won't even fit on Facebook. Gonna take some extra effort to tweet, so we're going to break this up into four amendments. The first part of the Fifth Amendment, requiring an indictment to prosecute, will become *Twitter's Sixth Amendment*.

It needs a sprinkle of interpretation, some real English, and a Twitter hashtag.

You need to be properly indicted except during war when the Militia can fuck with you and you need your gun. #comenearmeandIwillAK47yourass

The next part of the Fifth Amendment, double jeopardy, and life and limb, will be Twitter's Seventh Amendment. I am not sure where the limb part came from. Maybe that was before the cruel and unusual punishment amendment prevented cutting off arms for robbery.

You can't be tried twice for the same crime. #hahayoudumbassprosecutor

The third part of the Fifth Amendment, making it legal to avoid lying, becomes...

You don't have to testify against yourself. #ofcourseIdiditstupid

Finally, the last part of the Fifth Amendment has to do with Eminent Domain. Can't take my shit unless you pay me for it. Rephrased to be Twitter worthy...

If the government wants your house, you can't stop them. #dontflushthetoiletforamonth

AMENDMENTS TEN THROUGH TWELVE FOR TWITTER

The Sixth Amendment is just as wordy as the Fifth. The Fathers went from unintelligible to verbose over the course of two amendments. We will need three amendments here.

The current Sixth Amendment:

"In all criminal prosecutions, the accused shall enjoy the right to a speedy and public trial, by an impartial jury of the State and district wherein the crime shall have been committed, which district shall have been previously ascertained by law, and to be informed of the nature and cause of the accusation; to be confronted with the witnesses against him; to have compulsory process for obtaining witnesses in his favor, and to have the Assistance of Counsel for his defence."

Another run-on sentence, and that's before the first semicolon. It started out fine. Speedy trial, impartial jury in the place it happened. Period. That is all that is needed. Nine words, 53 characters, hashtag some stuff, move on. But no, we need some "district" stuff added. What does "which district shall have been previously ascertained by law" mean right after saying the jury must be from the district where the crime was committed?

IF I WERE GOD

I didn't know districts could "ascertain." Hell, I can't "ascertain." Or can I?

In any event, how can a district be a district if it was not previously "ascertained" by law to be a district?

A little redundant.

Seems to say the same thing.

Over and over again.

OK, I'll move on.

So the full amendment is the right to a speedy trial, to be confronted with witnesses, and the right to counsel. Free counsel, if need be. But what if you don't want a speedy trial. Maybe you're guilty as hell and there is no shot to get off (don't go there). You are out on bail and will never be out again. Let that trial take its time. Motion this and motion that. Fuck speedy. I want the right to drag this trial out until the cop retires. Where is that right?

Maybe we need to add the opposites to this amendment. Lengthy trial. And maybe you don't like the witnesses. You don't want to see them. There should be an opposite right. George Costanza once tried this.

It ended badly.

In any event, this is a long amendment that will have to be broken down as well. I did manage to describe the amendment in one sentence above, well under 140 characters, but it's the hashtag thing that will get me. It's way above my pay grade to figure out how to hashtag all that shit together.

Now we are ready for *Twitter's 10th Amendment*. But wait, why do we have to spell out the first nine numbers but when it comes to the next one, its OK to use the actual number?

Who made up that rule? Did Heloise get into number etiquette? Does anyone other than me really care?

Fuck it.

Twitter's 10th Amendment relates to the first part of the 6th Amendment, complete with run on, duplication, and incoherence.

You will be told why and tried quickly where you fucked up, providing it is a proper district. #youaregoingtohavetoextraditemyassfromEcuador

The next part of the 6th Amendment, the right to be confronted with witnesses and have compulsory process for obtaining favorable witnesses, becomes Twitter's 11th. This one is easy.

You have the right to be confronted by your accuser and get your own witnesses #myguysarebetterliarsthanyours

The last part of the 6th Amendment, to have the Assistance of Counsel, is now the 12th for Twitter:

You have the right to Counsel, any Counsel. #garbagecollectorsmakemorethanpublicdefenders #Imfucked

TWITTER'S 13TH AMENDMENT

To recap, we are up to the 7th Amendment as proffered by the Constitution. I have to admit, I had no clue what the 7th Amendment said. I am not sure I have ever heard it referred to on any *Law & Order* episode. I can't imagine Jack McCoy would lose an opportunity to show everyone that he even knows the inner workings of the 7th Amendment. But here it is:

"In Suits at common law, where the value in controversy shall exceed twenty dollars, the right of trial by jury shall be preserved, and no fact tried by a jury, shall be otherwise re-

IF I WERE GOD

examined in any Court of the United States, than according to the rules of the common law."

No wonder I have no idea what that means. Why "Suits" has an upper case S is unknown to me. It sounds like it might relate to civil suits as it refers to a controversy in excess of $20 (the Fathers didn't know number etiquette). It's a shame that I have to revert to the internet to understand the meaning of our basic rights. Maybe it's me. Wouldn't be the first time.

But if I try to understand this amendment from its written words, it seems to say that a Suit (capital S) based on common law shall be tried based on common law. As opposed to what? Did we really need a Right for this?

There are only 27 of these motherfuckers. At least until I get done with them.

Did we really have to take one of them up for a $20 lawsuit? Really, guys, you couldn't have found a better way to spend your time?

"Really, Really Important Constitutional Law for $20 please, Alex."

"The answer is: 7th Amendment."

"What is the dumbest fucking amendment ever made?"

"Right you are!"

Well, I can't change history, so I have to do something with this. Well, I can, but I have bigger fish to fry. By the way, did the Founding Fathers ever consider inflation? Such smart dudes, you would think there would be an "as adjusted for inflation" clause in there somewhere. Maybe inflation was not defined in common law yet. I can fix that too.

You have the right to a civil Suit. #whatawaSteofmyfuckingtimefor$20. #everhearofinflation #mypolyestersuitcost$20

TWITTER'S 14TH AMENDMENT

The 8th Amendment is actually quite clear, simple, and terse.

"Excessive bail shall not be required, nor excessive fines imposed, nor cruel and unusual punishments inflicted."

Based on previous amendments, I was expecting something along the lines of:

"Without probable cause and a sleep over with the Militia, bail cannot be set above a certain number outside the constraints of common law in the district in which it was deputized and more mumbo jumbo."

But while they defined a civil trial requiring a jury as one where the Suit was in excess of $20, there is no definition of excess here or what cruel or unusual punishment is. I can forgive them for that. But why the $20 in #7?

Anyway, all the Twitter 14th Amendment needs is a hashtag:

Excessive bail shall not be required, nor excessive fines imposed, nor cruel and unusual punishments inflicted. #hangthemotherfuckers

TWITTER'S 15TH AMENDMENT

The 9th Amendment reads:

"The enumeration in the Constitution, of certain rights, shall not be construed to deny or disparage others retained by the people."

Let me see if I get this. The bestowing of these previous 8, now 14 rights, do not remove any other rights, previously bestowed. Isn't that obvious? The Amendments do not say,

IF I WERE GOD

"These are your only rights." I am not sure why this needed to be codified. But they did it. At least it's good English.

Therefore, my Twitter's 15th Amendment reads (with only minor Twitter modification needed):

You can do whatever the fuck you want. #youcandowhateverthefuckyouwant

TWITTER'S 16TH AMENDMENT

Now to cover all the other bases, the 10th Amendment bestowed upon the states and the people everything else. Until they made more amendments later on. Indian givers. The 10th Amendment reads:

"The powers not delegated to the United States by the Constitution, nor prohibited by it to the States, are reserved to the States respectively, or to the people."

It says States (again with the capital S) or people. What if the people and the States don't see eye to eye? And if the people control the States, why the need to mention both? Makes things confusing. To me at least. What if a person sues a state because he was bestowed the "power?" Now what? What if each person exercised that "power" differently? And the State can't do anything, because it is made up of...the people. Oops.

Thank God for Twitter. We need to shorten this bad boy anyway. So we will kill 2 birds with 1 stone. And simply change "or" to "and."

To finish off the Bill of Rights, Twitter's 16th Amendment now reads:

*If the Fathers don't do it and don't say you can't, the States **and** their people shall.* #whopaysdamagesifyousueyourself? #canIbethejurytoo?

WE ARE NOT DONE

We are having way too much fun. There are another 17 of these bad boys. And there is plenty of room on Twitter.

Quick sidebar on Twitter. Maybe this has happened to you. Twitter is so fast-paced that a popular topic could create so many tweets that you miss most of them. Or your own. I was having fun on National French Fry Day and decided to tweet a joke about taking a date to McDonalds. Like "The only time it's OK to take a date to McDonalds is on National French Fry Day. #nationalfrenchfryday #noseconddate #loser." I was trying to sell my book about dating after 50 at the time, and this seemed a clever way to tweet something original. I was still a Twitter newbie and wanted to see my tweet posted. So after tweeting it, I tried to find it on the #nationalfrenchfryday hashtag. But there were so many being posted that I could not scroll down fast enough to find mine. So much for Twitter fame.

TWITTER'S 17TH AMENDMENT

OK, back to a much more important topic. So Amendment #11 goes something like this:

"The Judicial power of the United States shall not be construed to extend to any suit in law or equity, commenced or prosecuted against one of the United States by Citizens of another State, or by Citizens or Subjects of any Foreign State."

Adopted: February 7, 1795.

I have added the dates ratified to these for reference purposes, but I guess because it's different "Fathers" who were writing this shit, they apparently wanted to out-confuse the prior guys. Once again, I am mystified. If I read it r-e-a-l slow, it seems like the Supreme Court cannot hear cases of a Citizen (capital fucking C) suing a state he/she doesn't belong to.

And also it cannot hear cases of any foreign dudes suing a state. Sounds like the Supreme Court is telling the states, "You are on your own."

Not being comfortable that my interpretation was on point, I consulted a highly optimized website (it came up first) that appears to be an expert in interpreting the Constitution. It said, the "11th Amendment more clearly defines the original jurisdiction of the Supreme Court concerning a suit brought against a state by a citizen of another state." (https://usconstitution.net/constquick.html)

That didn't really help. So once again, my Twitter version must make things clearer to the common folk and allow the World According to Twitter to rule the day. Twitter's 17th Amendment would go something like this:

The Supreme Court will not get involved with all the crazies suing the states. #leaveusthefuckalone #wegotabortiontodealwith

TWITTER'S 18TH AMENDMENT (MAYBE)

The boys got a little verbose with the 12th Amendment. This will be really hard to tweet coherently. First the original version.

"The Electors shall meet in their respective states, and vote by ballot for President and Vice President, one of whom, at least, shall not be an inhabitant of the same state with themselves; they shall name in their ballots the person voted for as President, and in distinct ballots the person voted for as Vice President, and they shall make distinct lists of all persons voted for as President, and of all persons voted for as Vice President, and of the number of votes for each, which lists they shall sign and certify, and transmit sealed to the seat of the government of the United States, directed to the President of the Senate;--The President of the Senate shall, in the presence of the Senate and House of Representatives, open all the certificates and the votes shall then be counted;--The person having the greatest number of votes for President, shall be the President, if such number be a majority of the whole number of Electors appointed; and if no person have such majority, then from the persons having the highest numbers not exceeding three on the list of those voted for as President, the House of Representatives shall choose immediately, by ballot, the President. But in choosing the President, the votes shall be taken by states, the representation from each state having one vote; a quorum for this purpose shall consist of a member or members from two-thirds of the states, and a majority of all the states shall be necessary to a choice. And if the House of Representatives shall not choose a President whenever the right of choice shall devolve upon them, before the fourth day of March next following, then the Vice President shall act as President, as in the case of the death or other constitutional disability of the President. The person having the greatest number of votes as Vice President, shall be the Vice President, if such number be a majority of the whole number of Electors appointed, and if no person have a majority, then from the two highest numbers on the list, the Senate shall choose the Vice President; a quorum for the purpose shall consist of two-thirds of the whole number of Senators, and a majority of the whole number shall be necessary to a choice. But no person constitutionally ineligible to the office of President shall be eligible to that of Vice President of the United States."

Adopted: June 15, 1804.

Superseded by Section 3 of the 20thAmendment.

I would simply tweet #don't even try.

Let's see, electors and majorities and ballots and President and Vice President and what if no majority. Sorry, but I just finished watching *House of Cards*, Season 5, where this exact scenario came up. It was very cool! These Revolutionary fellows really thought of everything. I am very

IF I WERE GOD

impressed with this amendment. Of course, it is way too complicated. The House picks the President if there is not an electoral majority, but it's not based on a majority of the Representatives themselves, but a majority of states. Once again, the states are on their own. Justices are yukking it up in DC.

The Senate gets to pick the Vice President, but each Senator gets a vote. That sucks. The Representatives have to duke it out to see how their state is going to vote, but the Senators each have a vote. Of course, the Senators are only voting for the "heartbeat away" dude, not the main squeeze. Why is that? There are fewer Senators, implying more importance, but yet they get to pick number two. Maybe the Justices know.

But my favorite part is if the House doesn't pick a President by March 4, then the Vice President becomes President. Unless the Senate has also failed to pick one. Oh, shit, now what?! I am sure this has been addressed somewhere, probably in the above, but it escaped me.

Now for the tough part, Twitter's 18th Amendment:

Electors shall choose the Prez and Veep. If they can't make up their minds, all hell breaks loose. #whoseideawasthis #weneedafuckingking

Of course, there is a notation that a portion of the 12th Amendment was amended by the 20th Amendment. I am not going there. #lookituponWikipedia

TWITTER'S 19TH AMENDMENT

Now this next Amendment (#13) was a biggie. It had to be. The dudes in charge had been sitting on their asses for 60 years since they last did anything. The Supreme Court was so bored it was taking book on cock fights. This Amendment had better be a blockbuster, big budget, get DiCaprio and Tarantino at all costs, Oscar shoo-in.

It was.

"**Section 1**. Neither slavery nor involuntary servitude, except as a punishment for crime whereof the party shall have been duly convicted, shall exist within the United States, or any place subject to their jurisdiction.

"**Section 2**. Congress shall have power to enforce this article by appropriate legislation."

Adopted: December 6, 1865.

Now this day could have broken a record for tweeting back in the day.

Twitter's 19th Amendment can be simple:

Slavery is illegal. #finally

The reaction would be all over the place and could even include this as its pinned tweet:

Everybody's equal. #butwecanstillfuckwiththeIndians

20TH–23RD AMENDMENTS FOR TWITTER

Just as they were figuring out how to make amendments to the Constitution understandable *and* tweetable, along came the 14th Amendment. It included several parts, which makes one wonder why it was all in one amendment. The Bill of Rights had 10 Amendments, so there is nothing religious about adopting several differently numbered amendments all at once. Perhaps missing the confusion caused by previous amendments, they chose to make my life difficult again. I hate it when I have to search the internet to find out what a stupid amendment, written in fucking English, means. But

IF I WERE GOD

I did. For some of it at least. Here is the 14th Amendment, unabridged (read at your own risk).

"**Section 1**. All persons born or naturalized in the United States and subject to the jurisdiction thereof, are citizens of the United States and of the State wherein they reside. No State shall make or enforce any law which shall abridge the privileges or immunities of citizens of the United States; nor shall any State deprive any person of life, liberty, or property, without due process of law; nor deny to any person within its jurisdiction the equal protection of the laws.

"**Section 2**. Representatives shall be apportioned among the several States according to their respective numbers, counting the whole number of persons in each State, excluding Indians not taxed. But when the right to vote at any election for the choice of electors for President and Vice President of the United States, Representatives in Congress, the Executive and Judicial officers of a State, or the members of the Legislature thereof, is denied to any of the male inhabitants of such State, being twenty-one years of age, and citizens of the United States, or in any way abridged, except for participation in rebellion, or other crime, the basis of representation therein shall be reduced in the proportion which the number of such male citizens shall bear to the whole number of male citizens twenty-one years of age in such State.

"**Section 3**. No person shall be a Senator or Representative in Congress, or elector of President and Vice President, or hold any office, civil or military, under the United States, or under any State, who, having previously taken an oath, as a member of Congress, or as an officer of the United States, or as a member of any State legislature, or as an executive or judicial officer of any State, to support the Constitution of the United States, shall have engaged in insurrection or rebellion against the same, or given aid or comfort to the enemies thereof. But Congress may by a vote of two-thirds of each House, remove such disability.

"**Section 4**. The validity of the public debt of the United States, authorized by law, including debts incurred for payment of pensions and bounties for services in suppressing insurrection or rebellion, shall not be questioned. But neither the United States nor any State shall assume or pay any debt or obligation incurred in aid of insurrection or rebellion against the United States, or any claim for the loss or emancipation of any slave; but all such debts, obligations and claims shall be held illegal and void.

"**Section 5**. The Congress shall have power to enforce, by appropriate legislation, the provisions of this article."

Adopted: July 9, 1868.

Talk about a mouthful. Now each section is about a completely different topic. These should have been Amendments #14-#17. I am going to treat them as such for discussion as well as tweeting purposes.

Section 1 seems a bit repetitive. It seems to be telling the states not to fuck with people. Isn't that what the Bill of Rights did? Not sure I understand the need for this one.

Hello! In case you forgot, we got rights. # 🙂 # ☹️

Section 2 appears to provide for the arithmetic to determine the number of Representatives in each state. For the first time, a math equation appears in an Amendment. I am a CPA, MBA, spreadsheet nerd, and won a contest in 3rd grade because I knew my 12 times table. But I haven't a clue as to what the fraction described is trying to calculate.

Count all men except those you don't count. Or maybe, if you don't count all the men you are supposed to count, you don't get to count them. And what exactly is "whole number

IF I WERE GOD

of persons?" I didn't know persons came in the fractional variety. And the poor Indians. Fucked again.

Ultimately, Constitutional scholars and those willing to Google shit will tell me what it means. Probably send me a nasty tweet or two. That's OK. I am not trying to figure everything out. Just enough to tweet some semblance of what the Fathers were trying to tell us. I did figure out that it had to do with preventing the suppression of the rights of newly freed blacks.

So maybe we keep it simple:

Blacks are citizens now too. #andtheycankickyourass

Section 3 seems simple. If you committed treason, you can't hold public office. Seems reasonable, but isn't this sort of covered in the law elsewhere? Like, you get hung if you are guilty of treason. No running for office on death row.

So the Twitter Gods, who like short and simple:

If you screw us, we won't let you screw us further by running for office. #theguyswhodontcommittreasonscrewusenough

Section 4 says that United States debt is valid, but debt from the insurgents is not. Insurgents were basically the Confederacy. This was not spelled out as such, but certainly implied. So:

What we say we owe you, we owe you. What you say we owe you, we don't. #fuckMexicotoo

We are going to ignore Section 5. #duh.

TWITTER'S 24TH AMENDMENT

The 15th Amendment gave black people the right to vote. Black *men*, that is.

"**Section 1**. The right of citizens of the United States to vote shall not be denied or abridged by the United States or by any State on account of race, color, or previous condition of servitude.

Section 2. The Congress shall have power to enforce this article by appropriate legislation."

Adopted: February 3, 1870.

The Twitter version:

Everybody can vote now. Except women. #eatmypussy

TWITTER'S 25TH AMENDMENT

After a flurry of activity in the 1860s with the freeing of slaves, everyone took a breather for a couple of decades. Then came the IRS. Amendment #16:

"The Congress shall have power to lay and collect taxes on incomes, from whatever source derived, without apportionment among the several States, and without regard to any census or enumeration."

Adopted: February 3, 1913.

Even from women, who still couldn't vote, but could be taxed. Wasn't this the battle cry of the American Revolution? Taxation without representation. Boston Tea Party and all. About 140 years earlier, our Founding Fathers fought a war because of this and then wrote the world's most incredible political document in the history of man. And what did the descendants of the Founding Fathers do? They fucking taxed without representation.

Ugh!

The government can tax you based on income, and there is nothing you can do about it. #Itsonlythebeginning #wewillbefuckingwithyoufordecades

IF I WERE GOD
TWITTER'S 26TH AMENDMENT
Prior to this Amendment, the state legislature elected senators. The 17th Amendment changed that:

"The Senate of the United States shall be composed of two senators from each State, elected by the people thereof, for six years; and each Senator shall have one vote. The electors in each State shall have the qualifications requisite for electors of the most numerous branch of the State legislature.

"When vacancies happen in the representation of any State in the Senate, the executive authority of such State shall issue writs of election to fill such vacancies: Provided, That the legislature of any State may empower the executive thereof to make temporary appointments until the people fill the vacancies by election as the legislature may direct.

"This amendment shall not be so construed as to affect the election or term of any Senator chosen before it becomes valid as part of the Constitution."

Adopted: April 8, 1913.

Pure. Simple. In English. Sort of.

Twitter says:

The people shall elect Senators for terms of 6 years. There are no term limits. #oopsforgotthatpart #Mynewcareer

TWITTER'S 27TH AMENDMENT
Prohibition, or as the 18th Amendment put it:

"**Section 1.** After one year from the ratification of this article, the manufacture, sale, or transportation of intoxicating liquors within, the importation thereof into, or the exportation thereof from the United States and all territory subject to the jurisdiction thereof for beverage purposes is hereby prohibited.

"Section 2. The Congress and the several States shall have concurrent power to enforce this article by appropriate legislation.

"Section 3. This article shall be inoperative unless it shall have been ratified as an amendment to the Constitution by the legislatures of the several States, as provided in the Constitution, within seven years from the date of the submission hereof to the States by the Congress."

Adopted: January 16, 1919. Repealed by the 21st Amendment on December 5, 1933.

I wouldn't want to be the one tweeting this one. Highly eligible for delegation. Where's the new intern? Keep bad news terse. And women, who at least had enjoyed intoxication without representation, were losing that.

You got 1 year to buy as much storage space as possible and fill it with booze. #theregoesmygreygoose #wherestheweed

TWITTER'S 28TH AMENDMENT

Finally. The 19th Amendment is embarrassingly short because the boys did not want to acknowledge a century plus of terrible discrimination. The pussies said:

"The right of citizens of the United States to vote shall not be denied or abridged by the United States or by any States on account of sex.

"Congress shall have power to enforce this article by appropriate legislation."

Adopted: August 18, 1920.

Not when I tweet it. No beating around the bush (forgive the pun). Say it loud, say it proud.

We, men of the US, regret our egregious error of

IF I WERE GOD

denying women the right to vote and now agree to it. #wewillwatchOprahrerunswithyoufor1year

TWITTER'S 29TH AMENDMENT

The 20th Amendment states:

"**Section 1**. The terms of the President and Vice President shall end at noon the 20th day of January, and the terms of Senators and Representatives at noon on the 3rd day of January, of the years in which such terms would have ended if this article had not been ratified; and the terms of their successors shall then begin.

"**Section 2**. The Congress shall assemble at least once in every year, and such meeting shall begin at noon on the 3d day of January, unless they shall by law appoint a different day.

"**Section 3**. If, at the time fixed for the beginning of the term of the President, the President elect shall have died, the Vice President elect shall become President. If a President shall not have been chosen before the time fixed for the beginning of his term, or if the President elect shall have failed to qualify, then the Vice President elect shall act as President until a President shall have qualified; and the Congress may by law provide for the case wherein neither a President elect nor a Vice President elect shall have qualified, declaring who shall then act as President, or the manner in which one who is to act shall be selected, and such person shall act accordingly until a President or Vice President shall have qualified.

"**Section 4.** The Congress may by law provide for the case of the death of any of the persons from whom the House of Representatives may choose a President whenever the right of choice shall have devolved upon them, and for the case of the death of any of the persons from whom the Senate may choose a Vice President whenever the right of choice shall have devolved upon them.

"**Section 5**. Sections 1 and 2 shall take effect on the 15th day of October following the ratification of this article.

"**Section 6**. This article shall be inoperative unless it shall have been ratified as an amendment to the Constitution by the legislatures of three-fourths of the several States within seven years from the date of its submission."

Adopted: January 23, 1933.

Yikes! A lot of wind for not a lot of substance. Most of it is 'duh!' The primary purpose was to accelerate the effective date of the results of the election. This made sense since transportation had improved, requiring less time for people to travel to Washington, DC, and become prepared to take on their new Federal responsibilities. Tweeting Amendment #29:

The elected boys and girls have to show up for work in January; if Prez-elect doesn't make it, Veep-elect gets promoted. #Especiallyifheisabettershot

TWITTER'S 30TH AMENDMENT

Where would we have been without Prohibition? No Al Capone movies. Or Robert Stack as Elliot Ness. The 21st Amendment repealed Prohibition. It stated:

"**Section 1.** The eighteenth article of amendment to the Constitution of the United States is hereby repealed.

"**Section 2.** The transportation or importation into any State, Territory, or possession of the United States for delivery or use therein of intoxicating liquors, in violation of the laws thereof, is hereby prohibited.

"**Section 3.** The article shall be inoperative unless it shall have been ratified as an amendment to the Constitution by conventions in the several States, as provided in the Constitution, within seven years from the date of the submission hereof to the States by the Congress."

Adopted: December 5, 1933.

I'm not sure anything other than the first Section was necessary. Again, verbosity at times and illiteracy at others. Sometimes a middle ground would be nice. But I think only when under the influence.

Hi, guys. Let's have a drink. It's legal again. #oops #justkidding #nevermind #stilllliketheweed

TWITTER'S 31ST AMENDMENT

The 22nd Amendment limited the presidential term to either 2 elections or 10 years. For those who like the details:

"**Section 1.** No person shall be elected to the office of the President more than twice, and no person who has held the office of President, or acted as President, for more than two years of a term to which some other person was elected President shall be elected to the office of the President more than once. But this Article shall not apply to any person holding the office of President when this Article was proposed by the Congress, and shall not prevent any person who may be holding the office of President, or acting as President, during the term within which this Article becomes operative from holding the office of President or acting as President during the remainder of such term.

"**Section 2.** This article shall be inoperative unless it shall have been ratified as an amendment to the Constitution by the legislatures of three-fourths of the several States within seven years from the date of its submission to the States by the Congress."

Adopted: February 27, 1951

This one seems too easy.

Thepresidentialtermshallbelimitedtothegreateroftwoelections or 10 years. #iknewecalculuswouldfinallycomeinhandy

TWITTER'S 32ND AMENDMENT

The 23rd Amendment goes back to the days of gibberish. I think it gave the District of Columbia a say in the presidential elections. What do you think?

"**Section 1**. The District constituting the seat of government of the United States shall appoint in such manner as the Congress may direct:

"A number of electors of President and Vice President equal to the whole number of Senators and Representatives in Congress to which the District would be entitled if it were a state, but in no event more than the least populous State; they shall be in addition to those appointed by the States, but they shall be considered, for the purposes of the election of President and Vice President, to be electors appointed by a State; and they shall meet in the District and perform such duties as provided by the twelfth article of amendment.

"**Section 2**. The Congress shall have power to enforce this article by appropriate legislation."

Adopted: March 29, 1961.

More math and more confusion. These guy should have stuck to confusing us with words, something they are good at. Leave the numerical confusion to the accountants. Or just pronounce:

The District is awarded 3 electoral votes.

IF I WERE GOD

#wheredidcolumbiacomefrom #wtfcantbeatrhodeisland #thats3morethanguam

TWITTER'S 33ND AMENDMENT

No math, and not confusing, just boring, I guess. I wonder how much linguistic jockeying went on before they finally settled on the 62-word 24th Amendment.

"**Section 1.** The right of citizens of the United States to vote in any primary or other election for President or Vice President, for electors for President or Vice President, or for Senator or Representative in Congress, shall not be denied or abridged by the United States or any State by reason of failure to pay any poll tax or other tax.

"**Section 2.** The Congress shall have power to enforce this article by appropriate legislation."

Adopted: January 23, 1964.

By the way, I only word-counted Section 1. Every Amendment since #12 has a section giving Congress the power to enforce the Amendment. Whoop de damn do. Who else was going to enforce it? And if we were silent like we'd been for the first 12, what would we have? Anarchy?

But if you just consider the substance in this baby, you can really make good use of your knowledge of the English language.

Poll taxes are illegal. #youareverbosemotherfuckers

TWITTER'S 34TH AMENDMENT

There are a lot of theatrical references to the 25th Amendment. It is the one where folks can decree the President unfit for his role and relieve him of his duties. Maybe he is crazy, maybe he is incapacitated. Maybe the Democrats feel particularly spunky.

PA BROOK

It's a wordy one.

"**Section 1.** In case of the removal of the President from office or of his death or resignation, the Vice President shall become President.

"**Section 2.** Whenever there is a vacancy in the office of the Vice President, the President shall nominate a Vice President who shall take office upon confirmation by a majority vote of both Houses of Congress.

"**Section 3.** Whenever the President transmits to the President pro tempore of the Senate and the Speaker of the House of Representatives his written declaration that he is unable to discharge the powers and duties of his office, and until he transmits to them a written declaration to the contrary, such powers and duties shall be discharged by the Vice President as Acting President.

"**Section 4.** Whenever the Vice President and a majority of either the principal officers of the executive departments or of such other body as Congress may by law provide, transmit to the President pro tempore of the Senate and the Speaker of the House of Representatives their written declaration that the President is unable to discharge the powers and duties of his office, the Vice President shall immediately assume the powers and duties of the office as Acting President.

"Thereafter, when the President transmits to the President pro tempore of the Senate and the Speaker of the House of Representatives his written declaration that no inability exists, he shall resume the powers and duties of his office unless the Vice President and a majority of either the principal officers of the executive department or of such other body as Congress may by law provide, transmit within four days to the President pro tempore of the Senate and the Speaker of the House of Representatives their written declaration that the President is unable to discharge the powers and duties of his office. Thereupon Congress shall decide the issue, assembling within forty-eight hours for that purpose if not in session. If the Congress, within twenty-one days after receipt of the latter written declaration, or, if Congress is not in session, within twenty-one days after Congress is required to assemble, determines by two-thirds vote of both Houses that the President is unable to discharge the powers and duties of his office, the Vice President shall continue to discharge the same as Acting President; otherwise, the President shall resume the powers and duties of his office."

Adopted: February 10, 1967.

In Twitterspeak:

Incapacitated presidents can be replaced only with due process. #wehavealooneybirdintheWhiteHouse #whatelseisnew

TWITTER'S 35ᵀᴴ AMENDMENT

The 26th Amendment was real simple. If you can legally kill foreigners, you can vote. Finally, you get to vote for the motherfuckers sending you to war. But you can't drink.

It could have just said, 18-year-olds can now vote, but they had to do the negative assent thing.

"**Section 1.** The right of citizens of the United States, who are eighteen years of age or older, to vote shall not be denied or abridged by the United States or by any State on account of age.

"**Section 2.** The Congress shall have power to enforce this article by appropriate legislation."

Adopted: June 30, 1971.

Tweeting the happy news:

Citizens 18 and older can vote. #haveagunandaballotbutnotacocktail #howaboutajoint

TWITTER'S 36TH AMENDMENT

The last amendment requires a congressional election to pass before pay raises go into effect. This would seem to ensure that no self-dealing can be done, making members of Congress have to wait until the next election to get a raise.

First, senators do not have to wait to be reelected to get the raise. Just wait until the next House of Representatives election, which is every two years. And notice the amendment did not put any caps on raises.

Every House race since 1964 has resulted in at least an 80% reelection rate. For the Senate, the average rate is more than 75%.

The 27th Amendment states:

"No law, varying the compensation for the services of the Senators and Representatives, shall take effect, until an election of Representatives shall have intervened."

Embracing the true sentiment of those controlling their own salaries, Twitter's 36th Amendment says:

Congress shall set its own salary. #Wecanmakewhateverthefuckwewant #Hahahaha

#GOD2.0

#BelieveitornotEnglishisnotasecondlanguage

If only the Constitutional Amendments were more understandable in today's English and less subject to interpretation, we would have a lot less controversy about things like free speech, guns, and what a fractional person is. Bingo!

IF I WERE GOD

Now that the Constitutional Amendments are Twitter-friendly, how about making everything Twitter-friendly? We have judges interpreting laws, we need Tweedges interpreting the judges.

Or maybe just better English teachers.

Ouch.

CHAPTER 17

GUN CONTROL

(Is That an AK-47 Under Your Hat or Are You Just Happy to See Me?)

Look out. We already had a little bit of fun with this, but now I am walking a tightrope on a steamrolling treadmill. I am going to need my own bulletproof vest. Or maybe a semiautomatic weapon to protect myself. The NRA might be strumming its fingers, waiting to see where this one comes out.

Let's bash the Founding Fathers a little more. Who's going to sue me?

"A well regulated militia, being necessary to the security of a free state, the right of the people to keep and bear arms, shall not be infringed."

The 2nd Amendment is one of the most hotly debated issues in this country. And it's not even a complete articulate sentence. It has a noun and a verb, but it makes no sense. Read it again. It's missing something. What it's missing depends on what the writer meant.

Put an "and" in there and it is clear:

"A well regulated militia, being necessary to the security of a free state, *and* the right of the people to keep and bear arms, shall not be infringed."

Both a well-regulated (I think they also missed the hyphen) militia and the right of individuals to bear arms shall not be infringed. Perfect English. Maybe a semicolon or other manner of emphasis would have helped, but basically, no misunderstanding.

Add the word "eliminating" and again, no doubt:

"A well regulated militia, being necessary to the security of a free state, *eliminating* the right of the people to keep and bear arms, shall not be infringed."

A well-regulated militia eliminates the need for the people to have to bear arms. The militia will take care of the protection of the individual. No arms for the people. Sorry. Again, absent the helpful emphasis, this seems pretty clear.

Add another element and it makes the Constitution incredibly timeless.

"A well regulated militia, being necessary to the security of a free state, the right of the people to keep and bear arms *and text messaging*, shall not be infringed."

But in its original form—unintelligible.

So who were these dumb fuckers who wrote this Bill of Rights?

They were smart enough to create the most incredible of all governing documents in the history of man, but simple sentence structure eluded them. And 300 years later, we are ski racing downhill backwards in full throttle over this issue because they forgot a word!

James Madison is credited with the concept of the Bill of Rights, which includes the 2nd Amendment. He went to

PA BROOK

Princeton. Hopefully he engaged in the same practices of many lawyers of today. Dictation without proofreading. I can give him a mulligan for being too busy. I mean, that fucking Constitution was a bear to write. That Bill of Rights—who would come up with that shit back in 1790-something? As we saw in the previous chapter, according to the Bill, we can:

Say whatever we want,

Fucking shoot people who threaten us,

Kick a Marine out of our house if we don't have a convertible couch,

Prevent a search for my blowup dolls without due process,

Claim we knew nothing about shit because we go to jail if we remember,

Get speedy trials if we want; but if we fucked up, maybe that's not so good,

Get that trial by a jury, unless those in my neighborhood know I'm guilty,

Be assured we won't receive cruel and unusual punishment. But they used to burn women at the stake, so what did they mean by cruel and unusual? If burning was "usual," maybe I'm going back to England.

Be completely confused once again. "The enumeration in the Constitution, of certain rights, shall not be construed to deny or disparage others retained by the people." Hail Princeton.

Let the states figure out the shit we forgot about.

And that's only the first 10. But back to #2. Why didn't anyone ask these guys what they meant? I can't be the first person to read that and go "Huh?" Did not one of the Founding Fathers find something grammatically wrong with amendment number two? Several Fathers refused to sign for various reasons, but there is no record of poor grammar being one of them.

So where was my fifth-grade English teacher when all of this was going down?

I am having fun in advance of some really serious shit that needs to be discussed. Here we go (the sound you hear is me tightening the bulletproof vest).

I AM AN ACCOUNTANT, AFTER ALL

Let's start with some statistics and studies. A study found that the states with the highest gun ownership and weakest gun violence prevention laws had the highest rates of gun deaths. The same study noted the lowest gun ownership and strongest gun violence prevention laws had the lowest rate of gun deaths.

Of course, there may have been a lot more deaths by other means in the low gun death states and less in the others. But there is a clear correlation between gun ownership and gun deaths. Maybe that is a "duh."

Another study noted a similar correlation among countries. Guns per capita was directly correlated to the rate of gun deaths. The United States was at the wrong end of this study. High rates of mental illness in any country, on the other hand, did not predict more gun deaths.

Lots of guns, lots of gun deaths. Not so many guns, fewer gun deaths. Lots of crazy people, lots of Prozac. Minimizing the use of guns may lead to fewer gun deaths and fewer murders by guns, but will it lead to fewer murders?

One might logically conclude that this is true. Guns are

a relatively safe way to kill someone. No hand-to-hand combat. No need to look him in the eye. You don't even have to be in the same building. And it facilitates escape. Since all other means of killing someone have more risk involved, I would say that the simplicity of the kill makes guns a more appealing way to kill someone.

Take away the gun and other means are necessary. Hand-to-hand combat, maybe. Look him in the eye. This could lessen the number of murders since someone may think twice about killing someone with an alternate weapon. Up close and personal. Or maybe using an alternate weapon leads to the perp getting killed or the victim escaping. Both lead to fewer murders—a good thing.

So, in the extreme, what would happen if we eliminated all guns? It would not eliminate murders altogether, of course. There are many other ways to kill people. A primary concern for someone accustomed to using guns would be to keep proximity at a maximum when engaging in gunless killing. So while the gun lobby would be out of business, there might be many replacement industries that crop up that could use the lobbying talents of the NRA.

I introduce you to:

PBDAA

The Poisonous Blow Dart Association of America. Clearly, sales of poisonous blow darts would explode. They are simple to use; all you have to do is breathe hard. They are small and fit nicely into any purse or briefcase. They can be hidden snugly under one's coat. Of course, if they are deemed concealed weapons, there could be some issues. But that's where the lobbyists come in. And it will be a very long time before they correlate mental illness to blow dart sales or deaths.

Where do I invest?

IF I WERE GOD

CDABS

The Crocodile Dundee Aussie Boomerang Society. Those cute little L-shaped wooden toys that you throw and they come back to you. Now, it would not be a weapon if you threw it with the idea of it returning to you. No, that could be dangerous. But if it were just a piece of lightweight wood, what would be the harm in returning? None, but then that's not much of a weapon. That's where the CDABS comes in. They hook up with the metal industry, add some fun aerodynamics, maybe a rocket engine and, *voilà!* Another maximum proximity weapon. This one can come with its own pouch for ease of carry. And plastic safety edges to protect against unwanted surgery from the metal edges sharpened to cut through bone. Plastics get a boon too.

These little ditties come complete with instructions on how to throw and with toy boomers to practice with. The idea is not to return the boomerang, but to be able to attack from a distance, using an arced approach, so the victim does not even know from where the 'rang is coming. This will also impede the criminal investigation afterward, as trajectories can be programmed so no launch point can be pinpointed. Can't do that with guns. Bullets go straight. Maybe this can work even in a gun environment.

WTBABAA

The William Tell Bad Apple Bow & Arrow Alliance. "If you grow it, they will shoot" could be its slogan. Using a bow and arrow is clearly an art. Wind velocity, speed of target, feather capacity, bow tension, and number of vodkas are all inputs into the proficiency equation. OK, I made up the feather capacity shit. But an association is needed to teach all these things to help rookies learn how to be successful in bow killing. Thank you, *Hunger Games*.

Of course, most bow and arrow sets will not fit snugly into

one's purse and hiding the damn things will be problematic. Need to lobby for concealed weapons and really big coats.

WFNRAERSF

We're Fucked if the NRA Ever Resurfaces Slingshot Federation. We would probably need all the other associations to run afoul of the law before the slingshot dudes have a chance. They can always do their thing with rocks. Maybe even jerry-rig it to use poisonous darts. That will take some talent. But these guys are small. The slingshot thing is a little wishbone with a rubber band. That fits anywhere. Stick it in your crotch, and you avoid even a professional frisk. Of course, be a little careful it is not accompanied by a poisonous dart or two.

ARPOWAFP

The Association of Really Pissed-Off Wives of America Frying Pan. This is best used when a rush of adrenaline is in play. The petite frying pan may not require quite the Red Bull rush, but it will also not have as great an impact. It is best used when really pissed and no other options present themselves. Perhaps the knives are across the room, or you failed the most recent knife-throwing course at the local community college.

This particular version is best used by females who have found their husband officially atrocious, and who have made sure the life insurance policy is maximized and fully paid. Practice is encouraged, as this can only be used in relatively close quarters. If one misses when tossing the frying pan, the resultant reaction by the target could put the errant thrower in harm's way. Because training is not available at that lousy community college, the ARPOWAFP is well-suited to provide assistance in both strength and target training. It has also aligned with the PDBAA to strategically position a backup plan within striking distance of the target. Leave the windows open.

CTA

Chakram Throwers Anonymous. Picture a metal Frisbee with a razor-sharp edge. It is similar to the boomerang, but does not have the aerodynamics of a circular route to its target. The downside is the origin of the throw can be triangulated. The upside is accuracy. Any Frisbee player worth his salt can throw it and hit any target square on within its target range.

Motorized versions are available to increase the target range to up to 300 yards. This weapon can be camouflaged effectively. Think Odd Job aiming for James Bond in *Goldfinger*.

SPCT

Society for the Prevention of Cruelty to Tarantulas. Keeping with the James Bond theme and if you are handy at training spiders, this could be very effective. Simply give the tarantula a trail to follow to the intended victim. Best used late at night when said victim is sleeping and unaware of the spider infiltration.

Don't know how to train a tarantula? That is where the SPCT comes in. In an attempt to delay the extinction of this prized spider, the SPCT has created a cottage industry of training techniques that give these darlings of the spider species an alarming advantage over their brethren (whoever the fuck they might be). The beauty of the tarantula weapon is that it's virtually undetectable. Properly trained, it can be released hundreds of feet from its intended victim with no traceability. In addition, they have been trained to withstand intense interrogation, including those enhanced with drugs or torture.

When not used for murder, they make great Christmas gifts for the 7-year-old that has everything. Just make sure he does not hate you.

NPA
Fuck guns, these bad boys can protect you not only from the fucking militia, but also any and all Spartan spear chuckers, Colonial cannonballs, and Klingons.

The National Phaser Association. Hail *Star Trek* and its forward thinking at the time. Who knew?

BACK TO THE FUTURE
But we are here, not there. We still have guns, and we still have laws that govern their use. The 2nd Amendment is going nowhere. Those who are afraid that even the slightest infringement on gun ownership will lead to its repeal are simply smoking something. No one wants it repealed. The right to own a gun to protect oneself is a basic American right.

Ah, but now the fun begins. Is it a basic American right to own a gun to protect the entire free world? Is an automatic or semiautomatic weapon necessary to protect oneself? Guns of every description and killing capacity can and will be manufactured. If illegal here, their manufacture will be legal somewhere. Even if nowhere, someone will illegally manufacture them. So guns of all descriptions will be available for those who want to illegally get them. And they can be used against the legal pea shooters law-abiding citizens will have.

Do we need more than the pea shooter to do what the 2nd Amendment allows—protect ourselves? I do not think the owners of the illegal automatic weapons will be storming our

IF I WERE GOD

house to steal our milk. We, as normal citizens, do not have to worry about automatic weapons being used against us.

If something is illegal, there will be less of it than if it is legal. Yes, those who wish to break the law will still be able to get their hands on those items that are illegal, but there will be less of them and they will cost more. That is simple economics. We will still have our pea shooters to protect ourselves day to day, and that's what we are really worried about.

We read stories every day about how semiautomatic and automatic weapons kill large numbers of people. Pea shooters would kill a lot fewer. Make access to the semiautomatic and automatic weapons more difficult—not impossible, just more difficult—and two undeniable events must occur:

There will be fewer instances of semiautomatic and automatic mass killings. I did not say none. Just fewer, by definition. The perps often used legal weapons they owned. If they didn't own them, would they go out and find them, or use a pea shooter? Or maybe decide the carnage would not be great enough and try something different? Or nothing at all. Or maybe just off themselves.

There will be fewer deaths when a pea shooter is opted for.

This must be weighed against the benefit of an individual owning a semiautomatic or automatic weapon.

We have not yet touched on accidental shootings. These are perhaps the most tragic as they are clearly preventable. Guns are not locked or users are not taught how to properly use them. Sisters killing brothers. Toddlers killing themselves. Here, pea shooters can do just as much damage. The issue is not the 2nd Amendment, it is education and training. And consequences for not heeding the education and training.

GOD 2.0

There is no need or desire to eliminate guns from society. They serve a very useful and important purpose. However, having a gun is not going to prevent the militia from storming your house. Trust me, they will always have a lot bigger and better weapons than you will. And there will be lots of them. So forget that as an excuse for why you need semiautomatic or automatic weapons. You do not.

There is a need to keep all guns locked. If you must keep a gun under your pillow at night, make sure you lock it up during the day and keep junior in his room at night. All those who have access must be properly trained.

Instead of getting rid of guns, let's make the penalty for their illegal use very severe. As in overly severe. See Cruel and Unusual Punishment. Illegal possession maybe loses your hands. Illegal use maybe loses your eyes. Murder maybe provides a torturous death. Punishment is not always a deterrent, but even if it is only once in a while, that means fewer deaths.

If an unlocked gun is used in a crime or an accident occurs, then the owner will be charged with a crime as well.

Hopefully, eventually, if you want to kill someone, you will have to use your hands.

Or blow darts.

CHAPTER 18

PARENTS PUNISHED FOR CRIMES COMMITTED BY THEIR CHILDREN
(Sharing a Jail Cell with Junior)

A SEMINAL MOMENT OF MY RELATIVELY sparse parenting career came at the parental indoctrination about my daughter's ascension to high school. The parents were called in to the high school auditorium shortly before the school year began to learn what was going to happen to our former elementary students. The one statement by the high school principal, among all the wonderful things that my daughter had to look forward to as she entered another stage of approaching adulthood, which took my breath away, was the following:

"For the first time in her life and yours, her peers will have a greater influence on her than you."

Ayyyyyyyyyyyyyyyyyyyyyyyyyyyyyyyyyyyyyy

That was me jumping off a cliff.

Really? I'm even deader meat than I was in eighth grade. I thought the maturity of her entering a school with all older, more mature and parent-appreciating classmates would wake her up to the veracity of parent-provided advice. All the seniors would finally be worshipping their parents because adults are always right, and the exorcism of that grammar school Princess of Darkness would begin.

There was partial correctness there.

The seniors did prevail.

Ayyyyyyyyyyyyyyyyyyyyyyyyyyyyyyyyyyyyyy

My daughter entered high school as a nice young lady, quickly became Linda Blair, but then graduated a nice young lady. What happened in between is anyone's guess.

The point of all of this is to frame a conversation around the influence parents have on their children and whether (and, if so, to what degree) the parents should share in the responsibility if their parenting goes awry.

This reminds me of the story of the high school lad who needed a ride home from a party one night, but his father was not available. One of the other kids' dad was a cop and offered to take him to the police station until he could get a ride home. Wow, he could get a tour of an actual police station and compare it to what he saw on *Kojak*. If only his friend's dad was bald.

So, the young'un is being given a tour of the jail cells when his father finally shows up at the police station to pick him up. Dad goes over to junior and coldcocks him, slamming him against the wall. He turns to the nearest police officer and yells, "So what did he do this time?"

"Uh, nothing, sir. He just needs a ride home."

This was circa 1970, when authority was respected and assumed to be all-knowing, even to this extreme. Circa 2010, Dad would have been more inclined to coldcock the cop and then sue the entire police department for illegally imprisoning his son.

IF I WERE GOD

So what do these two stories have in common? Perspective. When I was growing up, there appeared to be less tolerance for a child's misbehavior than today. Witness coldcock Dad assuming his kid had screwed up and determined to punish him for it, versus today when many kids, certainly more than when I was growing up, are clearly overindulged.

I believe there are two reasons for this. Not based on any studies, not based on any real-life experience, just based on a little brain power channeled in the right direction. There are two major reasons that children in Generation Y and the millennial generation are less disciplined and more indulged than my generation.

Working mothers and broken homes. Ouch, I can hear the women already.

"Mothers have a right to have a career."

"You don't know what it's like if you haven't walked in my shoes."

"You just want to keep us barefoot and pregnant."

I am leaving out the many choice names I am being called. But please understand, this is not a judgment. I am completely in favor of equality between the sexes. Men and women should have equal pay for the same job, an equal chance at the same opportunity. There should be no glass ceiling.

What I am simply saying is that there has been a change in reality. I am stating a fact here, not making a judgment. It is a fact that there are more working mothers and fewer stay-at-home moms. And the number of stay-at-home dads is not on the rise. At least not at the same rate as the rise in working mothers. Therefore, by way of numerical calculation, the average number of hours in a day that a parent spends with a child is down. This by direct correlation means there is less supervision, guidance, and overall structure to a child's life by the parent. The child may be overseen by someone else, but nothing replaces a parent's caring.

Broken homes create the same lessening of parental oversight. There is only one of them at a time. With no one to help day to day. The natural tendency is to let Johnny get away with certain things when "Wait until your father gets home" is not available as a deterrent.

I have another theory, also borne of nothing more than too much time on my hands to think about stuff. One raises their children in the opposite fashion than how they were raised. The simplest example I can think of is strict/lenient. If your parents were very strict, there will be a tendency (likely subconscious) to be less strict with your children. Think about it. When they were preventing you from going to the neighborhood party because there was going to be drinking, you thought they were shitheads. You said to yourself, as you wallowed in your bedroom instead of imbibing, that you would never treat your kids like this. Look how it made you feel. Look at what you were missing out on in life. You would make sure your kid gets to go to every neighborhood party.

And you'll bring the vodka.

Once you have your own kids, you might not do the vodka thing, but you might be inclined to let them do things you were not allowed to. Or not allow them to do anything. Like my dad. He had no parental constraints. He was allowed to do anything he wanted. He liked to tell the story about getting caught doing 100 mph on the George Washington Bridge when he was 17. He was on his way to New Jersey with a 21-year-old. To get married. He might not have met my mom if he hadn't been stopped.

He also liked to tell me that he considered himself lucky to have survived his teenage years as he drank and drove all the time, drove very fast, and participated in various and sundry other activities that could have led to dire results. I looked at it and said, "Man, he had a lot of fun."

What was his reaction when it came time to raising me? I got to do nothing. I couldn't hang out at the local drug store a block from our home where my friends would gather to bullshit.

"Might be drugs."

I couldn't go to parties at friends' houses.

"Might be alcohol."

The driving age in New Jersey was 17, but I was not allowed to get my license.

"I know you will be drinking and driving just like me."

Then when it was difficult for me to go anywhere, "What am I, a fucking taxi?"

An extreme, but very real example of a parent raising his child the opposite of how he was raised.

How did I raise my daughter, you ask?

Her mother had more say than I did, but I was certainly somewhere between lenient and centrist. Not as extreme an opposite as my dad, but his strictness did have its effect on how I wanted to raise my daughter.

MOMMY MADE ME DO IT

Criminal children. Who is responsible? Parent or child? Or both? Does age matter? Once peers take over in high school, does the parent become less culpable?

Society makes laws initially to legislate what not to do, then more laws are created when folks don't listen to society's ideas. We need to create a punishment to deter the activity we are trying to prevent. I knew a spanking was at hand if I got too out of line as a kid. Now, a simple threat of no cell phone for a day will keep most preteens in line. If a significant enough penalty is exacted, then behavior can be modified. *Voila!* Society.

What if society said, "Hey, Mom and Dad, if your kids fuck up, you pay a price as well." If a significant enough penalty to parents is exacted, will their behavior change to more strongly control the actions of their children? If parents are found liable for their children's actions when they are young, will they do a better job at raising them? Will the children end up less inclined to commit crime? One would think so, but is it fair to hold someone (Mom or Dad) responsible for the action of another (Junior)?

There is a host of legislation out there that holds parents to some level of accountability. Most parental responsibility statutes punish parents for what they haven't done, rather than what they have done. The laws make parents criminally liable because they have not fulfilled their parental duty to keep their kids from breaking the law. These laws are based on a number of theories, including:

Parents have a legal duty to prevent their children from committing crimes.

Parental accountability is an effective way to decrease juvenile crime rates.

In many cases, the penalties are somewhat demure. Going for counseling, performing community service, and paying a fine are among the less severe consequences. Certain states will provide for incarceration of the parents for more heinous crimes by their offspring.

IF I WERE GOD

When should a parent be responsible for the criminal actions of their children?

Don't parents, by definition, give their child everything they can? When is everything enough? Is effort good enough? Let's face it, we were not taught how to be parents. Maybe it's our parents who fucked us up into being shitty parents.

Parents *are* the reason children turn out as they do as adults. Sure, the environment plays a part, but the parents have a lot to say about that environment in the beginning. Children only know what their parents allow them to. Catholics are brought up to believe in God and the church. If that is all they are exposed to, then that is what they will believe because they know nothing else. If they never met a Buddhist or an atheist, they would never know alternate experiences exist. If a child is brought up among wolves, it will never know about planes and cities and computers. If that child is told that there awaits a wonderful afterlife providing they always listen to their parents, then they will do whatever their parents say. Even if it means jumping off a cliff. Mom says junior will fly; Junior knows nothing different, so he jumps.

Even if it means putting on a suicide bomb and pulling the trigger.

The point to all of this is that parental influence is absolute. So parents must teach their children how to become responsible human beings and respectful of laws and others.

OR DID SHE?

But society does not mandate this. There is no law that says parents must raise their children a certain way. Nor is there a handbook that says "do this" and "don't do that." Parents rely on the tools they were given by their parents, who had no handbook. And so on.

So if parents were not armed by society with information sufficient to raise children, how can society fault them when they screw up raising their children and produce criminals? But wait, the environment can have a significant impact on their (mis)behavior. Ah, but the parents control that environment.

The argument can go back and forth, but we all agree parents bear many responsibilities, among them providing for their child's basic needs, ensuring the child is educated, and protecting the child from harm. In addition, parents are responsible for instilling moral values and social norms. When children are young, parents are able to exert a considerable amount of influence in compelling them to conform to the values and norms they have been taught. Parents reinforce positive behavior and punish those actions that do not conform to expectations. As a child ages and begins to develop his or her decision-making faculties, parental influence diminishes.

And those high school assholes take over.

Responsible parenting involves far more than taking care of a child's basic needs. It requires a genuine desire to raise a child from birth into adulthood by means of teaching responsible, acceptable behavior. This, of course, takes time, common sense, and a genuine love for the safety and future of one's child. In today's society, parents are consistently using other means, such as childcare centers, schools, X-Box, iPads, apps, or the internet to occupy a child's idle time.

No judgment, just facts. Working mothers and broken homes.

CAN WE GET AN A FOR EFFORT?

Studies have shown that parenting is related to delinquency

IF I WERE GOD

in their children. There are concepts such as positive parenting and negative parenting. And parental monitoring. Sometimes negative parenting characteristics, such as neglect, rejection, and hostility, can lead to an increased possibility of criminal behavior in children. Poor parental monitoring can also lead to increased risk. Lack of positive parenting characteristics (love, affection, and support) can lead to a heightened risk of deviant behavior. But to temper this thought, just because you don't give Jane a big hug every time she helps with dinner does not mean she will become Bonnie Parker.

But shit, if I can't avoid that negative shit, my child will become a criminal, and if I don't show enough love, my child will become a criminal. What the fuck do I do?

Do the best you can given the tools you have.

But we may be the best of parents, and things can still go wrong. We may do all we can to give our children the tools to keep them out of trouble and on the right path in society, and they still fuck up. Should Mom and Dad pay?

We are responsible for what our children do, because they are our children. We brought them into this world to become part of society—society did not ask for them. To cast blame onto others ("Oh, those high school assholes") or pretend we aren't responsible for neglecting to keep our children safe, and society safe from their criminal tendencies, is wrong.

Unfortunately, our society tends toward ignoring instead of punishing parents for irresponsible teachings or lack thereof and is OK with others footing the cost of their inadequate or nonexistent parental skills. Something is wrong with that society.

Regardless, think about this. If you were to be punished for the acts of your children, would you bring them up any differently? Would you take a few extra minutes a day to make sure Junior knows right from wrong? Would you be more inclined to protect them from risks that could lead them astray if you might go to jail with them? Does the prospect of sharing a jail cell with Junior affect your choices?

Unfortunately, the answer is "yes." Why is this unfortunate? Because many don't (won't) do it without the threat of going to jail. Wouldn't it be wonderful if we all did these things *without* that threat? Isn't that what parenting should be all about?

And if your answer is "no," then you really do belong in prison with your child.

Even if we do everything right, accidents can happen. They require responsibility and compensation. As a kid, if we throw the ball over our friend's head and break a neighbor's window, we (or our parents) have to pay for it. If, as an adult, we have a car accident that is our fault, we pay for it. It may have been caused by ice on the road or even a bolt of lightning, but our car was affected, and we rammed someone who was lucky enough not to be affected until they met us. So we embrace compensation for accidents.

Oh, that's easy. It's only money. Or most of the time, insurance. But if the penalty for little Sandy Koufax breaking the neighbor's widow was jail time for Mr. and Mrs. Koufax, guess what? Sandy is not throwing a ball anywhere near an abode.

UNWANTED CIRCUMSTANCES

Holding parents responsible for their children's crimes could have unwanted effects. For one, low-income families—particularly single-parent ones—would be targeted disproportionately. Poorer parents tend to work longer hours and have less time to look after their kids. Is it fair to hold

IF I WERE GOD

those who are less capable of acceding to society's norms to the same standard as those who have full capability? If yes, that means we are holding those who have not been given the tools to comply with those norms fully responsible despite a disadvantage. But if no, society is paying because a family unit was incapable of remaining together.

This is a tough one.

There can be extenuating circumstances and leniency when it is difficult to comply with the law. But should there be? When is compliance other than black and white? Either you ran the red light or you stopped. Either you pulled the trigger or you didn't. In criminal cases where intent can be illegal, perhaps we have an analogy. Conspiring to commit a crime is a crime. In some cases, passive ignorance of the possibility of a crime can be a crime. It is called criminal negligence. It is the crime of causing injury or harm as the result of doing something or failing to provide a proper or reasonable level of care. So we can go to jail because we failed to do what society thinks we should do.

But I have to go back to the single parent whose partner is gone and the remaining parent is being suffocated by financial woes. Do we punish people because they got pregnant and are unable to provide the proper parenting for their children? We need to recognize unforeseen circumstances when intentions are proper, but also must consider that, regardless of situation, a level of parental responsibility is required. And in this instance, such responsibility may only be defined by the lack or presence of delinquent behavior.

I'm sorry, but if you bring a child into this world, you have a responsibility to society to make sure that child brings no harm to society. Regardless of whether the dad or someone else has screwed with you. You drive a car, you have an obligation not to hurt someone else regardless of the distractions of your shitty life. If you can't handle that, don't drive. If you can't handle that, don't have a kid.

Comparing having a child to driving a car is almost scurrilous, but society allows us to have a kid with less restrictions than driving a car. We have to parallel park to get a license; we do not have to make sure a child goes to school to be a parent. We have to come to a full stop at a stop sign to get a license; we don't have to stop our children from hanging out with undesirables to be a parent.

So do we punish the mom who hasn't a husband as harshly as one who does? Here is where degree and repetition come into play. Punish, but allow circumstances to ameliorate the punishment. The first time. The second time, I'm sorry, but whatever your situation in life is, once you have been warned that you need to do something about your child and you don't, then you go to jail too.

WHAT'S A MOTHER TO DO?

It is human nature to do things to make our lives easier or to avoid making them more difficult. We pay our bills so we don't get charged interest and can get more credit when we need it. We don't go through red lights so we don't get mowed down by an 18-wheeler. Instinctively, we live our lives selfishly. Most of us, anyway. Bring pleasure, avoid pain. That is why we follow laws—it avoids pain. Most law-abiding citizens go out of their way to do this. But if there is no law, they may very easily engage in the activity. Even if it is dangerous.

I don't go 100 mph in my car because it is illegal. I have done it, and it was quite a rush and really scary, but my biggest motivation for not doing it is fear of losing my license. This is easy because it is a do-or-don't decision in which the choice is clear. And the law-abiding activity is clear—don't do 100.

IF I WERE GOD

Raising kids is completely different. One's definition of the right thing to do is someone else's belief that such thing will lead to bad things. If there were no speed limits, how fast would we go? I would certainly go faster than the current limits, but would I challenge 140? Where is that line that distinguishes appropriate behavior from harmful behavior? Cars are designed to go really fast. But how fast is "really?"

So let's say there are no speed limits, but the cops decide to give me a ticket for speeding. If I don't know how fast I am allowed to go, how can I be ticketed for going too fast? Does the cop get to decide that 80 is speeding? Maybe a different cop thinks it's 90.

The analogy here is to parenting. There are no speed limits to parenting. No laws that dictate proper parenting behavior. Yet there are laws that punish parents for harming society by not exhibiting proper parenting behavior. Where is the speed limit sign?

If parents know they will be responsible for their children's behavior, will it make a difference? Or will just those unlucky ones whose kids got caught be punished? Will that responsibility be an incentive to provide the kind of loving, supportive home necessary to reduce the risk of poor behavior? Or are genes (or the environment) at play here as well, creating the potential for even the most loved child to go astray?

Will it cause couples to think twice about having kids because they might go to jail if the little ones go astray?

It is like the parents who have two children who turn out very differently. Perhaps one is a rocket scientist and the other is experimenting too much with bad science. They claim to have raised them in an identical manner. They can't understand what went wrong.

PA BROOK

Duh.

Parents who have multiple children find it difficult to believe that they raised their children differently. But parents who have multiple children can easily identify how other parents have raised their multiple children differently. Of course, it is obvious. Just not for one's own kids.

One cannot help raise a first child differently than its sibling. Too many things subsequently change. As in it takes more effort to raise two children than one.

Where is this going?

You want to bring a kid into this world? Then, damnit, be prepared to take care of that kid. Be prepared to sacrifice to make sure that child is taught how to be a respectful and productive human being. If you don't, then you get to share a jail cell with your delinquent child. If you drive a car that is badly in need of brakes but choose not to take care of that issue and you run over someone, guess what? You are not excused because a car has a mind of its own. And guess further what? If it truly is an accident, like an icy road, then you still remain responsible for monetary damages simply because of your bad luck. Granted, you don't go to jail, but if a child is responsible for a civil tort, then someone has to pay. Sorry, Mom and Dad.

What about divorced Dad (or Mom)? While divorced dads may have 50% custody per the settlement agreement (witness mine), they often only have every other weekend and Wednesday nights (witness mine). If junior engages in criminal activity, does Dad receive the same punishment as Mom?

Yikes.

I know in my case, Mom had a much bigger influence than I did, but fortunately, our daughter turned out beautifully.

IF I WERE GOD

If she became an ax murderer, I would certainly blame her mother and her mother would blame me. But what should society say? Should Mom be more to blame than Dad? What if Dad was fucking around with Mom's best friend and that caused the divorce? Dad screwed up the family unit and forced Mom into a majority upbringing position. And maybe junior went on a murderous rampage out of anger that Dad was screwing the neighbor. It would not be fair to put a heavier weight on innocent Mom vs. asshole Dad.

Now what?

GOD 2.0

There is no one magic bullet for any issue. This is not golf. Parents do not get a mulligan for the crimes of their children. Legislators have enacted laws to address these untenable issues for a very long time. This is no different. With a hefty amount of latitude to adjust punishment, parents should be punished for their children's crimes at some fraction of the punishment meted out to the child.

For example, if that fraction is ½, then a child sentenced to 6 months in jail gets Mom and/or Dad 3 months. To allow for a myriad of reasons that could reduce the culpability of parents in their children's demise, a first offense can be mitigated to no jail time and no record. But after that, be forewarned.

This is way too complex, with way too many variables, to adjudicate with exactness. I leave it in the hands of smart people to figure out with healthy input from those who don't have and will never have children to eliminate parental bias.

I thought being God would be fun.

CHAPTER 19
INSANITY DEFENSE
(If You Are Full of Shit, You Must Acquit)

Damn, I have watched enough *Law and Order* reruns, I should know this topic by heart. "Not guilty by reason of mental defect" was a plea heard dozens of times.

I have lots of mental defects and can't get away with shit.

In English (or at least my English), an insanity plea means the perp either didn't know what he was doing or didn't know right from wrong. Maybe he was just stupid. The insanity defense reflects the generally accepted notion that someone who is "insane" should not be punished for criminal acts. A mental institution is the preferred treatment.

Inmates at *One Flew Over the Cuckoo's Nest* may not have agreed.

Most jurisdictions have some form of mental incapacity mitigating statute (say that three times fast). Even if judged guilty, evidence of insanity may be considered a mitigating factor for sentencing.

An insanity plea is rarely used and when used, rarely works. There are cases in which an insanity plea did not work, and the defendant received a longer sentence than if he hadn't pled insanity.

That's the way to tell someone he is full of shit.

Insanity pleas are only used in criminal cases. Some of the more famous ones follow.

JOHN HINCKLEY JR.
In 1981, Hinckley shot President Ronald Reagan and injured a police officer, a Secret Service agent, and Reagan's press secretary. Hinckley's defense claimed he was insane. He had become obsessed with Jodie Foster and her role in *Taxi Driver* and figured the best way to impress her would be to kill the president. I don't want to be near him when he gets on Tinder.

Hinckley was found not guilty by reason of insanity.

I'm obsessed with Charlize Theron. Who's pissed me off lately? Mmmm.

LORENA BOBBITT
Lorena Bobbitt and her husband, John Wayne Bobbitt, became celebrities in 1993. In a story unsettling to every male in the world, and as likely to keep them on the straight and narrow as *Fatal Attraction*, she cut off his manhood. She claimed insanity, citing a long history of sexual, physical, and emotional abuse at his hands. Or manhood. The jury ultimately accepted the argument that she'd snapped because of the mistreatment and ruled her not guilty by reason of insanity. She spent 45 days being evaluated at a state hospital, after which she was released.

She is currently someone's next-door neighbor. I wonder what her dating profile looks like.

DAVID RIGGINS

When pleading insanity, a defendant might not want to present the best possible image to the jury. Acting crazy can only enhance one's insanity defense. A defendant was charged with robbery and murder. After being taken into custody, the defendant complained that he was hearing voices in his head and having trouble sleeping.

Shit, that happens every time I have an internet date.

A psychiatrist at the jail prescribed drugs that kept this under control. By trial, he was taking 8 times the original dosage and acting like you would have brought him home to Mom. Just before trial, the defendant's attorney asked that he be taken off his meds so the jury could see the defendant in his natural, unglued state. He was denied. The defendant was convicted and sentenced to death. Eventually the Supreme Court overturned the conviction, noting that he had the right to be crazy in the courtroom.

Just like lawyers.

DANIEL SICKLES

In perhaps the first reported case that used insanity as a defense, Daniel Sickles, a politician back in the mid-1800s, at times exhibited poor judgment. Like the time he supposedly invited a prostitute into the New York State Assembly and subsequently introduced her to Queen Victoria.

That's back when politics was fun.

But that is not why he pleaded insanity. He shot and killed a man, claiming the proverbial next-door neighbor made him do it. Apparently, he was so distraught because his wife was having an affair that he had been driven temporarily insane.

Shit, if I'm killing anyone, it's her.

IF I WERE GOD

It appears he had powerful friends, or a bunch of hookers on the jury, as he was acquitted of murder.

JAMAICAN ME CRAZY

Insanity is only used in criminal cases. What if it were allowed in civil cases as well?

I don't have to pay alimony to the bitch because I was fucking insane to marry her.

You fell on ice on *my* sidewalk? Bummer. I am a New York Jets fan.

I'm obsessed with Hot Lips Houlihan. Too bad if I amputated the wrong leg.

Which reminds me of the George Carlin warning: "Someone, somewhere has an appointment with the world's worst doctor." Has to be. Right? Hope it's not you or me. And make sure Doc isn't a *M*A*S*H* lover.

But insanity is a real legal defense. There have been many other creative ways to get shitheads off. I chronicle some of the more interesting.

NEO MADE ME DO IT

Fans of *The Matrix* will recall how a computer hacker named Neo thinks he discovered that life is but a dream, created by some bad guy cyber-intelligence dudes for the purpose of fooling us into thinking it is not a dream, but real. Until we wake up, or is it fall asleep, and then realize it was (or was not) a dream. I am fucking confused, and I saw the movie.

Actually, I was not a fan. A little too "out there" for me, even though I am a science fiction buff. Or maybe I don't like Keanu Reeves. He is a monotone actor who got lucky because of his looks. It's like if I became a star of a commercial for hair removal just because I have the world's hairiest back.

PA BROOK

Genes, not talent, got me there. Although I did like *Speed*, but that's because I have always had the hots for Sandra Bullock.

My kind of genes.

While I am at it, Keanu Reeves is not the worst actor ever. That distinction belongs to Kevin Costner. Another monotone actor whose favored gene pool would have been destroyed in *my* science fiction movie.

As usual, I digress. *The Matrix* has actually been used as a defense for criminal trials. Neo made me do it. Possibly the most famous case was a woman who got a little too into *The Matrix*, believing most of life was a bad dream. This particular day, she must have had a really bad one. She thought her landlady was part of a scheme to brainwash her. She shot her. In the head. This is usually fatal. She could have just moved to another neighborhood.

Her lawyer told the jury (apparently suppressing a laugh the entire time) that the dreamer thought she was part of a computer simulation where she could kill anything she wanted. The jury found her crazy.

In another use of the Matrix Defense, some dude who was institutionalized in his home country before coming to the United States, unsurprisingly, hacked, chopped, and diced his landlady's body.

No wonder I can't find an apartment anywhere.

He claimed she was emitting "evil vibes," perhaps trying to brainwash him. He was afraid of being sucked into the Matrix. Killing the potential sucker seemed the only rational way to avoid that. He pled insanity and was quickly sent to his own kind of matrix.

One last Neo. This guy got dressed up like Neo, looked over

at his gun (he was 19; of course he had one in his room), checked out Neo in the poster on the wall, and filled his pockets with bullets. And then killed his parents.

His lawyer thought he was insane based on a bad upbringing, being adopted, and being dissed by the Marines. She had actually planned a defense that was based on Neo really making him do it. Luckily for the courts, all parties agreed to a plea deal and the kid got 40 years.

SLEEPWALKING

I remember those old horror films with the ghost walking around at night while sleeping and scaring the shit out of everyone. OK, maybe it was a *Three Stooges* episode. I have no idea. I just got this visual and had to express it. Hey, it's my book!

There are various schools of thought when it comes to sleepwalking. I present only those that are self-serving.

Sleepwalking is a sleep disorder in which the person appears to be awake and does shit, but is still really asleep. Or fucking with you. The stuff done can be harmless or harmful. We are here to talk about the bad stuff.

A couple of facts (I try to keep them to a minimum): Sleepwalking usually occurs soon after falling asleep (within two or three hours) and generally lasts less than fifteen minutes. Stories of longer sleepwalking episodes raise eyebrows. It *is* rather easy to fake.

Causes of sleepwalking are debated, with use of alcohol, drugs, and medication (I think that's a drug) frequently heading the list of voluntary behaviors. Stress, personal crises, and sleep deprivation have also been cited. Research suggests that people prone to sleepwalking can reduce or even eliminate sleepwalking episodes through simple lifestyle changes, such as reduced alcohol and drug consumption (duh), regular sleeping schedules (hello, ZzzQuil), and stress reduction (HELLO! Xanax). Oh, wait, that's increased drug consumption. Drugs can cure sleepwalking. And cause it. I'm confused.

I think I need a nap.

So some really smart, née sleazy, dude came up with a "sleepwalking defense." Its premise is that if one was sleepwalking while committing a despicable act, the defendant isn't guilty because he had no control over the act and no intent. Unless he was faking.

I'm stopping here with the technical shit. I think you get the point. If you are truly insane and don't know what you are doing, maybe you get some help instead of jail. If you are sleepwalking, do you know what you are doing? They say you can't do something under hypnosis that you would not do while awake. Who "they" are doesn't matter. Someone said it at some point. A corollary would be that one could not do something while sleepwalking if they could not do it while awake.

My corollary.

A couple of examples, please.

So the smart, née sleazy, dude first came up with this flash in the 1800s. His client slit a prostitute's throat, set fire to the brothel, and then took off. The lawyer found several witnesses that swore he exhibited weird behavior. Slicing a throat would qualify. After a six-hour summation (that's more than Jack McCoy summated in 20 years), the jury either got bored or bought it, as his client was acquitted.

In what may be my favorite malpractice case of all time, it was heard that the now free killer sued for half his legal fees to be refunded because the jury was so easily swayed.

IF I WERE GOD

In another case, a man stabbed his wife 44 times, then dragged her into a backyard pool and drowned her. I guess he had flunked out of Stabbing School. The widower claimed he had a history of sleepwalking and was sleep-deprived at the time of the attack. It didn't work. He found out what real sleep deprivation was like when he got to jail and his cellmate was Moose.

I DIDN'T MARRY THEM

A man got out of bed in the middle of the night and drove 14 miles to his in-laws' house. Without his wife. Seems a tad unusual to me. I had two sets of in-laws and never once came close to getting out from under the covers next to my naked wife to go pay a visit to her parents. Imagine me, not once. Shitty son-in-law I was.

I think I found a shittier one. This guy attacked his in-laws, strangling his father-in-law until he passed out and bludgeoning his mother-in-law with a tire iron, then stabbing both of them with a kitchen knife. Now that's passive-aggressive.

He claimed he was sleepwalking. According to one report, he was dreaming that his mother-in-law blew a huge lead on *Family Feud*. I dare you to look it up. They did some tests and found he had an abnormal brain.

Shit, the tire iron didn't convince you?

But he was diagnosed with some sleep disorder and the prosecution couldn't come up with a motive. Isn't "in-law" defined as a motive?

He was acquitted but won't be getting a sleepover invite from me anytime soon.

There are many other cases of sleepwalking defenses with varying degrees of success. There is a lot of debate on this issue, with some believing that if you were indeed sleepwalking, then you had no control and by definition are not guilty. Others believe there is at least some degree of volition involved as it was you who did it, and you are not insane. So the sleepwalker must bear some responsibility.

Is it worse if he snores?

PILLOW TALK
In what might be deemed similar to sleepwalking, research reports have diagnosed a behavior that includes sex while sleeping as sexsomnia. I would have preferred sleepboffing.

My kind of disorder.

Apparently sexsomnia is a recognized disorder that can cause unusual or perhaps even unwanted sexual advances while sleeping, including masturbation, fondling, intercourse, and sexual assault/rape.

I used to have wet dreams. Never killed anyone.

Sexsomnia may be caused by sleep apnea or sleep-related epilepsy. It may also be caused by the use of alcohol and sleep deprivation, both of which are controllable.

The results have sometimes been OK, with the affected person arousing his or her partner for consensual, enjoyable sex, even though the afflicted may not remember. One report had a woman describe her boyfriend as being a better lover with more effective technique while asleep than when awake.

Now that's a tongue full.

Sometimes, however, the results are not OK. Like the man who fell asleep at a house party on an L-shaped couch, with a woman sleeping at the other end. She awoke suddenly because he was on top of her, trying to have sex. He was arrested but used the sexsomnia defense. He had been sleep deprived, had taken drugs, and had ingested a shitload of alcohol. Sounds to me like he was just drunk and high. But at his trial, he claimed he had a history of sleep disorders, and this confluence of events led to its recurrence. He was eventually acquitted.

I think there was a confluence of sleep-deprived idiots on the jury.

THE PMS DEFENSE

A female doctor was stopped for driving erratically with her three children in the back seat. The doctor verbally abused a police officer and tried (but only tried) to physically abuse him (apparently her aim at the groin was a little off, owing to her erraticism). She also flunked a Breathalyzer test. She got a doctor to testify that her conduct was consistent with PMS. Raging hormones made me do it. Amazingly, she was acquitted.

I'm no woman, but I know when I am too drunk to drive. And I know not to drive drunk with kids in the back seat. And I certainly know not to yell at a cop who wants to arrest me. And if I am going to try to kick anyone in the balls, I am never going to be too drunk to miss.

If you think that one was bad, a woman got off a murder charge after stabbing another worker to death when she claimed she was not in control of her actions because of PMS. She claimed to turn into a "raging animal" each month. It appears she also kept a diary that documented how each of her prior 30 convictions and multiple suicide attempts occurred around the time of her menstrual cycle. That's one long menstrual cycle, or one crazy bitch.

I would think someone would have taken steps to keep her under wraps during "hunting season."

Her PMS defense led to a conviction for manslaughter instead of murder, with a significant reduction in jail time.

If O. J. Simpson had tits, he would not have needed the glove.

HOMOSEXUAL PANIC DEFENSE

The Homosexual Panic Defense (HPD) is based on a scientific and medical explanation of, and justification for, the behavior of defendants who murder gay individuals. The basic theory of this defense posits that a homosexual solicitation can cause a latently gay defendant to "panic," to become temporarily unable to distinguish right from wrong, and to severely beat or kill the solicitor. So if you think you might be gay but are trying to avoid the feelings, stay away from real gays, because you might kill them.

There is a variation of the defense that says, simply, a person is so disgusted by gays that any advance by them enrages the person and deletes control from his mind, providing a medical/psychological justification for the behavior. Such justification removes culpability of the perpetrator. He temporarily became insane and therefore should not be punished. The homo made me do it.

A couple of examples:

After finding out that a fellow male had a crush on him (on national TV no less), this dude went out and bought a shotgun, drove to his suitor's house, and shot him to death. Three days later. He claimed that the humiliation of being publicly pursued made him lose his mind. He argued that this "debilitation" should allow him to go free since he had no control. He sort of won, getting a lesser, though still severe, sentence.

In another case, a 17 year-old testified that he was urinating in an alley when an "old man" grabbed him from behind. The

IF I WERE GOD

defendant picked up a 4-foot-long stick, attacked the old man, and eventually killed him. The defendant pleaded not guilty, asserting that his actions were the result of an acute homosexual panic brought on by a fear that the old man was trying to engage in a homosexual act. Of course, flight wasn't an option. No way he would be able to outrun the "old man"...killing him was the only option. Fortunately, the jury found the defendant guilty of second-degree murder.

In another case, when the victim put his hands around the defendant's waist, the defendant lost his temper and stabbed him to death. In his confession, the defendant basically said the victim was trying to bring him over to the dark side and it made him completely insane. Once again, it was the jury that was insane when they convicted the defendant of a lesser offense, giving some credence to the "if he likes dick, I can kill him" defense.

In this next one, the perpetrator probably was gay. He agreed to spend the night with the victim and to share his bed. When the victim began to make a move on him, he jumped out of bed and went for a drink.

That's my typical reaction when the person I want to sleep with reaches for me. But I come back with some strawberries and whipped cream.

This guy came back to the bedroom with a meat cleaver and a roasting fork, and when the next advance occurred, he began cleaving and stabbing the victim. Apparently, as one who did not wield sharps objects proficiently, he felt he needed to choke him and jump on his head to finish the task. Apparently, he was a dropout from the Jim Bowie Lifetime Achievement Award competition.

He tried the HPD, but finally a jury saw the light and convicted this bastard to the full extent.

So let us summarize. One is allowed to offer as a defense to murder that one was solicited by a person of the same sex, which made one crazy. So to take this to another level, if someone makes you uncomfortable about anything, then you can kill him.

How about if you are solicited by someone of the opposite sex? Or so you think.

Two guys had sex with a woman, then found out after the fact (not sure how that was possible) that she was a transsexual who had more body parts than the guys expected. Instead of getting a couple of drinks, taking pictures, and cataloguing it for their next dating book, they murdered her. They claimed to have been enraged to the state of insanity when man parts suddenly appeared. It became known as the Trans Panic Defense. The first jury did not convict them, meaning at least one person thought it was OK to kill someone because of unusual genitals.

Takes hung jury to another level.

They were ultimately found guilty of murder at the second trial.

This could spin completely out of control...

The Annoying Spouse Panic Defense,

The Shitty Boss Panic Defense, or

The Bad Toupee Panic Defense.

I could kill almost everybody I know. Or they, me.

NEXT TIME ON... *SURVIVOR*

Some future cases may include:

My new girlfriend decides to put on *Fox News* and another

IF I WERE GOD

round of right-wing bullshit is being spewed at me, making me feel incredibly inadequate. Where's the meat cleaver?

My mother-in-law tells my wife, in front of me, how she wished her daughter had married Joe Captain of the Football Team instead of me. Where's my gun? Oh, the Democrats took it away.

And you thought I was going to get political.

My next new girlfriend (these women are not getting the picture here) thinks she is enjoying the strawberries, but when I am unable to extract them (yes, them—what was I thinking, using the whole quart?), she kills me with her curling iron.

And uses the PMS Defense.

I am not sure the visual is working quite right.

AFFLUENZA

The term "affluenza" (a combination of "affluent" and "influenza") has been used to refer to an inability to understand the consequences of one's actions because of financial privilege. In other words, you are so rich you become mentally incompetent to be held responsible for your actions. Seriously? Too many zeros and too little remorse. Sounds like a pretty good way to get away with a lot of shit.

Someone actually did.

Affluenza became a famous legal defense when a 16-year-old got drunk at a party and struck a group of people with his car, killing 4 of them and injuring others. The kid had been witnessed stealing beer from a store and speeding at 70 miles per hour in a 40-miles-per-hour zone. He was also under the influence of alcohol and a tranquilizer.

A psychologist testified that he suffered from "affluenza"

because he had a dysfunctional relationship with his wealthy parents. That dysfunction not only gave him a lifestyle others could only dream about, but also stole any sense of personal responsibility. I guess money can't buy happiness. Or at least not responsibility. His attorneys successfully argued that he suffered from affluenza and needed rehabilitation, not prison.

As a result, the teenager was given probation. He killed 4 people while on a drunken vehicular rampage and got no jail time. One would think one would count one's blessings and perhaps live a better lifestyle. No sense doubling down when you just hit the lottery. But no, he couldn't resist violating the terms of his probation, which included not being present in the presence of alcohol. He went to a party where alcohol was served. He was arrested and charged with violating his probation. He then had to serve 180 days in prison for each person he killed. Finally, some justice.

As a sidebar, while the family's wealth was a major part of his affluenza, his estranged parents were unable to pay for his court-ordered rehabilitation. So, the state picked up most of the nearly $200,000 that his treatment cost. Presumably treatment to cure him from affluenza.

Hopefully it included a lobotomy.

BIZARRE LEGAL DEFENSES
If that was not enough, here is more creativity.

BUSTED
A woman used her breasts for an interesting and different reason. To get off. No, not to get someone else off, but to get herself off. As in, out of legal trouble. She was accused of breaking and entering into a house via a hole in a door, however, upon further review, it was determined that her

breasts were so large, she could not possibly have fit through the hole.

If they don't fit, you must acquit.

LORENA BOBBITT SHE AIN'T
A woman was charged with vehicular manslaughter in the death of her boyfriend. She claimed she was not driving, but instead she was giving her boyfriend a blow job at the time of the accident. He was thrown from the car and found with his pants down.

But he was "intact." She was acquitted.

POLLY REALLY WANTS A CRACKER
An accused murderer attempted to enlist the testimony of... his parrot. Not your typical expert witness, the parrot was allegedly heard to say "Richard, no, no, no" right after the murder. The accused was *not* named Richard and claimed that this proved someone else did the deed.

I am not sure how he was able to prove that the parrot said this shortly after the murder. Unless he was there. He was convicted.

The parrot is serving time for perjury.

MY KIND OF SPEED
I was pulled over once for doing 80 in a 50 mph zone. It was just fast enough to put me into the "lose your license" paragraph of the statute. When the judge asked me why I was going so fast, I replied, "I guess I wasn't paying attention."

"Not the answer I wanted to hear," came the snotty judge's reply.

I lost my license for 14 days.

Had I been more original, perhaps I would have prevailed. Unfortunately, I was only married to one person at the time. She was also my attorney.

Apparently a man in Scotland was able to speed past the "lose your license" paragraph with a very unique excuse. Or rather, a need. He had two wives. He needed to commute between them each day in order to fulfill his husbandly duties.

Where was my attorney with that defense?

HE AIN'T HEAVY, HE'S MY BROTHER

With thanks to the Hollies, two guys actually carried each other. To freedom. Brother one was arrested for drug trafficking. He was caught red-handed, complete with DNA evidence. Brother two, however, looked like brother one. In fact, they were identical twins. At trial, they both showed up and confused the shit out of everyone. Since no one could figure out which one was the "caught red-handed" dude, there was no further prosecution.

HOMOPHOBIC BIGFOOT DEFENSE

A man charged with trying to do nasty stuff to a child claimed he was himself molested as a child. By Bigfoot (not the Howard Stern whack packer). He had already been convicted, but was looking to the court for leniency.

And this was the best he could come up with?

He got 20 years anyway.

GOD 2.0

If you do something bad, you need to be punished. Think of the other guy. He is dead, or maimed, or out of money. Clearly worse off than you. Even if you are insane, you need to be punished. You still harmed someone or society. Just

IF I WERE GOD

because you did not know it was wrong to shoot someone in the head or did not understand that one could die from a knife to the heart, you still killed him. He is dead; you are not.

The punishment should not be different. Crazy dude goes to maximum security prison along with sane dude for the same amount of time. Crazy dudes are segregated so they cannot be taken advantage of by the sane dudes, but they live just as harsh a life. Medication is available and administered as deemed appropriate. The difference comes at the time of parole. The crazy person is evaluated for sanity as well as rehabilitation. A crazy person will come up for parole sooner than a sane person, allowing society to mitigate the punishment at some point after extracting a punishment.

There will no longer be an insanity defense that can be used for acquittal. The only use of an insanity plea is for how the culprit is treated once inside jail. This will eliminate many court cases as this defense will no longer be available, making a plea bargain for a lesser criminal charge more appealing.

Remember, whether you are crazy or not, the guy you killed is dead. He would prefer insane.

THE PURSUIT OF HAPPINESS

CHAPTER 20

GOLF
(Is It Really a Sport?)

EVERYONE HAS HEARD OR MADE a joke about golf. Grown men (mostly) hit a tiny ball with a stick, trying to get it into an almost as tiny hole they can't even see three to four football fields away. Of course, in the old days, this was done in the midst of Mother Nature, well before manicuring was used to make something other than toes and fingers pretty. So, tall grass, the occasional (or perhaps frequent) tree, natural contours of the landscape, rocks, water, and I'm willing to bet, frequent dead animals, were all part of this surefire funfest.

At least dinner would be spoken for. I can imagine the guys telling their girls they were going hunting, when in reality they were going golfing. They were simply hoping to come across a "hazard" for dinner while they were gleefully chasing that little ball.

I bet par back then was 30 or 40, which likely equaled a fraction of the number of balls lost. Kind of like my golf game today.

THAT WAS THEN, THIS IS ANXIETY
So how did we get from the dead deer laden golf course of

old to the beautifully manicured golf course of today? As with most sports, you want to take as much luck out of it as possible, so the most skillful have the best chance to win. The original Golf Gods came up with the idea of creating an actual course to eliminate some of the luck. You know, get rid of the rocks and dead animals, cut down trees, mow the grass in certain areas, and place a flagpole in the hole so one can see something to aim for from far away. But they decided to make it a thin pole, small enough in circumference to allow the golf ball entry if it were stroked perfectly. Which happens once in a millennium.

On every par 3 ever played by anyone, the thought of a hole in one creeps into your mind. "Wow, my five iron is designed to go exactly 180 yards. If I get lucky…"

But it just creates anxiety.

See, when you hit the best shot of your life and it ends up 2 inches short of the cup, you get mad. Profanities fly, and sometimes, so does your five iron. And with each subsequent fantasy of being just 2 inches longer, you do this again and again, defying the definition of insanity. And damaging your five iron. Pharmaceutical companies are kept in business by the ingestion of psychotic prescription drugs because of the false allure of a hole-in-one. If the pole was just a little thicker, then a hole-in-one would really be impossible. *Voila!* Less anxiety.

PAR FOR THE COURSE

When they took the natural obstacles and subsequent bad luck of running into those things out of the equation, par went from 40 to 4 overnight. The wise Golf Gods said, "We just spent $7 million clearing away all that stuff so our guys can see the pin and flag and play without the impediment of obstacles. Hit the ball far and straight and you win."

IF I WERE GOD

But some diabolical genius said, "Sand traps."

Such was the genesis of shit us amateurs have to deal with every day. At least there are bikinis on a real beach. Weren't there enough "traps" before the Gods cleared them away? A dead animal or a natural marsh wasn't good enough? You had to get rid of that and import sand? What horror flick screenwriter came up with that idea? And why can't you touch your ball in the sand, but you can everywhere else?

Then you have to clean up after yourself with a rake. I came here to *escape* yardwork.

Water hazards. What was wrong with the natural ones? The Gods taketh away and the Gods giveth back. Bullshit! I want the natural ones. The Gods created some water hazards right in the middle of where you are trying to go. If you hit a perfect shot, you end up in the water. To miss it, you have to go out of your way to suck.

Rough. An area where the grass is not always greener but is always much higher. Sometimes there are tiers of roughs. Who knew roughs would be anointed with titles? Did someone measure the relative size of the fairway compared to the roughs so there was some symmetry and therefore, equal reward or penalty on each hole? No, it was random. The Gods said, "Let's make an expansive fairway with no rough on Hole 1 so we can really fuck with them on Hole 2." Guffaw. Guffaw.

The goal in golf is to get as low a score as possible. Without cheating. Golf is an honorable sport. You are not supposed to move your ball, and you don't. You are supposed to find your ball and play it, not discover someone else's stray shot and call it your own. You are honorable. You can count to 8 with the best of them and remember every shot. You sign a scorecard and no one checks it. Except narcissists watching on TV.

PA BROOK

HONOR AMONG THIEVES

Honesty. A virtue everyone should have. There are so many ways golfers can cheat, but for the most part, they do not. As a demonstration of this, a group of golfers got together to play in the World's Most Honest Golfer Tournament many years ago. At this tournament, the *highest* score won. Honesty and shitty became synonymous. The tournament was played at a famous golf course, one any amateur would give his favorite club to play. It was noted for an island par 3 on the 17th hole. The results went something like this.

The winner shot a 243.

On the famous 17th hole, he hit the water from the tee 15 times in a row, then putted up the cart path to card a 26 for the hole.

I want to play him in Liar's Poker.

WHO CAME UP WITH THAT?

As an amateur golfer, I have become familiar with the jargon. A lot of it makes sense, but for some, the genesis is far from clear. Many of the words have two meanings, and the connection is clear. Others not so. And some have different meanings for professionals versus amateurs.

Par, for example, makes sense. Par in English means level or even. In golf, it means the average score one should expect when playing a hole. For a professional, the reaction is one of resignation because a birdie was the goal. For an amateur, the reaction is "Cool!"

Birdie, however, doesn't make sense. I remember Conrad Birdie, but he wasn't a golfer. There are other Birdie people and, of course, badminton birdies. I am not sure how the Golf Gods determined this was an appropriate moniker for what pros deem par and what amateurs deem an outdoor orgasm.

IF I WERE GOD

Bogey has a natural negative connotation in golf, as in life. "The bogeyman caused my shot to stray into the next county." Some bad spirit took over my body for just the split second I was completing my swing. Of course. It can't be that I suck.

But look how golf treats worsening bad shots compared to improving good shots. If you do one shot better than par, you get a birdie. Tweet tweet. Two shots better, an eagle, and three shots could be a hole-in-one. But bad shots just get bogey. Then double bogey, triple bogey, etc. No cute names when you screw up. What, the Golf Gods couldn't spend a little time being clever on the downside? Soaring birds, flailing badminton thingies, and a "hole" to strive for. But just "bogey" if you fail. Well, I say let's liven this game up a bit and make it more fun for the announcers.

My offerings are twofold, one for the politically correct crowd, and one for those who don't give a shit about PC.

FOR THE PC CROWD

One over par would be a demerit. Simple. Denotes the loss of a stroke for an oxymoronically under par performance. It can even be named after Jimmy Demaret, a three-time Masters winner who played mostly in the 1940s and 1950s.

Two over par would be a snafu—a situation caused by errors or confusion. That can easily lead to two bad shots.

Three over par is now known as a gaffe—a snafu on speed.

Four over par is a bollix, which when spelled differently represents testicles, allowing someone to get a bollix and still have balls.

So, I can hear the golf announcers: "So, Jim, how do you think the tournament leader will recover after shooting 12 pars in a row, then a snafu and a gaffe after a bollix on the last three holes?"

That is so much better than all that bogey stuff.

FUCK PC

Now for the non-PC crowd, the following will be much more entertaining:

One over par would still be a bogey (maybe).

Two over par would be a boner.

Three over par is now known as a FUBAR (fucked up beyond all recognition).

Four over par is getting butt-fucked.

Now hear the golf announcers: "So, Jim, how do you think the tournament leader will recover after shooting 12 pars in a row, then a boner after getting butt-fucked?"

Now we're talking.

MORE GOLF LINGO

Dogleg has an unusual place in golf lingo. Do we really need pet analogies when playing golf? And why a dog? Why any animal? Where is PETA when you need them? Racing uses a hairpin turn. There's a visual. Right turn, 90-degree angle, gets the point across. I don't want to think of a dog's bent leg when I play golf. My shots go off in a 90-degree angle without having to give it a name. No more slice or hook. That was a "dogleg." Ugh.

Draw. A euphemism that pros use for a hook. Good golfers draw their shots; I hook 'em. A draw is intentional; a hook is a mistake. But are hooks really bad shots or just wind-altered draws? And are draws simply wind-aided hooks?

IF I WERE GOD

When does a draw become a hook? I think I am just a little pregnant.

The opposite of the draw-hook phenomenon is the fade-slice combo, with the much nicer sounding fade representing the good shot.

I say we give them all the same name—"not fucking straight."

"So, Jim, that was quite the not-fucking-straight shot."

Too bad there wasn't a dogleg.

"*Fore*" is what you yell when you hit a ball that you think might hit someone. It's like hearing thunder and thinking it's a warning to take cover. It's too late. We have all heard someone else yell fore and ducked for cover. There is just as good a chance that we duck into the flight of the ball as away from it. It's usually not meant for us, anyway, and often is an afterthought.

Like the time I was golfing with a bunch of business associates. I hit a beautiful shot from the fairway and, as I followed its lovely trajectory, I noticed my boss coming out from behind a tree and directly into the path of an oncoming pink slip. It was far too late, but I let out a feeble "fore" just as the ball hit my boss. Square in the ass. That night, he welcomed everyone to my "going away dinner."

So now let's add some golf words together to see what we come up with.

The *scratch* golfer *drop*ped his *knickers* displaying a *lofty putter tee*d up by the thoughts of a fantasy *foursome*.

An *unplayable lie* is like the song *It Wasn't Me* by Shaggy, in which he swears it wasn't him with another woman, even though his girlfriend caught him on video.

Notice that *wood* and *shaft* relate to something that, while golfing, we hold onto with both hands while fantasizing about our *stroke*. In real life, we only need one hand.

Is it really a sport?

GOD 2.0

As someone who is almighty and all-knowing and supposed to be all-kind, I should be sympathetic to the plight of the amateur golfer. But it is too much fun watching balls go flying in all sorts of different unintended directions, with the commensurate cursing by the propeller of such balls and the unmitigated hilarity unabashedly proffered by the observer of said wanton shots. It would be cruel and unusual punishment to discard golf from the ranks of "sport." Amusement and gaiety seem like better monikers, although joke and prank could be close followers. However, in the interest of athletics and exercise, we will continue to anoint golf as a sport.

But curling has to go.

CHAPTER 21

NEWBORNS
(The In-Alien-able Right to Be Ugly)

"He's sooooooooo cute!"

I prefer, "Yikes!"

The human birth experience is such an incredibly inexplicable event that no one can truly come to grips with it. Or at least I can't. A dose of sperm, which resembles an experiment of vanilla ice cream combined with Elmer's glue gone bad, chases down and sidles up to some microscopic ovum (whatever the fuck that is), and *voila!* Simon is born. Really? Does anyone really know how this happens? Most of my bad experiments end up somewhere in the bathroom. While not having first hand (no pun intended) knowledge, I have been told that there is a salty residue. What? Do ova taste like pepper? Surely, I have no clue how this all leads to little Simon. Or who the fuck Simon is. It just came to me as I was writing this. I know no one named Simon. Simon Cowell of *American Idol/America's Got Talent* fame notwithstanding. It's like the number 17. Everyone has had a thought that includes an imaginary made up number. Witness, "I smoked pot, you know, listening to the Dead, at least when I was in college, man, like 17 times."

PA BROOK

Like Simon, 17 came out of nowhere, but now it is an instinctive number that just shows up. Kind of like what happened with Simon. He just showed up. I was doing research, started typing, and when that moment occurred when a name was needed, Simon came out of my brain.

But I bet, whoever Simon is, he was fucking ugly when he was born.

No, despite all the relatives cooing over how cute Simon is, he is not. And this is just not the ramblings about the one baby who was born ugly. No, actually I was born with more hair than I ever had in my later life. It did not make me pretty when I was born, just less ugly than any other day in my life. Sad.

There is scientific evidence to back this up. We have to be honest. We don't have to tell anyone; it can just be our secret. But as you gazed into your newborn's eyes for the first (and second…and third) time, honestly, did you ever think: Why does my baby look like ET?

Let's see. Puffy eyes that match yours when you have had one (or two or three) too much, but hers are because of swelling from delivery. A flattened nose and cone-shaped head from navigating through a birth canal does not make for camera-ready child models.

More evidence. A newborn's head is very large in proportion to the body, and the cranium is enormous relative to his or her face. Talk about a swelled head. And at birth, many regions of the newborn's skull have not yet been converted to bone, leaving "soft spots" that could lead to unusual shapes. During labor and birth, the infant's skull changes shape to fit through the birth canal, sometimes causing the child to be born with a misshapen or elongated head.

IF I WERE GOD

A new meaning to fathead.

It will usually return to normal on its own within a few days or weeks. Well, after the "cuteness" wears off and has been replaced with screaming and diapers.

Now what are we going to be cooing about?

If you are not yet convinced, immediately after birth, a newborn's skin is often grayish to dusky blue in color. Newborns are wet, covered in streaks of blood, and coated with a white substance whose name is unpronounceable. A newborn may also have Mongolian spots, various other birthmarks, or peeling skin, particularly on the wrists, hands, ankles, and feet. This is my baby, and I want to take pictures? Ouch.

And while most relatives and friends won't get to check this out, a newborn's genitals are enlarged and reddened, with male infants having an unusually large scrotum. Oh, to be young again.

The breasts may also be enlarged, even in male infants. Females (and even males) may actually discharge milk from their nipples, and/or a bloody or milky-like substance from the vagina. Ugh. And we want Grandma taking pictures?

It is just not about looks with newborns. Can't judge a book by its cover. You have to look at the natural-born intelligence of infants. Witness my sister. Mom had just given birth and had a particular hankering for the name of Robin. She lifted my newborn sister to her shoulder, patted her rear, and asked, "How would you like to be named Robin?" Demonstrating more maturity and discipline than my most drunken college moment, my sister barfed all over my mother's blouse. To this day, Suzanne has not been allowed to live the moment down.

PA BROOK

WE ARE NOT ALONE

Whether we are is up for debate, but we have certainly seen the imagination of those who have written stories about them. Have you ever seen an attractive alien? Imagine what their babies look like.

Alien. The original 1979 movie featured a mama alien and her baby alien. The baby was actually incubated in a human and, in one of the best science fiction scenes ever, was born by busting through the stomach of its incubator. Alien Junior was quite cute, scurrying about the spaceship, dripping fucking acid from its mouth.

Klingons. Star Trek geeks like me were very familiar with their wrinkled foreheads and really funky hair. Although the wrinkled foreheads were not part of the original series because of a lack of a sufficient makeup budget. So we have early Klingons and later-day Klingons. Both would make wonderful baby albums.

ET. Everyone remembers an adorable ET riding in the sky with Elliott pedaling the bicycle, not an atypical ugly alien whose parents would surely not have brought the video camera into the delivery room. At least he had a finger that glowed.

Star Wars gave us many aliens, none of whom would have made the package of Pampers. There is a rumor that Yoda and Chewbacca had an off-camera romance and spawned...

Coneheads.

Alien babies are just as ugly as ours. Not uglier, just less familiar. Look at enough Klingon babies, and you might begin to think they are cute too.

Not.

IF I WERE GOD

GOD 2.0

Society says babies have to be cute. Science says they are ugly. If I were God, I have to go along with science. It is not only OK to call all babies ugly, it is expected. As a matter of fact, I would make it a badge of honor. The uglier the baby, the more ooooohs and aaaaaahs. Let's discharge some breast milk and swell some heads. And oh, Junior is making Dad proud.

Where's my iPhone?

CHAPTER 22
NOW, THAT'S WHAT I CALL FREE SPEECH
(Shit Is Gluten Free)

Cursing is generational. In earlier times, referring to deities was the worst. "Clubfoot Christ" or "Six-fingers Jesus" were heinous things to refer to. Sex and bodily functions were of little concern. Primarily because both were being done in public and no one cared. But don't mess with Jesus. You could fuck and shit wherever you wanted, but Goddamnit, don't take the Lord's name in vain.

Back in the Victorian days, it was all taboo. One could not even say "trousers" since it referred to "down there." When Clark Gable uttered, "Frankly, my dear, I don't give a damn," you would have thought all heck would break loose. But then it became fashionable to say "heck" or "damn," or dare I say, "hell." Of course, you would not hear that on "Leave It to Beaver," although "beaver" itself became somewhat taboo later on.

Damn and Hell became Bitch and Bastard, and then, oh, Jesus Christ, the "Goddamn." Oh, and did our parents cringe. Well, mine did as I laughed with glee. I still wasn't allowed to say any of this myself, but it did bring to mind the incredible oddity of cursing: in order for a child to learn

IF I WERE GOD

that cursing is bad, they must utter such a word and be chastised for such utterance, likely from the person she/he learned it from. Fucking irony.

So, one generation's curse words are the next generation's way to embarrass their parents. But by then, only the parents are embarrassed as the rest of society has accepted the new regime. Only no one told the parents. I experienced this firsthand. My daughter is a millennial. I was no angel and have always used my share of cuss words. I tried to be what my peeps would call civil and not use the worst of them in front of children, parents, or in business. But among friends, the fucks would fly. But not around my most innocent, precious, virginal, pure nun of a daughter. That did not prevent her from learning through her own devices. I would cringe when she used certain words, ask that she not repeat them, only to find that this egged her on. I finally gave up and wrote it off to the same thing my parents dealt with when I said "son of a bitch." It is generational. And as society keeps getting more liberal, bad words don't become so bad after all.

But the coup de grace occurred one night after a particularly horrible performance by a professional athlete on a team that we both loved led her (now 23 years old) to finish the description of the foulest of his sins by noting that "he can eat a dick."

For anyone other than my daughter, I might have responded with a typically testosterone-laden belly laugh. But it was my daughter. She knew about dicks? Fuck! Not knowing how to respond, I simply didn't, leaving poor shitty professional athlete stuck in that visual.

But think about this. There would be no profanity if no one was offended by it. As of today, there are only two words I can think of that remain truly offensive to the majority of the population. Words that almost no one can utter in the presence of strangers. I wonder how many of you would come up with a different combination from mine.

God bless imagination.

THINGS FOR WHICH SWEARING IS OK
There are certain things for which swearing should be OK regardless of generation and regardless of word. What are some examples?

Neighbors deciding to blow leaves or chainsaw trees early in the morning on the weekend.

The New York Jets losing another football game.

In the juxtaposition of the expletive with the activity, my upstairs neighbor during my early singlehood certainly met this criteria. She had a boyfriend who spent the night every Thursday, but their thing was not having dinner, watching a movie, and then screwing before going to sleep. No, they did the first two before going to sleep, leaving the screwing until 5 AM. And they knew how to enjoy themselves. And were very expressive. And he had porn star stamina. And the bed creaked. And she moaned. Loudly. Picture is complete.

Fuuuuuuuuuck!

Then there is the swearing based on the incredulity you feel about what you are observing. As in the first interracial kiss on TV. In almost every aspect of my verbal and writing career, I try to weave in some aspect of *Star Trek*. It is the most amazing television show of all time, given its social themes and futuristic looks at life, many of which turned out to be prophetic. In "Plato's Stepchildren," Captain Kirk kisses Lieutenant Uhura. Others had offered earlier interracial kisses, but mostly of a Caucasian with Asian variety. Nichelle Nichols, the actress who played the scantily clad communications officer, is African American. When one viewed Kirk laying a wet one on her, a "Holy Shit!" was the only possible response.

There are many who still shun cursing, and I have no issue with them. If someone tells me it offends them, I will be respectful and curtail my own use. But when someone says that I should substitute a mainstream epithet for a curse word, I beg to differ. I heard someone say that you should recognize when you are about to use a curse word and find another word that can equally express your thoughts and emotions. The theory: perhaps such a word can express your feelings better than profanity. Just take a breath and think about a nice word.

So when the hammer hits your thumb instead of the nail at 87 miles an hour, just stand there and internally debate the benefits of saying "Darn," think about the good of society, and come to the conclusion that saying something that won't offend a do-gooder is best. All the while your thumb is throbbing.

Sorry, but "Fuuuuuuck!"

I dated a woman in college who did not curse. When she got upset, she said "Pooh." Like Winnie the Pooh. That does not seem even mildly rewarding. I tried my best, but there is a level of satisfaction in cursing that is hard to describe. I have heard of studies in which it's asserted that cursing can be physiologically beneficial. One study noted that participants could keep their hands in extremely cold water longer if they cursed versus using some wussy word. Now, the word has to be provocative to the expresser. Theoretically, someone who never ventured past "Pooh" could keep their hands in cold water a long time just by saying "Pooh." But I need something just a touch stronger.

Some contributors to the profanity conversation use * so as

to not completely spell a word, while others spell it out. I am using both in my internet musings. But why? I am insecure and worried about what people think about me. So I can occasionally offend by saying shit, but then I get intimidated at the moment and use sh*t. But I am only fooling myself. Face it. When you read F*ck, do you say "F" "*" "c" "k"? No, you say "Fuck!" So who the fuck am I kidding?

My stepfather was from Belgium and spoke French fluently. My mother had a conversational knowledge of French. They used to speak French occasionally but never tried to teach me French or include me in those conversations. I always wondered what they were saying and, I am convinced, it was stuff they did not want me to hear. My parents frequently referred to an SOB in the midst of French conversation. They would spell it out, S-O-B. Initially, I thought they could not fool me. The poor slob they were referring to was a sob. I desperately wanted to know what that meant in French. I was dumbfounded. And eight years old.

So I decided to take French in high school. For four years. The best part of that experience was learning that my French teacher had a twin sister. And she and her twin sister had married twin brothers. At the time, it blew my mind. Now I think of the possibilities.

I never found out what sob meant in French. 'Cause it didn't. My diabolical parents were bilingually fucking with me, so I wouldn't be scarred for life by knowing what a son of a bitch was.

Lesson learned. Always learn the curse words first in a new language.

REAL NAMES YOU ARE GLAD YOUR PARENTS DIDN'T NAME YOU

We all know someone named Richard who goes by Dick.

IF I WERE GOD

Or the Fuchs that gets mispronounced on purpose. And the movie series about the 21st-century Beaver family, the Fockers. But there are some names that are even more debilitating. All of these are real names, as far as I know (visit your local website).

Willie Stroker

Ben Dover

Peter Bonerz

Mike Hunts

Mike Litoris

Chew Kok

Rusty Kuntz

Stanislav Seman

Alphonse Areola, the first ever nipple reference in a name

Andre Muff, whose sister Andrea married Bruce Driver and became...Andrea Muff-Driver

Brian Pinas

Argelico Fucks, almost sounds like a full sentence

Fabian Assman

Stefan Kuntz has embraced his name's brilliance since becoming general manager of a German soccer team by signing both Danny Fuchs and Florian Dick.

Except for those obvious foreign names, imagine giving your offspring a name that she/he is going to have to deal with his/her entire life. Imagine the odds of your family name being Litoris. What parent in their right mind goes through the book of 10,000 names and comes up with Michael? I understand if the last name is Fuchs or Bonerz, you are hindered no matter what. And if you are foreign, you may not get the childish torture you would be subject to here in the United States, so a Chew may be understandable for the Kok family. But do you give no thought to Dover and Stroker and the possibilities of Benjamin or William? I knew someone named Merry Christmas. Literally. Seriously, Mom. Did you really have to do that? OK, I give up, but my favorites really had no choice in the matter:

Simon Fuckebotere and Henry Fuckebeggar (and his rumored cousin, Sara Schtupahomelessperson)

But just what lineage got them there?

The "son" appendage to last names comes from the dad's first name and not wanting one's child to be confused with his neighbor's son. Ergo, William named his son, blah blah Williamson. But I don't think "botere" represented the same thing when Fucke Jones procreated.

Chew on that for a minute.

REAL PLACES YOU'RE GLAD YOU DON'T CALL HOME

Some of our Founding Fathers had quite the sense of humor. One must attribute it to that; otherwise, we never would have made it as a country. Of course, some of the towns have double meanings. I choose the fun one.

So you think living in Queer Creek, Alaska, is bad? At least you don't live on Gropecuntlane, a red-light district somewhere in ancient times. Aptly named, I must admit; although I am not sure which came first. And if groping doesn't suit your fancy sufficiently, how about some grooming in Shavecuntewelle, a lovely town in Kent circa 1275. After doing all that sculpting without electricity, it might make you yearn for Hungery Cunt, noticed on a Scottish map from around 1750.

IF I WERE GOD

But we live in the boring United States. Nonetheless, it does have its share of interesting towns.

HERE WE GO

You would not believe that in the state of Arizona you can find retirees living in Santa Claus, getting involved with the residents of Three Way. Those in Surprise were not.

Arkansas has its own Three Way, but this one includes Three Brothers. We are not surprised. We are surprised that the boys (or other critters) from Hog Jaw didn't join in. Of course, Four Gums houses the only two desirable women in the state.

Illinois had the residents of Fruit and Gays surrounding the barricaded in Normal.

Beaverlick is a favorite destination for those visiting Kentucky. After some good moonshine, they might find real beavers. Or Deer Lick. When they run out of beaver, there is always Monkey's Eyebrow. After enough moonshine, Possum Trot could be mistaken for something else. Ultimately, when they get bored (or run out of moonshine) they get in their pickups and go to Camel Hump, Wyoming. If they overstay their welcome in Camel Hump, they risk being thrown out and ending up at Humpatulip, Washington. Ouch.

The Kentucky Lick clan actually includes the following cousins: Beaver, Bee, Big Beaver, Deer, Knob, Mud, Wolf. Now that's a party!

Maryland is just Boring.

Chargoggagoggmanchauggagoggchaubunagungamaugg Lake, Massachusetts. I think I spelled it right. Thank God for copy and paste, but who knows if the fucker I copied it from got it right? Does anyone not competing in a spelling bee really care? Imagine paying bills and having to write that on the back of your envelope several times a month? Thank God for online bill pay. Or those charities that send you address labels for a contribution of $10. Talk about money well spent. Of course, the charity might be out of business by the time it prints your address labels.

In an attempt to outdo Illinois, Faggot Hill and Gay Town sandwiched Assinippi, Massachusetts. However, the Assinippians welcomed the Faggotites and Gaysters. Cox Corner and Cummaquid round out Massachusetts's contributions. Cummaquid, which implied you could finish for a British pound, was almost named Cummaquick for the typical experience in Boston's Combat Zone in the day.

In my home state of New Jersey, I could not ignore the juxtaposition of Convent Station and Dicktown. For their residents, it's probably a good thing they are at opposite ends of the state. It would be fun if they were in the same zip code.

In New Mexico, there was a lot of confusion as Elephant Butte Estates competed with Twin Buttes for settlers, butt they were soliciting folks from Lesbia who had very different ideas. Queen would have offered more fertile recruiting grounds. Unless they were all under the influence of the Weed-ites.

A lot of people think New Yorkers are assholes. And killjoys. Kentucky has Beaverlick, New York has Beaver Kill. Talk about a downer. However, their liberal bent created Butts Corner (is that a hiding place or a 90-degree ass?), Gayville, Gayhead, and of course, the egomaniacal Horseheads.

Which was settled first in North Carolina, Horneytown or Jugtown? No one knows, but both spawned Erect. Nags Head had to arise from the desire to shut up a bitchy wife. Or perhaps a horse blow job. Residents of Whynot chose not to weigh in on the debate.

IF I WERE GOD

In North Dakota, townsfolk from Mott and Hoople formed a band.

Do you think LeBron would live in Pee Pee, Ohio? What do you call the residents? Peepeeites? I'd rather live in Nags Head with my horse.

Ohio also boasts of Pussy Creek, where all the Seaman flows after the spring thaw. Swimming is a Novelty in Ohio.

There is a lot of irony to Hookers neighboring The Holy City in Oklahoma. In response, the city council of The Holy City has annexed Cox City in preparation for war. Hookers responded with its invasion of Beaver. It appears to be a stiff standoff.

With Dork Canal, Poop Creek, Shitepoke Creek, Tilicum Beach (read that one real slow), and Wanker's Corner, no one in Oregon is drinking the water.

I must pay homage to Beaver Falls, Pennsylvania. Fortunately, there is a double entendre that allows me to digress here. My most revered sports hero, Joe Namath, is from Beaver Falls. And now that the Cubs have won a World Series, it eliminates a fan base that had suffered even more than the Jets. I remember the day when I was a mere youth and Joe Willie executed the impossible dream. Super Bowl 3 (before there were Roman numerals attached to the event).

Thank you for your indulgence.

Let's get back to beaver. Or the lack thererof, as in Virginville. Maybe not lacking beaver, just experienced beaver. Which means once they get some Desire, they can visit Intercourse. And once the Desire becomes insatiable, Needmore is just around the bend.

Finally, to this day, every time I pass by a sign that tells me I am near Scotrun, a different word forms on my lips.

PA BROOK

I have nothing against the South, but why name a town Ninety-Six (South Carolina) when there is a perfectly acceptable opposite?

Is there really an Eagle Buttes in South Dakota? Hard to picture, but then again, I never had an incentive to contemplate this. If not, how does the shit that falls on my head escape?

Digressing from sexual references for only a moment, I present Bison Bonesteel, South Dakota. Sounds like a UFC fighter.

Only, Tennessee. As in what? Only women with all their teeth need apply? Or if you are missing a few, please have Sweet Lips. If you are not from Sweet Lips, it will be helpful if you can be Wetmore than the Only-ites. And if you can't get with the program, stay the hell away from Horny Head Creek.

Texas could be the scariest state. It starts with Bushland. It doesn't matter which Bush. Fortunately there is no Cheneyville in Texas. Good thing Dime Box wasn't named Dime Bag, as its residents could end up spending 20 years in Glasscock County Jail. Or Gaylord Penitentiary. Oops for the residents of Coke. There is always the Gay Hill wayward school for wannabe priests.

Despite the allure of Nipple, Utah, its antithesis, Virgin, allows me to move quickly along the alphabet.

Butts, Virginia—at least these guys spelled it right. Then there is Fagg—so much for the spelling bee. Now it gets fun. Mouth of Wilson. Is that a male or female? Or wait, maybe my horse. And does it imply what my dirty mind thinks it does or is that something else?

That's what blogs are for.

IF I WERE GOD

But we have more. Virginia is such a giving state. Onancock. Like Onatopp, the Bond girl from *GoldenEye*. Bad English, but maybe the Brits are fucking with us. Whose cock? Faggites? Or Wilson-ites? Nah, that doesn't make any sense. Who came up with that shit?

But we got a couple of cool towns left. Threeway, but we have been there before and Virginia is not quite ready.

The Tightsqueeze townspeople felt, well, rather cramped. See, I can keep it clean once in a while.

Just where is Cheat River, West Virginia? What about Frazier's Bottom? Just ask Lilith. Or the residents of Gay. But then Mount Gay interceded. Did Moses favor his Left Hand? Me too.

I hear folks from Dykesville, Wisconsin, vacation on the West Coast, at Big Beaver Valley, Washington. If they wish to spend their free time locally, Spread Eagle offers some of the best hospitality in the state. Residents from both towns along with Mount Gay and Gays Mills often frequent Imalone when companionship is needed.

LET'S NOT FORGET OUR FRIENDS TO THE NORTH

Come By Chance is in the province of Newfoundland and Labrador in Canada. Good for them, but I guess the founding fathers were looking for a euphemism for premature ejaculation, which was any town I lived in until I graduated college.

Creativity by Canadians continues. Also in Newfoundland and Labrador we can find Dildo. I am not sure what was on the Board, or perhaps Bored, of Governors' minds at the time they named this town, but perhaps some leeway can be granted. Their brethren to the south chose to ignore creativity entirely, spawning South Dildo. Northerners were not much better in Upper Dildo.

PA BROOK

That's a three-county sex toy. Talk about some happy women. And that was before they made the vibrating kind.

In the end, the settlers of Come By Chance and Dildo came (ugh) to understand that they needed to think about the future of society and moved to Conception Bay.

Saskatchewan (whose Roughriders have always been my favorite Canadian Football League team) may consider merging Big Beaver into Climax, although if they instead merge with Dildo, Climax may be left hoping that Venus Butterfly is available for merger. Of course, Venus Butterfly is not yet a city, but I am sure someone will rectify that shortly. You do know what a Venus Butterfly is, right?

In the meantime, residents of Fairy Glen are marching in protest.

INTERSTATE RIVALRIES

Not everything needs to be about sex. I am grateful to the residents of Enterprise, Mississippi, and to our northern neighbors in Vulcan, Alberta, who likely stole their town name from Vulcan, Michigan, to allow me to bring a modicum of decency to this rambling. And get in my *Star Trek* plug.

To honor interstate rivalries, we note that the people of Sugar Tit, South Carolina, left town to help enlarge the population of BraSwell, Georgia.

Neighboring Hopeulikit lived up to its name, pleasing those from Kiester, Minnesota, and providing much needed relief to Blue Ball, Arkansas.

Tarzan, Texas, and Krypton, Kentucky, give our superheroes their due.

When forced to leave their home, many of the men from Mars, Pennsylvania, relocated to Lovelady, Texas. Others

IF I WERE GOD

went to Fairy, Texas. And I hear a few went to Black Bottom, Kentucky.

The entire lot of Why, Arizona, were just as confused as the citizens of Nowhere, Colorado.

Internationally, the flight from Crotch Crescent, United Kingdom, to Middelfart, Denmark, included plenty of Fuckings from Austria. The Wetwangs took the bus. Not even their suburban brethren from Titty-Ho could get them up.

GOD 2.0

Cursing is controversial because it is taboo. But there is less and less taboo about the current curse words. Younger generations are not even put off by the worst of the four-letter words. It looks like they may become mainstream words sooner rather than later. Cursing could become obsolete, unless...

We create new ones!

So let's accept all the old ones and make up some new words that I will decree as curse words. I always wondered who invented "fuck" and made it a bad word. Well, I am embracing the challenge of creating the next generation of curse words. I have a couple of rules. They have to be harsh sounding and have to begin with a letter that has no other English curse words associated with it. Might as well spread the good cheer.

My thoroughly exhaustive research left the following letters uncursed:

E	Q	Y
I	R	L
K	V	U
O	X	Z

PA BROOK

We can debate what is a curse word, and that may add or delete certain letters, but this is my list, ergo my left-over letters. Keep in mind these new words are not going to sound good. No new words do. They only roll off your tongue after they have been used a bunch. You think "fuck" flowed naturally in the beginning? "Selfie" sounded really stupid just a short time ago.

After having given this a lot of thought and counseled with many similar-minded, time-available brethren, I have come up with the following modest list of new curse words:

Kout replaces fuck. Iterations will work well over time. Motherkouter. Smooth.

Qarm (pronounced "karm") replaces shit. Represents all the nasty stuff you don't want to step in, have dumped on you, or have to eat. "You're in deep qarm." Bingo, you know you are in trouble.

Zectu. Most curse words are one syllable. We need a little variety in the new regime. It doesn't replace any one curse word, but represents a really horrible person. Instead of calling someone a "piece of shit" just call him a "zectu."

Ogglecust because I wanted to get a vowel in there. They are the poor cursing stepchildren. This represents all the bad words related to body parts and functions. Dick, cock, cunt, pussy, piss, tits, ass, shit, etc. This makes cursing much more efficient as one word fits all. You don't have to spend any time trying to figure out whether "you know who" is a dick or a pussy; whether you want to shit all over him or piss all over him. You can now do both.

If we keep this our little secret, you can get away with a lot of qarm for a while, especially with kouted-up relatives and bosses.

CHAPTER 23

LEGALIZING DRUGS
(We-ed Shall Overcome)

I ENTERED COLLEGE IN NEW JERSEY never haven gotten drunk, high, or laid. Luckily for me, I met some cool people the first weekend. When it was over, I actually was no longer virginal in two of the three. Unluckily for me, guess which I was still a virgin at?

My dorm mate across the hall had a navy jacket with huge pockets that enabled him to hide a full bottle of Muscatel so we could drink while wandering around campus. Muscatel, you ask. Ouch. Ever hear of Boone's Farm? You may be too young. It was cheap fruity wine. They had Strawberry Hill and Apple wine, both disgusting but perfect for college kids. Muscatel was no different, just not fruity. Yuk!

Next door to me was a rather large pothead. He wasn't a big person; he just smoked *a lot*. Of course, he told me that I wouldn't feel it the first time, but since *I* smoked a lot that first weekend, it wasn't too long before I felt my first buzz.

Since I wasn't particularly cool at that time of my life (which implies coolness arrived at a later time—up for debate), I didn't become hangout friends with the pothead. However, it almost cost me a disaster.

PA BROOK

I went home on weekends my freshman year of college, and my parents would come and pick me up Friday afternoon. I was waiting for them, dutifully sober, on this particular Friday shortly into my first semester. Sis was seven at the time and very cute, of course. I never knew of this story until well into adulthood, but on this fateful afternoon, Mom and Sis were on their way to my dorm room when Mom got a whiff of my next door neighbor's favorite pastime. Only she thought it was coming from *my* room. That would have created a firestorm of shit.

Mom confessed that she stood outside my dorm room for a full 30 seconds thinking about how she would react if the odor was emanating from my room. Scold me, tell my father, pull me out of college, join in. OK, not join in. She was also concerned about exposing my innocent sister to the evils of weed. While she was contemplating her next step, Sis became impatient and started pounding on the door. Mom was paralyzed, until I opened the door to the most pleasant aroma she could have hoped for.

Dirty laundry.

So college passed with just an occasional indulgence, beer being much more available and prevalent. This led to many other stories, but beer is legal, and we are here to proselytize about that which is not.

Fast forward 5 years. I survived college, no untoward parental discoveries. And I finally got laid. Thank God it was before my sister. I now had an MBA in accounting and was getting ready for my first real job with an accounting firm in New York City. Conservative me in a conservative profession. You know, green eye shades, pocket protectors, only white shirts. Working for a prestigious New York accounting firm oozed integrity and honesty. Do the right thing.

I was right at home.

IF I WERE GOD

Only not all accountants are stuffy and boring. My job began with a five-day training program so we could learn how to be good accountants. Follow the CPA rules. I have always been a rules follower.

Until my first day as an accountant.

In the training room environment, especially an interactive one like this was, it doesn't take long for participants to find like kind brethren. We are all strangers at 9 AM, nervous and wondering if we stack up with the rest of the class. By lunch, we begin to get comfortable. Dave accosts Debbie, who is sitting next to Doug, who role-played with Eileen, who shared a joke with Joe, and *voila!* Six of us are going out for pizza.

Six nerdy, fresh-faced, enthusiastic accountants wandered 42nd Street in Manhattan, searching for pizza. In Manhattan, that task takes all of 5 seconds, but we found ourselves on 43rd Street, not nearly as busy a street. Well, it turns out at least one of us was not as nerdy as the others.

He whipped out a joint.

Really. 43rd Street. Manhattan. Lunch time.

Only five of us nerds left. What is the accounting world coming to?

They all took a puff.

Only one nerd left.

Alternating between horror that I would be arrested on my first day, on my first real job in my life, and a tingling excitement about doing something taboo, I said, "Fuck it," and gleefully toked.

Look at me, a cool accountant.

PA BROOK

In a juxtaposition of the ironic and oxymoronic (I dare you to ask an English teacher, or a Founding Father), the owner of the joint and I became good friends. I called him Source. Talk about going from 0 to 60 in record time.

We hung out quite a bit for the first few months of my career. He sold me the only ounce of pot I've ever purchased in my entire life. In a brown paper bag. It was the '70s. He put my college pothead dorm mate to shame. We would regularly get high, although we would not necessarily put it to good use, like in chasing women.

Until one night.

The year was 1977. The place was New York City. The time was October. The sport was baseball. The late '70s were magical for baseball in the Bronx. The Yankees made it to the World Series in 3 of 5 years, winning it twice. At a point almost smack dab in the middle of all of this, there was a Game 6 about to be played at Yankee Stadium. Source and I decided to get high and try to figure out a way to get into Yankee Stadium for the game. A World Series game. Game 6 and the Yankees could win the whole fucking thing. No ticket. No friends with benefits (as we defined them back then). No relative of Craig Nettles. Having no way of conjuring up a solution straight, we toked up, taking us to the only place that this fantasy had a chance.

High.

We hatched a plan. Yeah, this had a chance.

I was preparing for the least conservative event of my entire life. I called Source to discuss our options as game time approached. Oh, shit! He was toking up to a rock star level and was now almost comatose.

"What plan? Huh? Lucy in the sky with diamonds." He was officially done.

IF I WERE GOD

Shit. Flying solo now. Best-laid plans. And it was such a good plan. Oh, well.

But wait. What did I need Source for? Maybe to give me balls, but wasn't that what the fucking pot was for? Where's the lighter? I dug into my paper bag.

Newly equipped, I was ready to execute the plan solo. Balls in hand, so to speak, I headed for the subway.

Unless you have ever been there, the excitement of a Game 6 when your team can win the World Series is an incredible high with no embellishments necessary. I had embellished. At first blush, the plan did not seem realistic, but with each additional embellishment, it gained credibility. That's how pot works. Start with a fantasy.

Embellishment #1 – Fantasy becomes something you heard on Twitter.

Embellishment #2 – Twitter becomes a YouTube sensation.

Embellishment #3 – Holy Fuck, I can do this!

But I was in the pre-internet phase, remember, so embellishment turned the 50-year-old hag on the phone sex line into Christie Brinkley. Or in this case, my incredibly stupid plan of getting into Game 6 of the World Series into a mythological piece of cake.

So what was this plan?

Simple—bribe my way in. You know, grease the ticket taker. Sweet talk him a little. High five for Ron Guidry. How's the kids? We are BFFs. Then hand him $15. So I went to Yankee Stadium to execute my plan armed with a 10- and a 5-dollar bill folded in my hand. Foolhardy! Illegal!

After embellishment #4. Genius!!

PA BROOK

I imagined an orderly, single file line to the turnstile and entrance. If the ticket taker had not embellished himself and declined my inducement, I could meekly slink back and recede into the night.

My imagination was under-embellished. When I got there, it was a crush of people, all vying to get in at the same time. Think New Year's Eve at Times Square. I found myself eventually pushed to the front of the line with no chance at slinking or receding. If Source and Ticket Taker were not of the same cloth, I was fucked. What would I do when unembellished Ticket Taker announces to the world, "Are you kidding me? Get the fuck out of here!" But I have nowhere to go. What happens now? My accounting career was careening to an end before it got started. They would take a urine sample and arrest me for being an idiot as well.

But here I am, unblemished by arrest or positive urine test. Ticket Taker took the $15 and HOLY SHIT! I was in Yankee Stadium for Game 6 of the fucking World Series. Did I say "Holy Shit?" I was very high and "a kid in a candy store" understated my reaction by infinity to the nth degree. But the story does not yet end. Not that pot had anything more to do with it.

I didn't have a ticket, so I wandered for a while and settled in the upper deck with a couple of cool dudes who decided the three of us would share two seats. At this point, anything went for me. As the game progressed, Reggie Jackson, Mr. October, hit two home runs, helping the Yankees to a lead late in the game.

In the day, one could go onto the field after a baseball game. This was my first World Series game, and it was about to become an immortal game. I wanted to be on the field after the game ended, but I was in the upper deck. I decided in the eighth inning to trek to the lower deck, to prepare for

IF I WERE GOD

the on-field celebration when the Yankees won, as they were surely destined to do. So between the top of the eighth inning and the bottom of the eighth inning, I decided to head downstairs. And it was not even stairs. It was a long and winding ramp to get to the lower deck. It was going to take longer than the commercials, so I began to run.

I had forgotten that the leadoff hitter in the bottom of the eighth was going to be Mr. October. He had already hit two home runs, a historic feat for a World Series game. He could not possibly hit another one. Not even Mr. October can do that. I heard the public address announcer introduce Reggie. "Now batting for the Yankees, number 44, Reggie Jackson." I increased my gait on the most embellished ramp in the history of stadiums, but no sooner did the roar for his introduction fade than the unthinkable happened with me still many yards from a view. He hit another fucking home run on the first pitch, forever embellishing his place in baseball history and forever embellishing my place in fucked-up pot stories. Oh, and by the way, his home run iced the World Series. I read it in the paper. And yes, I did get to walk on the field. I think.

I soon thereafter stopped weed and never went back, except for the very infrequent indulgence. Perhaps my experiences speak to keeping pot illegal, as it could keep others from the unsightly outcomes I have had. But remember I am the accounting nerd. Otherworldly types will engage in its full benefits. And the government could engage in its full taxation and regulation.

DO WE REALLY HAVE TO SPOON, HONEY?

I only tried something stronger once in my life. At a good friend's wedding, after much beer ingestion, we decided to take a walk to a nearby restroom to do a different kind of embellishment. This one involved a spoon. Who the fuck came up with that? It was easy to inhale a joint. Now I had to have other accoutrements. I was destined for failure.

Friend and I entered an unoccupied public restroom. He was quite the experienced embellisher and quick to impart his knowledge on my newbie ass. I went into a stall with instruments in hand, and he was giving me instructions from the other side of the wall. All was going well until I had some difficulty executing his precise instructions and someone else walked in the bathroom. Discourse had to discontinue for fear that the Marriage Police were now peeing, so I was left to my own devices. I was clearly unsure as to how to proceed, and I could not hear his continued whispered help. Do what with the spoon?

Get me a fucking beer.

But with steel will, I did not allow my spoon insecurity to take me down, and I emerged victorious from the stall, reengaging Friend, his bride, and, oh, by the way, my girlfriend. She noticed no difference, and unfortunately neither did I. It did not seem to have much effect on me. To this day, I do not know if I am disappointed or not. I'd embellished once before and narrowly avoided arrest. Two times is a charm. Or whatever the fuck they say.

So how does this support legalizing drugs?

It doesn't. It's just several stories that all of us can relate to because we have had similar ones. And we survived. No jail time.

But should drugs be legalized? Let's look at alcohol as a proxy.

Alcohol gets you high and feels good. You do things you should not. Sometimes you remember. Sometimes not.

What about marijuana or cocaine? Mmmm. Same? Maybe.

IF I WERE GOD

I am not an expert, so I will couch my comments in the veil of opinion derived from an inflated sense of knowledge. Feel free to dispute.

But is alcohol that much different from marijuana or cocaine? I will let the experts answer that technically. Let's start with some facts. Or pseudo facts, which is how you define the internet.

THAT'S A LOT OF PESOS

About $108 billion was spent on illegal drugs in 2010 in the United States alone. Or maybe it was $200 billion. Or $750 billion. These are all numbers I have read, so no one really knows. But it's a big fucking number. And illegal, as in not taxed. The highest US tax bracket at the time of this writing was 39.6%. Now, the fact there is a decimal in this tax rate and the others are whole numbers is why they pay those Congress dudes the big bucks. There must be some logical reason. As in someone's lucky number was .6. Yeah, point 6. Hey, if you had to make such worldly decisions as Congress deals with, you might gain some eccentricities yourself.

I might have understood 39.9%, as in selling something for $99.99, as if that makes a big deal versus $100. But I guess it does. There might be a study about that somewhere whose cost was probably $249,999.95.

Anyway, I am presuming the drug dudes would be in the highest tax bracket. Let's take the mid-point between $108 billion and $750 billion. That would be $429 billion. Lost tax revenue comes to about $170 billion. Yeah, there are 9 zeros after 170.

(Editor's note: The highest tax rate has changed since the original writing of this, but revising it would have left no room to bitch about point 6. The new politicians have lost their point envy.)

SOMEONE CALL 911

In 2012 there were approximately 1.6 million people in jail, of whom 330,000 were there for drug-related offenses. It is estimated that the average annual cost per inmate is $25,000 per year. I'll do the math for you—$8.25 billion spent on drug offenders. But that's only those in jail. Since the drugs are illegal, we are spending taxpayer dollars on law enforcement trying to put all bad guys in jail. Some estimates put drug usage in the United States at around 9%. More fucking math. That's 24 million felons. There are 330,000 in jail, but another 24 million awaiting capture.

Imagine if law enforcement was a lot more successful than it currently is. Isn't society's goal to create incarceration as a disincentive to crime? In order for it to be a real disincentive, law enforcement has to make the prospect of capture real. So let's imagine capturing every single person breaking the law. Well, at least the 24 million pot/whatever heads. We will leave the murderers alone for this conversation.

So now 24 million really bad motherfuckers go to jail. At the cost of $25,000 per year. Fuck, I need one of those super computers. It's a 6 with a lot of fucking zeros. I think its $600 billion. Everyone will check my math, and if I am wrong, I will get a lot of nasty emails, tweets, blog posts, or whatever. But they say bad press is better than no press.

So where are we? We desire to capture all the bad guys, which means we, as a society, want to capture the 24 million illegal drug users and send them to jail at a cost of $25,000 per year. So society would find it beneficial to spend $600 billion to have the right to lose $170 billion in revenue.

Huh?

And this is just the United States. Assuming the US is 5% of the world's population and the world's most affluent country, how do we extrapolate just the lost revenue of $170 billion to the rest of the world? More math geek shit. I'm going to keep this simple. Let's say we are triple the wealth of the rest of the world, so the 5% becomes 15%. If the lost revenue is $170 billion for 15% of the world, the total for the world is $1.1 trillion. The one with 12 zeros.

Damn!

So should we just legalize drugs and tax the shit out of them?

THE OTHER SIDE

But of course there is another side. The side that wants to avoid addiction and crime caused by addiction or the need to fund addiction. If no drugs are available, no one dies of an overdose. Or kills someone because they need money. Or just because they are high. Those who do not use drugs because they are illegal might very well use them if they were legal.

Look at alcohol. Kids can't wait until they are old enough to drink and begin at ages earlier than are legal. If the drinking age were 14, do you think more kids would drink and drink more? I think the answer is obvious. Society has mentored us to some degree on how to handle alcohol. Don't drink and drive. We have all done our share of drinking and can usually tell if we have had too much. That does not always translate into an appropriate reaction, but we have a history to draw from.

If we suddenly make drugs legal, then those who experiment will be doing so without a history of how it will affect them. Moderate drinking is deemed acceptable social behavior, especially if it does not negatively affect the drinker or those around them. We cannot yet say the same for drugs. We just don't know. Do we really want to take that chance?

Legalizing drugs may not decrease the amount of illegal

activity. It may decrease the amount of illegal *drug* activity, but those in the illegal activity game will likely find a different illegal outlet for their expertise. Did organized crime go out of business when Prohibition was lifted?

Clearly, the use of drugs would be lower if they remain illegal.

And there would be less chance of stupid accountants trying to bribe their way into World Series games.

GOD 2.0

As a society, we have decreed certain things that are bad for us as legal and certain other things that are bad for us as illegal. There is the concept of degree of harm that should factor into the decision. Something that could kill us will be more harshly viewed than something that can only cause us to get sick.

Cigarette smoking is known to cause cancer. It is legal.

Alcohol is known to cause liver cancer, violence, and potential harm to innocent people. It is legal.

Anyone can buy sleeping pills. Take enough of them and you can off yourself. They are legal.

These are all legal because they were here before all the harms were discovered, and they have a rather large lobbying effort to keep them legal. Not so for illegal drugs…yet.

But let's give it a try. Let's legalize, regulate, and tax the shit out of all drugs. This will also create lots of jobs here in the United States. There will be less of a necessity to grow all this stuff somewhere else and smuggle it in. We can grow it ourselves, creating jobs for lab workers, farmers, marketers, and migrant workers.

And lobbyists.

CHAPTER 24

LEGALIZING PROSTITUTION
(The Pimp and the Pauper)

YOU MEET A NICE WOMAN and ask her out to dinner. You order a bottle of wine, enjoy a nice meal, and maybe have some tiramisu. Maybe you then find a place with some music or even some dancing. A couple more pinot grigios later and you invite her up for a nightcap. She agrees.

You are officially excited. You turn the lights low, put on some soft music, excuse yourself so you can freshen your breath, pour the wine. Conversation continues, but on the soft contours of your couch with her inches away from you, no longer across the table. You waft in her feminine aroma. You ask her what she wants in life. She purrs.

You have exhausted the verbal aphrodisiacs. You go to kiss her.

You have probably invested $200 at this point. Yes, I know you are looking for a relationship, but at this point, that has decayed to basic testosterone. You are a guy. She wants cuddly, you want sex. We will worry about a relationship tomorrow. But she ends the night with a nice kiss and that alluring look that says "maybe next time." But you want it now and are left hanging.

PA BROOK

If only it were legal. Where's *that* app when you need it?

* * *

You come home from work on Friday pumped about having the weekend, but you have no plans. Your internet date cancelled at the last moment, and none of your single buds are free. What to do? You can go to the local bar, but that has rarely produced results. You can troll the dating sites, but your disappointment with the cancellation has you less than excited about internet dating at this point.

What you really want is some female companionship. Yes, that kind of companionship. Tonight it's just about immersing yourself in the physicality. You can do the internet porn thing, but you want shared physicality. Choices are slim.

It was not always the case. I remember the old days in New York City, when choices roamed the streets unabashed. There were certain street corners where you knew a selection was available. They were quite aggressive. Coming up to you or your car with no shame. Some would even give you a sneak preview of what they possessed.

But Mayor Giuliani screwed that up for good.

Even if you weren't interested, it made for a good story when you got home. Not sure the wife appreciated it.

But here you are. No street corners. You would certainly trade your situation for a $200 date and waft of aroma just for the possibility. But you are stuck at home. Wouldn't it be nice to call up and order a pizza for dinner?

And a hooker.

If she only costs $190, you are ahead of the game. And happy. But it's illegal. Oh, well, pizza and porn.

IF I WERE GOD

* * *

Of course, my story has a "happy ending" but not the kind you would think. In the 1980s, my girlfriend lived on the Upper East Side of Manhattan. I would take the subway and then walk a few blocks to her apartment. One night I noticed a quite attractive woman standing in front of a building that looked like a hotel. I wasn't quite sure why she was just standing there. She caught my eye and smiled at me. I began to get the hint.

I passed her on another occasion, and she waved me over. I had never chatted with a prostitute before, so I chalked this up to my continuing adult education. I went over and said, "Hi." Wasting no time, she asked if I would like to go upstairs. Being completely honest and ridiculously nerdy, I replied, "No, but I never spoke to a hooker before and wouldn't mind just chatting." Her retort, with a bit of a smile was, "Sorry, honey, but I have to pay the rent." We both laughed, and I left on good terms with my sort-of newfound friend without benefits.

One night soon thereafter, I was walking home from dinner with my girlfriend, and we happened to pass the same hotel with the same young lady standing in front. Unabashed, as I guess salespeople must be, she hollered out, "Why don't you drop off the girlfriend and come see me for a while?"

I am pleased to say the only reason I still have my testicles intact is because I'd had the good sense to tell my girlfriend the original story of how we met prior to that night. Her response was simple, "Is that the one...?" We both laughed, and I waved to my FWOB. See, happy ending, testicles intact.

But what is prostitution like in real life? Should it be legalized? Should it be regulated? Should it be taxed? There are opinions on both sides of this debate, some passionate, some clinical. Mine are simply logical.

But before we get into that, let's look at some statistics. Compiled from various and sundry quasi-intellectually reliable websites and opinions, I offer you the following.

PROSTITUTION STATISTICS

Here are some interesting statistics about prostitution from statisticsbrain.com:

> The average annual income of a US prostitute is $290,000. Presumably tax-free. Pre-tax, they would have to earn around $475,000 to still take that home. Hookers would have to raise their prices to compensate. That's $185,000 in tax revenue lost. I might be getting ahead of myself here.
>
> 22 countries have legalized prostitution.
>
> 80,000 American citizens are arrested annually for soliciting sex. I would have to think the total that engage in soliciting sex is a multiple of that number.
>
> The cost to taxpayers annually, in court and jail fees, to prosecute prostitutes is $200 million.
>
> Some experts estimate there are 1-2 million prostitutes in the United States, 40-42 million worldwide.
>
> You want some more statistics (from The Prostitution Statistics You Have to Know)?
>
> Prostitutes are beaten on average 12 times per year.

Prostitutes have unprotected sex 300 times per year.

10% of men in the world have purchased a prostitute.

Murder rate for prostitutes is 20 times the national average in the United States.

75%-95% of prostitutes were abused as children.

$58 billion is estimated to be produced annually by the sex-trafficking industry.

The average age of entering prostitution (male or female) is 14.

20% of johns were robbed by prostitutes.

92% of prostitutes say they want to leave prostitution but cannot because of lack of money or food.

90% of New York City prostitutes had to give away at least one child to child protective services.

These statistics make the current state of prostitution appear to be a devastating profession. Would any of that change if it were legalized?

Before we answer that question, a brief history of prostitution is not only in order, but entertaining.

HISTORY OF PROSTITUTION (ACCORDING TO PROCON.ORG)

The first notation of prostitution on a list of professions was in 2400 BC. Other female occupations were noted (lady doctor, scribe, barber, cook), so perhaps prostitution is not the oldest profession. But probably the most fun. And profitable.

Legal brothels appeared in China in the 600s BC. The idea was to increase state revenue. It may have just increased the state population. After China, various jurisdictions both legalized and criminalized prostitution along the way to the ADs.

In the 1500s, the courtesan made a renaissance. The courtesan was considered a classy woman who was very selective in her clientele. She was desired by the high-class district. Perhaps this was a forerunner of the escort service (with or without sex).

In the early days of America, prostitution was not always illegal. There were laws against "sexual deviants" who could be punished for, among other offenses, night walking. Women who strolled the street for immoral purposes were subject to arrest. I'm not sure if screwing in public was considered sexual deviance. That would certainly advocate for getting "down" to business quickly.

Prostitution flourished in New York City in the late 1700s as its seaport identity brought in many from other areas looking for comfort. Imagine what Indians could have gotten for Manhattan had they factored in that business proposition.

New Orleans criminalized prostitution on the first floor of buildings in the late 1800s. But only the first floor. The law was soon declared unconstitutional. Apparently floor discrimination was not to be tolerated.

In New York City in the early 20th century, a committee of 15 was formed to study how New York should treat prostitutes. I wonder how many were johns. The results of the study were inconclusive, as the committee opposed regulation and favored improved work conditions for prostitutes. But it also favored higher wages, so I guess not all of them were clients.

In 1918, legislation was passed that allowed the government

to quarantine (and take other remedial steps against) a woman suspected of having a sexually transmitted disease. Note the term "suspected." Not "found" or "proven" but simply "suspected." That monumentally discriminatory legislation was followed 2 years later by women being given the right to vote. Was remorse at work? Hopefully just common sense.

Other examples of mid-20th-century prostitution-alization:

Japan created brothels in WWII for the use of Japanese soldiers. Wives weren't happy.

"Entertainers" in Hawaii were licensed and expected to pay taxes in the 1940s. Another reason to retire there.

Germany regulated brothels during the pre-WWII years. Republicans claim this is an example of how regulation can bring down an entire civilization.

After WWII, there were many instances of decriminalizing, legalizing, or regulating prostitution. Nevada and the Netherlands are the most well-known stories. Then there was the First World Whore Congress (WWC) in 1985, an international conference of prostitutes and supporters to champion rights of prostitutes. Many believe Congress had been whoring way before then. The World Charter for Prostitutes' Rights, which includes provisions for legalization, working conditions, and health education and testing, was born from this movement (no condom use there). There was a Second WWC the following year, but I could not find a record of a third. Perhaps the Pimp Union intervened.

TO LEGALIZE OR NOT

Isn't prostitution just two consenting adults who are not married or in a relationship but are having sex? The only difference is the exchange of money. Is a $200 dinner an exchange of money for sex if sex is expected? What about adultery? That often excludes even the dinner, so it is purely the same thing but no money is exchanged. Why isn't adultery illegal?

Mail order brides. This is not illegal, but is it any different? Actually, it's worse as it can turn into indentured slavery, and marriage is a commitment, not a one-night stand.

If you pay her, it's illegal; if you buy her dinner, it is not.

If you pay her, it's illegal; if you enslave her, it is not.

Of course, the difference is the manner in which the activity occurs. Despite consent in all instances, the surrounding environment is potentially horrific for the prostitute. What if we cleaned up that environment?

There are passionate arguments on both sides of the legalization of prostitution debate.

PRO-FESSIONALS

Proponents of legalizing prostitution argue the following:

Tax revenues could be significant. Nevada brothels collectively make around $50 million per year. Using the statistics from above, there's $185,000 per prostitute in lost tax revenue. Suppose there are 1-2 million prostitutes in the United States. Let's use the midpoint, 1.5 million. The sound you hear is my calculator asking for a raise. There could be $277.5 billion in tax revenues from legalizing prostitution. That would feed a lot of poor people.

Health standards can be instituted. There would clearly be a reduction in sexually transmitted diseases for both prostitutes and johns.

Prostitutes can be protected. They may be more liable to report crimes against them if there is no fear of prosecution for themselves.

IF I WERE GOD

Legalizing takes organized crime out of it. Look at alcohol and Prohibition. Once Prohibition ended, organized crime had to look elsewhere for revenue.

Some believe government intervention into consensual activity should be unconstitutional on its face. Prostitution is simply the provision of services for a fee. Whether that fee is cash secured at first meeting or provided through weeks of expensive courtship is inconsequential.

Others argue that money spent trying to prevent prostitution is wasted. Money spent prosecuting prostitution includes:

Cops arresting prostitutes.

The district attorney's office prosecuting prostitutes.

The public defender's office defending prostitutes.

Medical costs for the results of cat fights among prostitutes in detention. Although ticket sales to the event could offset that.

Legalizing prostitution reduces human trafficking (an opinion supported by different studies).

It is vulnerability that creates victims, not sex work. Remove the vulnerability by legalizing it, and victimization is lessened.

CON-DOMS

Those against legalizing prostitution argue the following:

Legalizing prostitution leads to an increase in demand. Yeah, baby! If it is legal, then more men may participate. This can lead to increases in human trafficking. This argument is used for both pros and cons.

Prostitution is dehumanizing to women.

Prostitution takes desperate women and further abuses them.

Rape flourishes in an environment where men sexually control women. Women are loathe to report it since they may then be arrested.

Prostitutes do not benefit from any kind of labor rights.

Even when legalized and regulated, women who would be required to report as a legal prostitute do not report as such because of the stigma.

There is a blurred line between forced and voluntary prostitution even where it is legal.

Imagine an unemployed woman in an environment of legalized prostitution. When unemployed, someone must seek a job for which they are qualified, and accept it if offered or risk the loss of unemployment benefits. Clearly any woman is "qualified" to be a prostitute. Could society unintentionally force a woman into prostitution who cannot find a better alternative and who would otherwise lose her unemployment benefits? A cynical corollary could muse whether government would abdicate its responsibility for making decent employment available for women because prostitution is always available.

The pros and cons, and passionate opinions, do not stop with the above. It is just a sampling of considered thought that has gone into the debate. Some supported by studies, others just opinion.

RESULTS OF LEGALIZATION

There are many studies of the aftermath of legalization or decriminalization of prostitution, with results on both sides

IF I WERE GOD

of the argument. Here are some interesting tidbits that I came across:

Rhode Island unintentionally legalized prostitution in 1980. This was brought to the public's attention based on a criminal case in 2003. The law was corrected in 2009, criminalizing it again. During the 6 years prostitution was publically legal, the number of rapes in the state declined by 31%. Gonorrhea infection among women dropped by 93%.

New Zealand had no increase in sex trafficking or number of sex workers 5 years after decriminalizing prostitution.

Germany incurred a decline in sex trafficking after legalizing prostitution, but the results also included a lack of any measurable improvement in the social coverage or working conditions for prostitutes or their ability to exit the profession. Perhaps a wash.

Australia's attempt to legalize did not meet its goals, as it failed to maintain regulations and standards to keep the women safe and healthy.

In Sweden, the law was changed to make it illegal *to buy* sex. Ingenious. Reduce the demand, and the problem is mitigated. Street prostitution declined by 50% and the number of prostitutes declined by a similar number. The number of men who visited a prostitute before the law was enacted was 12%. The after was 8%.

In Germany again, Flat-Rate Brothels became in vogue. One price for everything, for a day or evening session. Complaints from patrons that the women were no longer fit for use after a few hours were common. No shit!

Streetwalkers in Bonn, Germany, could purchase a ticket from a machine that was valid until 6 AM the next morning to ply their trade. Like a parking meter.

GOD 2.0

Let's start with money. I know there are studies out there on how much prostitutes make, but I am going to make my own study. Let's assume one works on her own, can make $200 for an hour, works 5 nights a week with an average of 5 clients per night. Factor in a healthy 4 weeks of vacation, 5 sick days, and all federal holidays. That leaves 226 days of work or $226,000 in salary. Not far off from the $290,000 noted above. And still tax free. Yes, medical expenses will be higher and there might be some hazardous conditions from time to time. No commentary here, just my facts. I am avoiding a pimp situation. Not a bad salary if you can handle the working conditions. Of course, there will be those who can make a lot more (anyone see *Pretty Woman*?), but also those women who are working for pimps or on drugs or in other dire straits.

Ah, but those working conditions. And the pimp thing. And the perceived degradation. Many women are in prostitution because they have to be. They do it to make ends meet or support a habit.

But the real reason that legalized prostitution has not worked as well as its proponents hoped was not because of a flawed concept. It was because of the flawed execution of the concept. Since prostitution was illegal for so long, its stigma did not disappear simply because it became legal. Since the stigma was still there, there remained lack of respect for the women and, therefore, protection of the women. Men have ruled most societies from the beginning. Men still dominate law enforcement. You can't just change the law. There must be changes in perception and education. Women have been fighting for equal rights for centuries. This fight is no different. Because it has not been won yet does not mean it should not be fought.

IF I WERE GOD

Therefore, the best solution is to legalize prostitution but also incorporate the following concepts:

Build a business model. Marijuana businesses have sprung up and are successful despite being a formerly illegal business. Have prostitution follow suit. Make it profitable to be a company that sponsors prostitution. It will not be hard.

Crack down on pimps. Seriously crack down. Significant jail time if you pimp. More if you abuse the women.

Arrest men if they engage with unregistered prostitutes. Follow the Swedish example of making the purchase of sex, not the selling of it, illegal. Here, it will be the purchase of illegal sex. With an option to purchase legal sex, this should lessen the effect of the black market for prostitution.

Create a union. Follow some of the principles of the First Whore Congress.

Enforce the principals of safety, health, and acceptance.

I will leave execution of these concepts in the hands of those expert in law enforcement and the issues of prostitution. I am not going to fix everything myself.

What would I need people for?

CHAPTER 25
CITIZENSHIP WITHOUT ENGLISH
(Needing an Interpreter for the Pledge of Allegiance)

Press 1 if you want to read this chapter in Spanish.

Oh, don't have any buttons? Just read below then.

Si usted quiere ser un americano, puta aprender inglés.

First of all, if you only speak Spanish, how are you going to know to press 1 to read this in espanol?

TONGUE-TIED

It is uniquely human to be able to talk. I was not aware of this, as I hear animals make sounds all the time. Like those damn birds tweeting at 5:30 in the morning and owls hooting in the middle of the night. But they are not talking. And those stupid little tiny dogs that yip yip yip all the time. I love dogs, but those bastards are just obnoxious.

So while animals can make sounds and some can even mimic human languages, they do not have the necessary anatomy to create speech. And not only can humans talk, they have the capacity to understand multiple languages. Including English, the predominant language of the United States, but not its "official" language. The United States does not have an official language. Some have argued that we should have an official language, and everything that relates to the federal government should be in English, including speaking only English in the execution of all federal government business. This would have made Ellis Island an unfriendly place.

A financial argument for having an official language and limiting official communications to English is that this would surely save the government a lot of money by eliminating the need to translate so many forms, instructions, websites, etc., into multiple languages. One report had the IRS translating 500,000 income tax forms at a cost of $113,000. Only 718 of the forms were filed. That's a lot of money to be saved.

Still others believe an English-only society would create more harmony and diminish our differences.

But wait. Isn't this the land of opportunity for all those from around the world? Embracing different cultures has been a hallmark of our development. Why not embrace all languages?

Many who come to this country learn English as a second language, and their dual-language abilities benefit them. And us. In this ever-globalizing world, many English-only US citizens would benefit from learning a second language, so we do not wish to discourage the use of multiple languages in the United States. Actually, multilinguists should be encouraged.

Certainly immigrants who learn English will have the benefits of additional employment opportunities as well as enjoyment of the US culture.

But should it be a requirement?

What about...

BECOMING A US CITIZEN

Per the US Citizenship and Immigration Services (USCIS) website, in general, applicants for naturalization must demonstrate an understanding of the English language, including an ability to read, write, and speak words in ordinary usage.

Sounds like a requirement.

They must also demonstrate a knowledge and understanding of the fundamentals of the history and principles and form of government of the United States.

Sounds reasonable that a citizen should have some basic level of knowledge of the history of their country of allegiance. Together, these are known as the English and civics requirements for naturalization. However, there are exceptions to these rules. Bear with me, as it appears an ape could become a citizen.

NO SPEAKA DE ENGLISH

Per the USCIS website, you are exempt from the requirement to know the English language, which means you can take the citizenship test in the language of your choice, if:

You are age 50 or older at the time of filing for naturalization and have lived as a permanent resident (green-card holder) in the United States for 20 years, or;

You are age 55 or older at the time of filing for naturalization and have lived as a permanent resident in the United States for 15 years.

If you are age 65 or older and have been a permanent resident for at least 20 years at the time of filing for naturalization, you will be given special consideration regarding the civics requirement.

IF I WERE GOD

Not sure what those considerations are. Maybe they give you an abacus and a civics professor.

If you do take the test in your native language, you must bring an interpreter with you to your interview. Your interpreter must be fluent in both English and your native language, but you don't have to be. And your interpreter does not have to be a citizen, but he speaks English and you don't.

Huh?

So let me get this straight. You have come from a foreign country, managed to stay here for 15 or 20 years, made a living in the United States, and have not learned English. That is almost impossible. And where it is possible, you would have had to have tried really, really hard not to learn the language. You must have worked in a job where they speak your native tongue only and don't wish to speak English. You must have family and friends who speak your native tongue only and don't wish to speak English. You must have searched for entertainment in your native language...only.

So, clearly, you did not *want* to learn the language.

So, clearly, go the fuck home.

We'll take the ape.

MEDICAL DISABILITY EXCEPTIONS TO ENGLISH AND CIVICS

Again per the USCIS website and related form instructions, you may be eligible for an exception to the English-speaking requirement as well as the requirement to take the civics exam if you are unable to do so because of a physical or developmental disability or a mental impairment that has lasted, or is expected to last, 12 months or more. To request this exception, there is a form to be filled out by a licensed medical professional.

PA BROOK

So you can be crazy and become a citizen.

We have enough of those in Congress.

In simple terms, the medical professional must establish and certify that you have a physical or mental abnormality that has impaired your functioning so severely that you are unable to learn or demonstrate knowledge of English and/or US history and government. So you could abnormally not give a shit about becoming a citizen because of a mental impairment, and still become one.

What does that do for us? Isn't citizenship a two-way street? You get the benefits of being an American, and we get the benefit of your allegiance to America. Oh, wait, if you are insane, you do not have to pledge allegiance to America. No, you do, you just don't know what you are saying or what it means. You are, after all, crazy.

Guess what, we don't want you. We won't deport you; we just won't give you citizenship.

But it does say physical or mental impairment. Crazy is mental. What about physical? There is no definitive list of physical impairments noted as a cause for exemption. But what kind of physical impairment would prevent you from learning English or civics? I could certainly understand an impairment if one or more of your senses was affected, e.g., hearing or sight, or if you are incapable of speech. I support that accommodations should be made to facilitate the learning of English and the civics. But what other physical impairment would prevent you from learning them?

Hangnail—imagine not cutting your nails for 12 months. Just to get an exemption from learning that George Washington crossed the Delaware. In bare feet. Well, he didn't, but don't tell Hangnail Man.

I am still at a loss.

IF I WERE GOD

So you can have a mental or physical impairment, not learn English or anything about the country you are becoming a citizen of, and you get the benefit of our freedoms and social services (perhaps more so than you can comprehend, especially because you are disabled in some way). What do we get? A feel-good moment that we have contributed to the life of someone less fortunate than us? We have enough of that without you.

However, you do need a doctor's note to claim either mental or physical impairment. Nothing fancy, apparently. The same doctor who wrote you a note to excuse you from school in fifth grade because of a hangnail can write you a note to help you become a citizen.

Presumably the doctor's note has to be in English.

Or does it?

OATH OF ALLEGIANCE
An Oath of Allegiance is required at the ceremony of citizenship. It is administered in English. However (ugh), an applicant may have a translator to translate the oath during the ceremony. Seriously.

The Oath includes swearing to uphold the Constitution of the United States along with "to renounce and abjure absolutely and entirely all allegiance and fidelity to any foreign prince, potentate, state, or sovereignty of whom or which the applicant was before a subject or citizen."

In other words, if you are from France, you can tell your former BFF to go fuck themselves.

In French.

There seems to be something wrong with that.

Finally, having been accommodated with your native

language throughout becoming a citizen of a country whose language you do not speak, one would think you could memorize a few lines to show some sincerity and thanks that you get to afford yourself all the benefits of being an American citizen. One would think you would want to. But it's OK, you don't have to.

Not in my Kingdom.

GOD 2.0
Beta God proclaimed that we do not have to know English to live here and some accommodations will be made at the discretion of those around you. That sounds reasonable and laudable. And best for a country that prides itself in diversity and opportunity. But to gain citizenship, you have to know English. Well, maybe.

God 2.0 is both compassionate and fiercely patriotic. (Yes, he is a man and an American.)

Let's be humane here but also have a sense of pride for our country. For immigrants who are here legally trying to make a better life and assimilate into society, we should make initial attempts to assist them in their native tongue. Basic health and human services, police protection, job searches, etc., can all have other languages available to assist those in need. There should be a strong encouragement to learn English and availability of classes to do so.

But to become a citizen, learn the fucking language.

The basic rights of citizenship include voting, trial by jury, freedom of speech and religion, among others. If you avail yourself of these rights, you will have to do it in English. Sorry, no ballots in Spanish. No interpreters in court. No federal tax forms in German.

IF I WERE GOD

By the way, the Pledge of Allegiance in Spanish sounds something like:

Yo prometo lealtad a la bandera de los estados Unidos de America, y a la Republica que representa, una Nacion bajo Dios, entera, con libertad y justicia para todos.

That is just not right.

This is real simple. If you want to be a citizen of the United States of America, learn English. No speaka de English, no passporta de US. I don't care if you have 27 personalities, have been raised by monkeys, or even fucked by monkeys—no English, no citizenship.

CHAPTER 26
GOVERNMENT WASTE
(It's Fun Spending Other People's Money)

WE CHATTED EARLIER ABOUT BULLSHIT studies. Many of them are funded by Uncle Sam. Oops, wait. That means many of them are funded by you and me. We are going to discuss a lot of areas of government waste. Not a new topic, but certainly a new spin. To get the ball rolling, how about these studies the government laid out money for:

A $400,000 study on how humans make decisions, using online dating as its premise, concluded that men like thin women and nonsmokers prefer...nonsmokers.

A related study found that 77% of all women preferred dating a man who was...

Alive.

Just my luck, I find the 23%.

A study entitled "Understanding Age Related Changes in Relationship Maintenance Strategies" should have been entitled "How to Date Grandma." It wasted $375,000 of government money.

In what could have been a classic *Survivor* food challenge, young children were asked if they liked food that was sneezed on better than food that was not. This was part of a $2 million grant by a government agency to study what influences kids' views on food. Anyone want to guess "sugar?" But this study was complete with visuals of actors actually sneezing on the food. As all studies do, incredibly complex terms were used, including describing the un-boogered food as "yummier." The study both acknowledged similar studies from the past and recommended future studies.

Achoo.

But at least it was about humans.

MONEY DOES GROW ON TREES

So why is there government waste? Why can't governments make money like normal corporations? Let me count the ways.

Corporations don't give their money away to foreign countries to help them do shit they don't care about and that doesn't help their customers. The government does.

A government agency allocated $250,000 to what many would call a worthy cause—the green movement. Environmentally friendly this, environmentally friendly that. Good cause. In Morocco.

Of all the gin joints in all the towns in all the world, let's solar panel Rick's Café.

Another government department allocated $5,000,000 to reduce wanton killing and trafficking of wild animals. In Africa. Maybe they are pissed that Rick let Ilsa get away. I was.

Sorry, but $5,000,000 is much better spent on humans in the United States.

Finally, another government agency set aside a measly $25,000 for the creation of a workshop in India on media ethics. Is that the pot calling the kettle black or an oxymoron?

Depends on the content.

MAKING MONEY THE OLD-FASHIONED WAY

How about just making money? The government funds private companies and industries that are not making enough money to survive by themselves. Well, blow them the fuck up!

Government subsidies include help for the sugar, dairy, and peanut industries. What happened to capitalism? Only the strong survive? If an industry cannot figure out how to make itself profitable, then it isn't important enough to exist. If it is important enough to exist, people will pay what it takes to make the industry profitable.

If I refuse to pay $5 for a bag of peanuts (which, by the way, is OK if it is at a good concert) and that is what it takes to make the peanut business profitable, then the peanut industry goes away. Walnuts will be fine. WB&J has a ring to it.

Amtrak. The train people. You would think it's a profitable business, right? The government subsidizes Amtrak to the tune of more than $1 billion per year. They would shoot it if it were a horse. Maybe we go back to horses. No nasty conductors or fat people sitting next to me to deal with. If Amtrak lost its subsidy, it would figure out a way to make things work. Perhaps people would be willing to pay more to take the train than they are. Perhaps Amtrak would figure out ways to save money. Or Mr. Ed sales would skyrocket. But life would go on and folks would get from here to there. And the government would have a billion to spend elsewhere. Or pay off the national debt.

Novel idea.

IF I WERE GOD

CAN YOU EAR ME NOW?

Earmarking is a controversial practice of adding local-level spending to appropriations bills to benefit a particular Polly's local constituency. Frequently, earmarks have been used as a means to sway Polly to vote for a particular bill. That is called bribery. Earmarks at their best are attempts by a Polly to get something legitimate done in his district. To fund a much needed new road in town, for example. Government dollars are meant for that. At their worst, they are attempts to make friends and get reelected. A big corporation that supports a local candidate has some power. Its CEO likes opera and *voila!* A $250,000 grant for the local opera company is slipped into the Defense Department appropriations bill.

Or Polly Joe is trying to impress his new rich in-laws and creates an earmark so his father-in-law's construction business can repave a new road.

There are better ways to get into the will.

Maybe not for Joe.

If you want to use earmarks as negotiation tools or as a way to generate cohesiveness, at least make the expenditures have universal application and appeal. Don't fund a $3 million project to study the DNA of bears in Montana. Fund a study that helps poor people in Montana. The most prominent earmark is probably the infamous "bridge to nowhere" that would have connected the Alaskan town of Ketchikan to an airport on the nearby island of Gravina. After a $223 million earmark was secured in 2005, the failed project was scrapped 10 years later.

Earmarks were actually banned in 2011, but a rose by any other name still pricks the same.

Activist groups like the Citizens Against Government Waste have attempted to identify and eliminate waste, fraud, abuse, and mismanagement in government. Despite the ban on earmarks, they continue to identify the thorny roses that Pollys tried to identify as carnations (ask any woman, that is not hard to do). Earmarks continue to exist.

WHO YOU GONNA CALL...LANDSCAPERS?

The federal government owns about one-third of the land in the United States. Once again, I am going to use some fancy math here. You can skip a paragraph or two if you blanch at numbers. I get it. I can't change a light bulb without a close call with electrocution.

Various estimates exist for the value of land. One estimate put an acre of land at $3,000. Another looked at it differently and estimated that the total value of all the land in the United States was $23 trillion. There are 2.3 billion acres of land in the United States.

Abacus, please.

Multiply those 2.3 billion acres by $3,000 per acre. Golly gee, Batman, that's a big number—$6.9 trillion, to be exact. If you don't want to take that as gospel, then consider the total value of all land in the United States of $23 trillion and divide it by 3 since the government owns one-third. Don't need superpowers for this one. It's $7.7 trillion. Not far enough away from the $6.9 trillion to think somewhere in the middle might be at least in the ballpark. The US national debt at the time of this writing was in the neighborhood of $18 trillion. We could pay off more than one-third of it just by selling the land the government owns.

Sell some fucking land.

I want to be a real estate broker.

It will not be that easy, since a lot of the land is used. But that which is not, bye bye. And sell some of it to private industry. They know how to make a profit out of land.

EARLY TO BED AND EARLY TO RISE...
Makes me boring and tired. Public service will suit me fine.

Governments play with other people's money. How fun is that? Give me a boatload of cash and free rein to spend it on anything I want. And I chose to become an accountant. Actually, I was a financial adviser for several years and did indeed have other people's money to play with. I took that very seriously. More seriously than my own money. But few are like that.

Give a politician someone else's money to spend, and he excels at that. Why can't a smart (most are lawyers), articulate, charismatic person champion a good cause? If you are smart enough to talk people into voting for you, or maybe voting against the blithering psychopath who was your opponent, then why can't you do the right thing?

And why do we keep voting for these motherfuckers?!?!?!?

What, me, cynical?

But why does this happen over and over and over again? Let's think about the psychology of government waste. What is it in the human condition that makes politicians and others not care about waste?

The government has a job everybody wants. Spending lots of money—other people's money—with no real consequences. There is no profit motive in government. There is not even a reduce spending motive. There are only motives to spend more money because...

Politicians get reelected when they do good things for their constituency. Even if the constituency does not deserve it or it is not an effective way to spend money. But the locals get a benefit, and Polly gets reelected.

In an ironic twist of fate, because the government is spending other people's money, it tries to do a good thing. Craft some rules to make sure it is not spent inappropriately. But they let the cow out with the nipples, or however the fuck that goes. They can make it so difficult to get things purchased that ease trumps efficiency.

Government workers are not paid top dollar. There has always been a discount for lifestyle and benefits. But who does that attract? Not Bill Gates. I do not wish to disparage government workers, but if they could have gotten a job at Apple, they would not be processing Social Security applications. Think of it this way. Private industry has decided to hire the best and the brightest, and the result is that we have an economy where a lot of private companies make a lot of money. The government loses money. Do you think the people who run things have anything to do with that? If the premise is that hiring the smartest people and paying them a lot of money will result in a better bottom line, then maybe the government should get on board.

Now, I will have to fuck with unions. I do not have a problem with them. Actually, it is the fault of the business for giving unions too much power. I can't fault a union for trying to get all of its constituents high-paying jobs with no fear of being fired no matter how badly they perform. I would negotiate for that as well. But it's the dumb employers who signed up for that who are to blame. Some of them are private companies, but those who signed the bad deal probably got fired. I am not so sure about the ones who negotiated the government union contracts. As noted above, they were negotiating with other people's money. We know where that is going.

IF I WERE GOD

POLLY APPOINTEES

Many high-level government jobs are appointed by the Polly in power. This leads to unqualified folks in charge of shit they know nothing about. And perhaps only while Polly is in office. No reelect, no job. So this dude has no job security and doesn't know what the fuck he is doing.

Ouch.

This reminds me of the mutual fund business in the old days. Funds are public companies and are required to have independent boards of directors. Directors are charged with overseeing companies and protecting shareholder interests. Oftentimes, the directors were chums of the guy running the money for the fund. He might have been a sculptor. Perhaps a musician. Not exactly qualified to oversee a financial company that invests the public's money, but what most of these directors did have in common was no knowledge of what the SEC stood for.

Lest you think I am talking out of my ass. Again.

In many government agencies, there are no repercussions for bad behavior. That means it's really hard to get fired. So people who could not get jobs at Apple, for some reason, now work where they know they won't get fired. Mmmm, is that sudoku I hear being played in accounting?

WHAT, ME WORRY?

What about fraud? If there is no incentive to do the job right, there will be cracks in the process that can be exploited. And they are.

One of the most glaring areas is Medicare. You can do your own research here, but what gets me is that they publish a report on "Improper Payments" each year. An improper payment is any payment to the wrong provider, for the wrong services or in the wrong amount. This includes overpayments and underpayments. These improper payments are most often caused by lack of any or insufficient documentation, lack of determining medical necessity, and incorrect coding. In 2017, according to a government agency, there were $36 billion of improper payments. That equals almost 10% of the total Medicare payments. Yikes.

Now, yes, some of those could be because of legitimate human error, but it could also be because of fraud. First, a 10% human error rate would cause someone permanent unemployment (perhaps with lifetime benefits if that agency is as inept as Medicare). Second, if we know $36 billion is being paid "improperly," why would we not do something about making that better? In 2016, it was $41 billion (11% of total payments), so it's not getting better.

I do not even want to guess how much is spent each year on producing a report that tells you things are really screwed up. The 2017 report is 90 pages long. I wonder how much is spent on trying to fix the issue. Obviously, not enough.

The Social Security Administration does not seem to be much better. Because of a breakdown in officially recording death certificates, it appears that there are about 6.5 million people over the age of 112. That's not a typo. This does not mean that these 6.5 million supercentenarians (who knew that was a fucking word?) are all getting Social Security payments, but how many are?

In private industry, one would hire a consultant to come in and figure out what the fuck is going on and come up with a way to fix it. It would cost way less than $36 billion. Those who screwed up would be given a nice severance and a recommendation, but they would be gone. Other consultants would come in to install new systems, new processes would be put in place, and *voila!* We are making money again.

Auditors would be hired, consultants paid a fortune. But

in the end, there would not be any more fraud or "improper fucking payments." And the company would make money again. Given the amount of money the government gives away to fraud, hiring a forensic accountant from time to time and implementing his fucking recommendations would cost a shitload less than what is being lost to fraud and waste.

USE IT OR LOST IT

This is the theory that if you don't spend your budget, you will have the excess taken away and next year, you will have to live on less. Somehow, not spending your entire budget might be a good thing. If you spent less than you budgeted, perhaps you should be rewarded. Now, if you just didn't get everything accomplished that was in the budget, you don't get a bonus. But if you legitimately did a good job, why waste the money on buying some shit you don't really need just to spend the budget? How about spending it on a bonus for those who did a good job?

That would be corporate America. Capitalism at its finest. Save money, get rewarded.

Pollys spend money and get rewarded. Or not. But no one cares.

So how do we fix it?

Unfortunately, only Pollys can fix the system, and it is not self-serving to fix it. Pollys always want a cracker.

Incent government workers to make a profit. Or save money. Or just be efficient.

And we need to create a position of power for someone to make this happen. And he needs an authoritative title. Like president or CEO. How about Grand Poobah Motherfucking Budget King? OMG, what a concept. How unique and original. Have someone with authority and an incentive to make budget decisions. One person. Grand Poobah Motherfucking Budget King. We pay him a lot of money to balance the budget for real. No hidden ball tricks or disappearing revenue. President can't fuck with him. Congress can't fuck with him. Christ, even Kevin Spacey can't fuck with him. Although he may want to.

We'll even have a nickname for him. My favorite was always the accounting oversight board that was known as Peekaboo. Now that's a name for someone overseeing numbers. Actually, it was the Public Company Accounting Oversight Board. Peekaboo. I loved it. They did not. It is no longer referred to as "disappearing money." But that should not stop us from creating our own. It does have to be politically correct, especially since the real name is not. So it will always be referred to as this in the press and on Fox News. Howard Stern will come up with a way to get someone to say "motherfucking" at some point. But for now, we will go with…

PoMoFo

But we still have to work on the cause. PoMoFo can't fight the totality of city hall. So what else can we do? If the cause is Polly, you need to get rid of Polly. Or at least make him more reasonable.

TERM LIMITS

Obviously this is not a reality show because this would never happen. If only a few Pollys were good people, we could get things like term limits done. It doesn't mean you have to retire from being a Polly. Just take a break.

If you can't get term limits, let's try campaign finance reform. Rich people should not have an advantage when it comes to running for office. I'm not implying that poor people would make better Pollys, but it is a club that is populated with rich people.

Now wait a moment. So we have mostly rich successful businessmen as Pollys. That seems like something desirable. They know how to build profitable companies and run successful businesses. Perfect to be the fiduciary for our tax dollars. But something happens on the way to the state capital. It's called power. And their incentive has now changed. They were elected to represent the people and do the best for them they can. But what is a Polly's overall goal in life? Reelection. Not make a profit. Not reduce expenses. Not discover fraud. Get reelected.

We are humans, and we respond to positive and negative reinforcement. Unfortunately we are providing the wrong reinforcement to our Pollys.

But what else do Pollys have? They do not get paid a lot of crackers to be a Polly. So the profit incentive is not there. There is no bonus for a job well done. So why does a Polly embark on such a life? Power. Replace power with dollars, and the Polly will not complain. Reward Polly in a way to make him do the best job possible for the people. What is that? Since nothing else has worked, here are some ideas:

Bring back Monica Lewinsky. A good blow job has been known to alter behavior.

Host the *Apprentice*—look what it did for Donald Trump.

Bang Stormy Daniels—look what it did for Donald Trump.

GOD 2.0

So let's see how we fix this.

The government stops spending money on bullshit stuff. Uh

oh, all the people who worked on the bullshit stuff are out of a job.

But as with most important things in life, there will be some philanthropist or rich guy to take up a good cause. Of course, if the cause sucks, oh well.

Now the newly unemployed go on unemployment for a while. Paying unemployment is certainly cheaper for the government than paying their salary or funding some stupid project.

With the government saving so much money, they can cut taxes.

Private companies make more money.

They invest some of it and hire some of the unemployed.

The formerly unemployed now work harder and are more productive because if they don't, they might actually get fired.

Companies use these newly productive employees to build their business to even bigger heights and larger profits.

And pay more taxes.

Everyone is ahead. Folks are making more money in private industry; companies are making profits.

Maybe some rich guys are frustrated because their formerly government-funded projects don't seem too worthwhile or are executed poorly.

And some monkeys have time on their hands. Maybe they can collect unemployment.

Oh, and the government is ahead.

I think.

CHAPTER 27
MY TRAVEL BAN
(Give Me Your Tired, Your Poor, Your Huddled Masses Yearning to Breathe Free and Throw the Smelly Ones the Fuck Overboard)

TRAVELING IS USUALLY NOT FUN. Regardless of means, getting from one place to another is usually more work than play. When strangers are added to the mix, you have the potential for conflict.

LEAVING ON A JET PLANE

Cramped quarters, recycled air, shitty food. Forget about jet lag. Entertainment choices have gotten better over the years, and there has always been one constant, alcohol. There has been a second constant as well. Inconsiderate fellow travelers.

Who gets the armrests? It is easy for the aisle and the window occupants. They have monopolistic rights over one each. But the two middle ones are up for grabs. Three people, two armrests. If I am in the middle, I say, you have your own armrests, lean the fuck away from me. If I am in the aisle or window, I try to figure out how to make it fair.

It is rare when you have no contest. No one ever sits demurely in the middle seat and crosses their arms or puts them squarely and unequivocally in their space. But I am not asking them to do that. Just be fair.

That leads to the three middle seat types: flexor, extender, or jackass.

The flexors bend nicely and try to find a spot on the armrest so they can be comfortable but don't leak into your space. I usually give them first dibs on a spot and fit into the remainder. There is plenty of room on an armrest for two elbows. Ceding the preferable elbow spot is a small price to pay for having the better seat. Sometimes they take my second choice, and I have a good seat and comfortable elbow spot. These are the nice people.

The extenders set their elbows defiantly on as much of the armrest as they want, leaking at least an elbow into your space. Most normal people will react with accommodation if their elbow is touched, readjusting their position so that both elbows can fit. Not extenders. They are rigid and almost seem to dare you to touch them. If you do, stiffness is their usual response.

But jackasses are the worst. Not only do they take complete control of the armrest, but their knees wander as well. Really. I understand people having a leg issue in the middle seat (I am one of them), but you got dealt a bad hand with the middle seat—deal with it.

What if you are the one in the middle? How do you react to the flexors, extenders, and jackasses who sit in the aisle and window seats?

Take the bus. Or a Xanax.

So did you ever do this, pick an aisle seat on the two-seater side with an empty window seat in the seating chart when you make your selection, instead of the very small single seat on the other side? I did and was surprised when the seat became no longer unoccupied. By a 400 pounder. I took the cramped single seat next time.

This does lead to a very politically incorrect subject. Self-inflicted travelers. I have a solution. Have "obese" rows that cost a little more. Just like the premium seats with more legroom that cost more. Tall travelers are as inconvenienced by small seats as heavy passengers. They have the opportunity to upgrade, so should the huge. Perhaps require them to.

There will be an outcry from many minority groups that will claim discrimination and targeting against a disabled segment of the population. But if a segment of the population is causing harm to the mainstream population, why is it an issue to address it? We are too politically correct these days. We need to stop the euphemisms and call fat fat. If you are pissed at me now, read a few more pages.

CHATTY CABBIE

It was a long day at the office. I need to catch a plane to meet some client or prospect for dinner or breakfast or get to the spa for a facial. I am trying to catch up on emails on my way but run into a stone wall. Chatty Cabbie. I understand cab drivers do not interact with other humans except their customers during the day. That is different from most of us who work with others and have a natural need to converse frequently during the day. But cabbies only have their customers to talk to.

Lucky us.

I have had my share of cab rides where I engaged the cab driver in an interesting conversation. Where are you from? Why are you a cab driver? Do you know where the hookers hang out? But it was always at my beckoning. If I want a conversation, I will engage you. Otherwise, leave me the fuck alone.

Cab drivers should learn from their customer-focused brethren, bartenders. Bartenders are great listeners and will often engage a customer in conversation. This is different in two very distinct ways. At a bar, I am now in leisure mode and may very well want a conversation. Often, when I have traveled and gone to a bar or restaurant for dinner and am by myself, I enjoy a conversation with the bartender/waiter. But I have chosen to go to a bar, and I am usually looking to relax. Ergo, I do not mind the approach. If he gets out of hand, I can leave. Not so easy with a cab. The other major difference is that the bartender usually has several customers and can chat away with someone else if I am not receptive. The cabbie has only me and can sometimes be relentless.

THE WRONG KIND OF BUZZ

The bronze medal goes to barbers. I have never enjoyed haircuts. There were necessary evils that couldn't end soon enough. Perhaps part of my issue is the most unusually shaped bald spot that developed randomly like lava cooling and forming Australia. It started at 30. When the barber took that mirror so I could see how the back of my head looked, all I could focus on was how my follicle genes must have been smoking way too much pot.

Once again, you are a captive, just like the cab. Only this time, you have a razor blade at your throat. Responsiveness becomes a seeming requisite for continued existence. But I only want to get out of there. So, Mister Barber, please just buzz me and shut up.

HOT WATER IS FREE

I know I am going to piss off a lot of people with this one. We have all run into that guy on the plane who hasn't showered since the Jets won the Super Bowl. Seriously. I knew a flight attendant who had a request from a passenger to deplane a particularly stinky fellow passenger. The flight attendant was skeptical at first, but when she got a whiff, the perpetrator was actually forced to deplane. This was in the '80s. Imagine that happening today. Lawsuits, twitter bombs, discrimination charges, and excuses. Rumor has it a lawsuit ensued but was snuffed out.

Their excuse: "Oh, it's not in my culture to shower." But it's in mine to breathe, so take one if you travel.

Another excuse. "Oh, I did not notice."

Even I could smell the smoke in my clothes when I was a smoker. I know when I need a little extra deodorant. If you stink, you notice it. If you don't shower frequently and think you don't stink, you need more than deodorant.

My favorite: "I am being discriminated against because of my body order." Goddamn right you are. "Smelly" is not a protected class under our discrimination laws.

I know it is not easy to tell someone they smell. Bad breath is the same. Having had an occasional bout with less than stellar oral emissions, I was always incredibly embarrassed when someone told me to brush my teeth. But since they already knew what I did not, me finding out should not make it any more embarrassing. Now, at least I had a chance to fix it.

I had a couple of dates with a lovely young woman in high school—couple being the operative word. Back then, I was a complete nerd and did not even go for anything more than a goodnight kiss on the cheek on the first date. But since the second date was going real well, I fantasized that a good make-out session might be in order. She was kind of shy, and I knew she was not one of "those" girls, so I tempered my hopes. As I began to make my move, I realized she wasn't that shy. Damn, maybe I could get a feel too. I wondered what those things felt like.

Now, I had kissed a girl like "that" before, so I knew what to do. And I executed it flawlessly. And she responded. Flawlessly. Unfortunately.

And I never got the feel. In retrospect, if only I could have held my nose.

Yes, I was that big an idiot back then.

Should I have told her she had less than ideal breath? Perhaps if we were in a relationship (or she'd just given me a blow job), I might have let her know so we could continue the relationship. Or perhaps, depending on how good the blow job was...

But that was then. What do we do now? Again, if you know someone who smells, they will be embarrassed to find out you know. But since you know already, why not tell them so they can fix it? Their embarrassment will be justified, but not telling them and "laughing behind their back" is clearly not a better alternative.

So to summarize, if there is an unfriendly odor, let the odorant know. If you think you smell, do something about it. If someone tells you there is an unpleasant scent about you, fix it, and don't get all bent out of shape.

REALLY SHITTY FOOD

I do not expect airline food to be good. I do expect to recognize it. When trying to feed 150 total strangers, one would think you would choose something mainstream. Grilled chicken with a small potato and a sprig of broccoli. Recognizable. I am not expecting tasty, but at least I can identify the participants. But chicken with some weird cheese on top of it and some leftover Papa John's something stuffed inside with strain of polenta that looks more like a placenta? Or something called mushroom pizza (I still don't know what is wrong with plain pizza) that is a couple of shit-ake mushrooms on top of a pile of dough? No cheese, no tomato sauce. It was like eating a loaf of white bread.

If I want to experiment in a fancy restaurant with a world-famous chef and take my chances on his creating an exquisite dish, I am all for that. But whoever cooks airline food is 7,000 cookbooks away from being a famous chef.

KISS.

BABIES

Is procreation really necessary? Maybe we can do without it for just a little while. I have nothing against babies. If it weren't for them, the world would literally grind to a halt. I was actually one once, but I am not sure it was a pleasant experience. For anyone.

Taking a baby on a plane is likely to be a lousy experience for the parents and the other 148 passengers trying to identify dinner. Babies do not do well in strange environments, forget ones with air pressure changes and close quarters. Parents need to recognize this and leave the babies home unless it is absolutely necessary to bring them. And if they do bring them, they should be required to purchase a conditional ticket. Conditioned upon how much the baby cries during the flight. I don't care if this is difficult to monitor. Who thought a watch could count my calories? Figure it out.

An alternative could be to charge a premium and let the extra revenue go towards an open bar on the flight. And very big ear plugs.

SNORERS

Not much different than babies from a noise standpoint, but

oh, so much easier to remedy. Just wake the motherfucker up! I was on a long flight coming back from Europe and some dude was understandably sleeping, but what was not understandable was why his flying companion refused to give him a little elbow when he started snoring. That's all it takes. Dude stops snoring, remains asleep, everyone is happy.

Shit, the snoring caused some baby to start crying.

GOD 2.0

We should not discriminate against types of travelers based on race, nationality, sex (as a matter of fact, I encourage sex), sexual orientation, or whatever else you want to add to the list. But we should definitely discriminate against the assholes and inconsiderate. We can institute an asshole levy on all public transportation. It will be like a rebate program. Everyone has to pay a little extra for their ticket. If they act appropriately, they can get their ticket punched and redeem it to get a portion of their fare back. No promo code needed.

You can even create rewards points for those who are particularly nice.

"Here, have my pretzels. I know you hate mushroom pizza." – 10 points

"Please, use the entire armrest." – 25 points.

"I'll kidnap the crying baby in row 17 so you can sleep." – 100,000 points

There, much more civilized traveling.

CHAPTER 28
MEDICAL RESEARCH
(Funding Nurture vs. Nature)

BULLSHIT STUDIES ASIDE, THERE IS also some very important non-bullshit research going on. Like trying to cure cancer and a host of other diseases. Stuff that kills us. For perspective, most research funding comes from two major sources, corporations (approximately 60%) and government/universities (30%). How they spend their research dollars is the subject of much debate.

One might posit that corporations spend research dollars for self-serving purposes. A pharmaceutical company working on a pill to cure sex addiction might very well spend money on research regarding prostitution. Hoping to make it more popular, so there are more people to cure.

Regardless of what the decision makers are deciding, one would also posit that research dollars should be spent on the most important projects for society. Like how to save the most lives. Like how to make sure the prevalence of bad shit happening to good people is minimized. Like in spending research money to fund cures for shit people had no choice in getting. As opposed to lung cancer, where not smoking could have solved almost the entire issue.

So should research money be spent on the most prevalent

diseases or the most prevalent *unpreventable* diseases? Having that filter disses the plurality. But if the plurality had a choice in getting its affliction, should that matter?

One might think the shit that kills us the most would be the same shit that most of the research money is spent on. Taking it a step further, one might think the funding of shit that kills us that is genetic or otherwise unavoidable would be far greater than the funding of shit we could have avoided by not doing related bad shit that caused it (e.g., smoking).

One might.

But corporations fund most of the research. What is their motivation? Certainly not curing anything. Corporations don't really want a cure. No, they want a treatment. If they cure the disease, no one has it and the drug they invented is rendered useless. So treat the symptoms, don't cure the disease.

The National Institute of Health (NIH) publishes statistics on the amount of money spent funding research for various health issues. Their statistics note both the amount spent and the death rate associated with the issue.

My exercise attempts to match funding with death rate and further examine the preventability of the related affliction. One might think the results would make sense.

One might.

Below are several examples of bad shit that happens to people. The focus is on preventable bad shit. It is openly acknowledged that even the most preventable of diseases cannot always be prevented. And there is no lack of sympathy for those who are unlucky enough to contract any disease, whether they contributed to it or not, but when it comes to spending money trying to find cures, should those who had no choice be given research-funding preference?

IF I WERE GOD

I smoked for 20 years. If I get lung cancer, shame on me. Someone who gets some cancer because of bad genes should have a better chance of survival than me. Bad luck trumps bad behavior. With that in mind, let's proceed and start with perhaps the poster boy for funding research of preventable disease.

AIDS

Per the NIH, of all the diseases that had related death statistics, AIDS-related deaths were 40th on the list; that is, 39 other diseases caused more deaths. However, the amount of money spent on AIDS-related research was the second most of all diseases that had deaths associated with them. Some afflictions do not cause death and are ignored for the purposes of these statistics.

Per the Center for Disease Control and Prevention, there were 39,782 new HIV infections diagnosed in the United States in 2016. Of those, 67% of those diagnosed were either gay or bisexual men and 9% were drug users.

Taking a leap of faith that some may dispute, I am going to say that most of the gay/bisexual men contracted the disease from some form of consensual sexual activity, and the drug users contracted the disease from some form of consensual drug activity. That's 76% of the infected. I am assuming the other 24% contracted the disease from some really, really bad luck. Like a blood transfusion. Or other reasons over which they had no control.

Not from voluntary activity.

So the second most research-funded disease is the one in which 75% of the deaths were avoidable.

I will fund all future AIDS research with a paltry $6.99.

Condoms.

SMOKING

Cigarette smoking is the number one risk factor for lung cancer. In the United States, cigarette smoking is linked to more than 80% of lung cancers. People who smoke cigarettes are 15 to 30 times more likely to get lung cancer or die from lung cancer than people who do not smoke.

Lung cancer's funding rank is 17th and its death rank is 12th. So at least it is not funded more than it kills. But at 17, it is funded significantly higher than many diseases that kill a lot of people involuntarily. Once again, a disease from a primarily voluntary activity is heavily funded.

LIVER CIRRHOSIS

One of the most common causes of liver cirrhosis is chronic alcohol abuse. I am beginning to sound like a broken record. Liver diseases, including cirrhosis, rank 20th in funding and 16th in deaths. In addition, there is a separate category of funding for alcoholism. That ranks 12th and 17th for funding and deaths, respectively. There is no evidence that the two overlap. If you combine the two "diseases," you get ranks of 9th and 15th for funding and deaths, respectively. We are not counting general liver disease, which is another separate category that we are assuming is not alcohol- or cirrhosis-related.

At least drinking is fun.

DIABETES

Type 2 diabetes is by far the more common type of diabetes and is caused by overweight, even more overweight (obesity), and physical inactivity. Except for those who have some genetic or medically unpreventable reason, being overweight is caused by eating more calories than expending. A lot more. It ranks 5th and 7th in funding and deaths.

But wait, obesity has its own category as well. Let's do a

spreadsheet. Combined, diabetes and obesity rank 3rd and 7th in funding and death. Again, there are other diseases (e.g., heart disease, certain cancers) that may be caused by diabetes or obesity or to which they may contribute.

Have another cupcake.

HYPERTENSION

Hypertension, or high blood pressure, afflicts about one in every four Americans. It is a major risk factor for heart and kidney diseases, stroke, and heart failure. A list of causes of high blood pressure include:

Smoking

Being overweight or obese

Lack of physical activity

Too much salt in the diet

Too much alcohol consumption (more than 1 to 2 drinks per day)

Stress

Older age

Genetics

Family history of high blood pressure

Chronic kidney disease

Adrenal and thyroid disorders

Sleep apnea

There was no notation that the list is in order of prevalence, but the fact that the first 6 are voluntary was noted. I could interpolate that, at worst, half of the cases would be based on voluntary actions. At best, a significant majority of high blood pressure is based on controllable behavior.

Oh, and what kind of behavior can we exhibit to decrease the chances of high blood pressure? How about...

Don't get fat. Or do get regular exercise. Or don't drink so much. Or do reduce salt intake and stress.

Or you can take drugs and do whatever the fuck you want.

Oh wait, where does this fall? Hypertension ranks 30th in funding but 5th in death rate. That actually sounds about right.

PROSTATE/COLON CANCER

Both of these have a prevention care regimen that is easy to follow. Early detection prevents many deaths and many deaths occur because of a lack of the prevention care regimen. That is truly a shame. But those statistics are as follows:

Prostate cancer – 24th in funding, 23rd in deaths

Colon cancer – 21st in funding, 18th in deaths

DEPRESSION

Ranks 14th in funding and 31st in death rate. I am not sure how you die from depression. Guess there are a lot of shrinks not doing a very good job. And drugs too.

WHO COMES UP WITH THESE NAMES?

I always wonder where the technical names of diseases and drugs come from. Maybe from smoking some. Drugs, that is. Every drug commercial has the official name of the drug noted parenthetically with its brand name highlighted. Sildenafil is Viagra. Fluoxetine is Prozac. Not sure how they got that. Perhaps a contest. That would make working at a pharmaceutical company a little more fun.

"To all employees. We got this new drug for limp dicks and need a name for it. Submit your entries by next week. The winner will get a lifetime supply."

Now we are going to see some employee productivity.

Actually, there is a naming protocol and an approval process that goes into creating both the generic name (e.g., Fluoxetine) and the brand name (e.g., Prozac). I like the naming contest better.

Mis-prescribed drugs are one of the most common errors in health care. Names can be confusing, and there are some that sound alike. A couple of simple examples are Celebrex and Celexa, and Losec and Lasix. Such a mistake can be a deadly one. It makes me think we should be a little more proactive in naming drugs so there can be no confusing them. Sildenafil comes from combining sulfonyl, phenyl, and pyrimidine in some form under a significant amount of hallucinogenic drugs. It has no meaning relative to what it does. Which is make-penis-hard. Bigdickafil would be a much better name for this drug. Embraces the form and substance and will never be confused with any other drug on the market.

Another example is Fluoxetine. It is made up from (maybe) fluor+oxy+methyl+amine, but who really knows what goes on in those labs at midnight on a Wednesday? Did you ever wonder why it takes 20 years to develop a drug and only 30 seconds to figure out my cell phone number and bombard me with 30 calls a day? Some major experimenting going on. These are the fun drugs to work on. Hard-ons and highs.

But this Fluoxe-thing can potentially be confused with something else. So we need to bring a dose of reality to it.

Its principal use is to un-fuck you. Now most of the time fucking is a good thing. But sometimes getting fucked is not fun. And this drug can help when you feel you are getting fucked, but not in the good way. So let's be a little more practical.

Fuckolatime.

There are tons of drugs with weird names. Actually, all of them have weird names. I don't think they are the result of a naming contest.

Maybe a bunch of bored scientists experimenting with them.

IF AN ERECTION LASTS MORE THAN FOUR HOURS

How come it's never the woman who has to go to the hospital?

The most famous side effect of all is the butt (aptly placed) of many jokes. But what is with these side effects? Every drug has side effects. They are so numerous that it can scare you from using the drug. Of course, they put every possible bad thing that can happen to you in the disclosure small print section so they can tell you they warned you and you can't sue. But some of these side effects are seemingly ridiculous. Some appear to be a side effect of every single drug.

In order to be deemed a side effect, it must have shown up in at least 1% of the test population.

Below are some of the most interesting side effects.

Muscle stiffness is a side effect of Prozac. That does not sound like a side effect to me. A hard-on is a sure way to combat depression.

A side effect of Xanax is altered sexual interest and ability. Not depleted. Not enhanced. No muscle stiffness. Just altered. Xanax is for anxiety. Further altering that state is

IF I WERE GOD

likely not a good thing. Don't take it with Prozac and keep the fuck away from Viagra. Just in case.

Speaking of my favorite recreational drug, one of the more unusual side effects was breast enlargement. On guys. So along with your big dick, you get big tits. Lovely.

Pupil enlargement was another rare side effect. I think it was simply getting wide-eyed when you looked in the mirror at your new DDs.

More Viagra nonsense. Many users of Viagra find that they can't visually distinguish the differences between the colors blue and green. Whose idea was it to manufacture a little "blue" pill? Talk about self-defeating. A good red could mean more than a quality cab.

A side effect of Flomax is a decrease in semen. Talk about your oxymoron.

Zoloft, another depression medication, can also produce an erection lasting 3 or more hours, but it can also cause what is known as an "ejaculation failure," meaning you can't come. Combine it with Viagra and you can enter the Guinness Book of World Records. Combine it with Flomax and you may get what my old friend Lance used to call SSB. Severe Sperm Backup.

A side effect of Percocet is unpleasant breath odor. Only scientists can make bad breath sound scientific.

Ofloxacin, the most common of ear infection drugs, has a strange side effect: It can cause genital itching. Not exactly moving uptown.

Apparently using Requip (I never heard of it either) to treat restless leg syndrome or Parkinson's disease could lead to compulsive gambling and sex. Twitching during sex is not recommended.

There are several drugs that can cause blue urine. The blue color comes from artificial colors in these drugs. I can handle blue, but I wouldn't want to be pissin' pink in the men's room at a UFC match.

My favorite of all time is Anafranil, an antidepressant that was documented to have caused people to have an orgasm every time they yawned. Puts boredom in an entirely different light. In three documented cases, Anafranil was administered to depressed patients with remarkable results. In all 3 cases, depression disappeared, making the use of the drug a resounding success. Little did they know. All 3 experienced sudden urges to yawn, accompanied by an actual orgasm. Two of the 3 wanted to continue the medication well past the dissipation of the depression. Like, forever. The male began wearing condoms all the time lest a bad joke be bestowed upon him unwittingly. I will now always wonder whether someone is tired or...

And I am going to look for a different type of friends.

IF YOU SURVIVED THE SIDE EFFECTS
In addition, certain drugs have published signs of an overdose. Percocet notes that a change in consciousness is a sign of an overdose. Not loss of consciousness, but any change. So waking up could mean trouble.

Vicodin is worse. It notes that a sign of an overdose is no pulse or blood pressure. Mmm, I'm not a doctor but I think that is a sign of death. Perhaps there could be an earlier warning sign provided.

GOD 2.0
The above is only a small sampling of the diseases that have funding and death rate statistics. This may not have been a fun topic, but it is an extremely relevant one to our society. There are billions of dollars each year allocated to

researching hundreds of diseases at the discretion of folks who may have their own motives. That needs to change.

More money should be spent on illnesses for which the afflicted had no choice versus those that are self-inflicted. There should be a line drawn between funding Nurture vs. Nature.

That does not mean to say one cannot get AIDS without living a dangerous sexual lifestyle or lung cancer without smoking; however, the odds are greatly increased when such behaviors are embraced. This means certain diseases are brought about by voluntary activities of the afflicted, knowing the risk that the disease may occur. In these instances, cures for these illnesses should use up less of the research dollars than those that the afflicted have no control over.

Despite the intent of a donor to support a personally affiliated charity, such donations will not be allowed. Many people donate to a charity that funds a disease a loved one was afflicted with. If they can only donate generically, they may not donate. And we need the donations. Therefore, all donations, whoever they are made to, will secretly become generic and subject to an algorithm that correlates personal responsibility for becoming afflicted with a disease with its cure funding.

Only I would know.

Maybe it's already happening.

Wink.

CHAPTER 29

GETTING LUCKY WITH THE TEACHER
(When Algebra Was Fun)

THE AVERAGE TEENAGE BOY LOSES his virginity at 17 years old, and teenage girls lose theirs at 17.3 years old, according to Wikipedia. We all know Wikipedia is not the official source for anything but simply a compilation of postings of what people think is fact, but it does come up real high in the results when you google "age when virginity is lost." Actually, Wikipedia comes up high when you google almost anything. According to its website, it is "written collaboratively by largely anonymous internet volunteers who write without pay." Lovely! We know how reliable people are who work for nothing and troll the internet all day.

So, the average person loses his/her virginity at about 17. Most of the time, it is likely with someone their own age or at least close, but society realizes that before a certain age, you should not be allowed to do some things. Like vote, drink, go to war, etc. Sex is one of them. While it cannot prevent two people from having sex, it has created laws to protect those it believes are too young to make their own decision as to whether sex with someone else is appropriate. Someone who is too young has yet to reach the "age of consent." Generally speaking, if one has sex with someone under the age of consent, he (or she) is committing statutory rape.

IF I WERE GOD

Even if she/he is younger. Huh?

According to the US Department of Health and Human Resources website, each state has its own statutory rape laws and virtually no two states are identical in their laws. In 11 states, the age of consent is 18; in six of them, it is 17; and for the rest, it is 16. Since the average teenager is having sex by the time he/she is 17, in 11 states she/he is getting raped. And if both are under that age, then they have raped each other.

That's going to fill up a lot of jails.

In addition, some states have a minimum age of the victim under which sex becomes child abuse, not statutory rape. Many states also have an age differential provision. In other words, if the age differential between the "defendant" (the older party) and the "victim" (the younger party) is greater than some number of years, it becomes statutory rape. If the age differential is less than that number, it's just a couple of teenagers having some fun.

I am not suggesting all teenagers investigate the law before engaging in sexual activity, although there have been stories of dad filing charges of statutory rape because his daughter was having sex with someone he didn't like. Or maybe he would not like anyone having sex with his daughter. And it would not matter that they were boyfriend and girlfriend, in love. If the ages don't work, the boy could be in trouble.

Decades ago, many state laws only protected females from older men through statutory rape laws. Now most of them apply regardless of sex. So if Mom does not like the girl sonny boy is banging and the ages don't work, she may be able to file charges against her. Ouch!

SOCIETY HATH SPAWNED WHAT IT SEEDED

What is wrong with men? They have been in charge since

the time of Adam and Eve. Well maybe since Adam. Mmm. I wonder who came first? Is that specified in the Bible?

But men have been in charge. Why? Because they are bigger, stronger, and Dad. Women are meant to bear and nurture their children. So in the early days, guys were in charge because Mom was too busy taking care of Junior. And men made all these rules, which became better known as "society." Since they (men, aka society) didn't want Mom to be straying when they were out hunting, they made it a crime if she had sex with anyone else. (Remember the *Scarlet Letter*—OK, that was adultery, but *he* didn't have any letter around his neck.)

But man didn't make it a crime that said *he* couldn't have sex with another woman. If he was boffing a woman who was boffing illegally, he wasn't even in trouble for contributing to the delinquency of an illegal boffer. Man wanted to keep his options open because, well, he could. If, while out hunting, he came across a neighboring camp where Mom was bored with Dad because he hunted too much and/or angry because Dad never woke up to feed Junior in the middle of the night, maybe he could have some fun. It was OK for him, but she might get arrested.

You get the point. Men have made the rules about sex and created this double standard. Guys who have lots of sex are studs, and girls who do the same are sluts. Society shuns women who engage in sex too early or too often. Girls are brought up to be wary of sex; men are brought up to chase it. My mother actually told me it was OK if I had sex before marriage but did not think it would be OK for my younger sister. Dad almost tried to get me laid when I was 16. Almost. Too bad.

IS IT RAPE?

For all you *Law & Order: SVU* fans, we know when there is a

IF I WERE GOD

suspected rape, the first thing the police want to do is get a "rape kit" to check for signs of rape. What are those signs? Basically that there has been some physical damage that is evidence of the use of force during a sexual encounter. And in the case of a male raping a female, there will usually be signs. If there are not, it becomes a "he said/she said" affair, where the credibility of each party is the only evidence to deliver to a jury. In many cases, it will be difficult to get a conviction. If there is physical evidence, the story is much different.

But what evidence can there ever be of a female raping a male? Maybe there is bruising from being beaten because he didn't want to have sex with her, but that is battery, not rape. What can a rape kit check for in a male? Nothing. It becomes "he said/she said." But wait, if she said it wasn't rape, what's he going to say? Exactly. Guess what? If they had sex, it was consensual. Half of you reading this know that we can't get an erection under undue stress; the other half should know this as well. So if we can get it up, it is not rape.

Some of you may have seen the movie *Disclosure* released in 1994 with Demi Moore and Michael Douglas. At the height of sexual harassment training and attention, primarily because of men sexually harassing women in the workplace, this movie was about the opposite. She allegedly sexually harassed him. Ah, but they did have sex, and he did get it up, so could it be harassment? In this case, the answer was that it was harassment, but it certainly was not rape.

But that was in the context of consent, not whether you are mature enough to consent. And that is where this is all leading. An older man having consensual sex with a female teenager probably includes some kind of emotional involvement by the female. Likely some undue influence as well. Society has said this is wrong behavior by a female, so there is more likely to be guilt and remorse. The emotional scars are likely to be much greater than if the roles were reversed.

I agree that we have to protect young females from this in some way. Do we have to protect young males to the same degree? While there still may be emotional involvement and undue influence, it will likely be to a (much?) lesser degree. And not so undue.

In my (complete lack-of-psych-training and based-on-my-ability-to-get-an-erection-when-my-teacher-wore-a-short-skirt) humble opinion.

IS HE LUCKY OR A VICTIM?

Finally, we get here. If a teacher has sex with a student, should it be a crime, and if so, what level of punishment should be meted out? I read differing research and studies that in some instances supported the need for sentencing to be identical for both male-perpetrated statutory rape and female-perpetrated statutory rape, and in other instances noted that such was not the case.

In one case, a 43-year-old female teacher pleaded guilty to having sex with a 13-year-old boy. The judge gave her probation, saying in effect that there was no harm done and society need not be worried. She was not a sexual predator, and it was consensual. But is this type of sentencing and belief fair?

STUPID FOR $20, ALEX

Before we proclaim final judgment, I have to admit to googling my brains out for stories about female teachers having sex with their male students. I came across some crazy ones. They seemed to be fitting into categories like a *Jeopardy!* game. So I decided to make a *Jeopardy!* game out of it. Unfortunately, it won't be pure as there will not be an answer in the form of a question; they will just be stories grouped into categories. There is some embellishment here (and plenty of opinion), but the basics are all factual. Well, as factual as the Internet can be.

The categories are:

Is This Really a Crime?

Stupid

Really Poor Taste

Can We All Chip In for a Hotel Room?

You Can't Make This Shit Up

Potpourri

We'll begin with real-life definitions of crimes that make one scratch one's head.

"Is This Really a Crime" for:

$10 – *Unlawful transaction with a minor.* In this jurisdiction, sex is deemed a transaction. Like trading baseball cards. But what do I get for my Mickey Mantle rookie card? A blow job? Damn, I'll throw in Joe DiMaggio.

$20 – *Annoying or molesting a minor.* I get the molesting, but annoying? Every parent would be guilty, as would teachers who keep their clothes on. And what about annoying minors, why do they get a pass when they annoy us adults?

$30 – *Sexual interference.* Is this a spot foul?

$40 – *Third- and fourth-degree criminal sexual conduct.* This does sound ominous, and apparently third-degree criminal sexual conduct involves penetration. So is fourth degree worse or better? Am I happy or sad?

$50 – *Failure to report a reportable offense.* If someone knows that a sexual offense has occurred, there is a legal obligation to report it. Failure to report it is a crime. A woman was arrested for sexual conduct with a minor and charged with failure to report a reportable offense—hers. She got arrested for not telling the cops she committed a crime. This can become circular very easily.

Daily Double – *Penetration with a foreign object.* Am I happy or sad?

"Stupid" for:

$10 – A 41-year-old teacher emailed nude pictures of herself to a 15-year-old who…guess what…sent them to all his friends. And so on and so on.

$20 – A 28-year-old teacher admitted to having sex with two students under 18 years old. She described her relationship status on social media as complicated, noting that one of her difficulties in teaching her students was to teach them how not to get caught. Where was she when I was in high school?

$30 – A 24-year-old teacher had sex and a baby with a 17-year-old basketball player. She was introduced to his parents as his teacher with neither of them feeling the need to hide the relationship. Dad wanted to know if she could hit free throws.

$40 – A 24-year-old was accused of molestation and indecent exposure with a 12-year-old. The 12-year-old actually had a babysitter who taped the entire thing. She is not winning "Babysitter of the Year" anytime soon.

$50 – This one was 27 and had sex with 5 students…at the same time. That's a lot of inputs. The whole mess was videotaped. Guess the camera guy drew the short straw. And I thought being the designated driver sucked.

IF I WERE GOD

Daily Double – A 33-year-old teacher was pulled over for a minor traffic violation with her student in the car. She proudly told the police officer they were having an affair, and she was taking him home. He proudly handcuffed her.

"Really Poor Taste" for:

$10 – A 30-year-old teacher had sex with a 16-year-old in her car...with an infant child strapped into a safety seat inside the car, during the act. You are not getting that education in nursery school. Finally, something more fun to watch than Barney.

$20 – A 29-year-old teacher groomed her 16-year-old student for sex. After the affair ended and when she got caught, she made up a story that she was beaten up by two friends of the victim. She claimed that the beating was payback for taking advantage of their friend. For excluding them would have been more believable.

$30 – A 32-year-old had sex on the floor of a hotel room with a football player student from her school. Meanwhile her two children, ages 4 and 8, and their 17-year-old babysitter slept on a separate bed in the same room. Maybe the babysitter pretended. Seems Teach was celebrating, as this occurred the day after her divorce was finalized. Talk about moving on.

$40 – When your daughter's trash becomes the object of your affection, you know you are in trouble. This 39-year-old teacher decided to have sex with the 13-year-old former boyfriend of her own daughter. I wish my ex-girlfriends were that accommodating. Take a moment.

$50 – I don't think this is technically incest, but it depends on what the definition of "is" is. A 50-year-old had sex with an 11-year-old *and* his father. Dad actually compared his son's relationship to that of Bill Clinton and Monica Lewinsky. Take a moment.

Daily Double – This is really, really poor taste. A 46-year-old teacher arranged group sex with underage kids in a hotel room. She bought alcohol and also let the kids have sex in the back seat of her car while she drove around. The group of kids included her own daughter.

"Can We All Chip In for a Hotel Room?" for:

$10 – Classroom. Probably a popular spot for teacher-student sex because of its logistical plusses. A 27-year-old teacher was caught having sex with a 14-year-old in a classroom at her school. She allegedly told the student not to tell anyone, but the boy's cell phone had hundreds of calls and texts to and from her. In probably her one moment of sanity, she urged the student to erase the messages on his phone. Not sure how that turned out.

$20 – If you can't find a classroom, there is plenty of other acreage to explore. A 42-year-old teacher had sex with a 16-year-old three times in the press box at the football stadium. Touchdown!

$30 – Is it Black Friday? A 37-year-old had sex with a 17-year-old in her minivan in a Target parking lot. In an unrelated story, sales at Target increased significantly after the event was reported.

$40 – A 41-year-old teacher had sex with a 13-year-old student more than 20 times, including behind a curtain in the school's cafeteria. I hope they wore hairnets.

$50 – Is there a bibliography in here? A 29-year-old teacher had sex with a 15-year-old in the women's restroom in the public library.

Daily Double – If only *she* were God. A 32-year-old was

IF I WERE GOD

found in a van with a 16-year-old in a church parking lot. An unconfirmed rumor out of the church office notes an increase in tithings in recent weeks after the event. And Target shoppers became religious.

DOUBLE JEOPARDY

"You Can't Make This Shit Up," Alex, for:

$20 – Twin sisters aged 26 were involved in lewd acts. One committed them while the other watched. The one who watched was charged with failure to report a reportable event. The arresting officer asked the other one for a date.

$40 – A 30-year-old school nurse received a grant allowing her to start a school-based health clinic study. Apparently, she started it off by sharing a beer with a 17-year-old. Oh, and some sex. He was not in the placebo group.

$60 – A 28-year-old teacher faced 39 criminal counts relating to illicit sexual behavior with 14- to 15-year-olds. Also, she supplied alcohol, marijuana, crack cocaine, and condoms. In a plea agreement, she was charged with 11 counts of various indiscretions. I guess 28 guys were really happy.

$80 – A 42-year-old teacher engaged in sexual conduct with a 17-year-old student. She was a former "teacher of the year." Rumor is the vote was by the male students.

$100 – A 31-year-old teacher had sex with two 16-year-old boys. They broke up with her when she asked one of them to kill her husband.

Daily Double – Speaking of disgruntled spouses, a 30-year-old teacher became sexually involved with an 18-year-old student. Her husband got wind of it and killed the 18-year-old. If that wasn't bad enough, the couple's kids were given to the wife for custody. Wasn't there an aunt or uncle somewhere in the country who could be a better role model?

But wait, it gets even better. She was then hired by another school (so much for checking references) but was dismissed after a parent complained of her attention to a 17-year-old boy. She subsequently disappeared with her kids.

Hope they're not home-schooled.

"Potpourri" for:

$20 – A 23-year-old teacher pleaded guilty to one degree of sexual assault against a minor on Valentine's Day. I guess hubby didn't buy her flowers.

$40 – Dad blew the whistle on this 32-year-old teacher who sent inappropriate photos to his 16-year-old son. He was pissed he wasn't copied.

$60 – A 29-year-old teacher had consensual sex with a 16-year-old over 300 times, beginning when he was 13. Dad turned her in when he found letters the teacher had written to his son. Bummer, no pics. The irony—the teacher was a tutor to the alleged victim's younger brother. But he never got "any."

$80 – And speaking of numbers, a 34-year-old had sex with an elementary school student 26 times in one week, plus a blow job. That's a year's worth for me. When I was 20.

$100 – Maybe this should be its own category: "Forgiveness." A 29-year-old had multiple sexual encounters with a 17-year-old that included alcohol. When this came to light, she was immediately fired by the principal. Who was her husband. Later, when she was paroled, she had sex with another parolee. She remains married to the principal.

Daily Double – Police wanted to question a 32-year-old teacher about her relationship with a 15-year-old student, but she had taken off to Disney World with him. The two had had romantic encounters at the apartment the boy shared with his mother. Not the teacher's place, but home, with Mom presumably within earshot. According to a police statement, the mother found nothing wrong with it, calling the teacher a nice person and a good influence on her son.

That's in the "How to Win Teachers and Influence People" Chapter in the *Bad Parenting Handbook*.

FINAL JEOPARDY

A 37-year-old had a relationship with a 15-year-old friend of her son. Under Georgia law, where this occurred, underage individuals may marry if the female is pregnant. She was. They did. This may have cemented their vows but did not mitigate the gravity and illegality of the "relationship." She was charged with statutory rape, child molestation, and enticing a minor. Under a plea agreement, part of her sentence was that she agreed not to communicate with the victim, her husband, until he was 17.

GOD 2.0

There are dozens more stories like these, and while I present them with a somewhat sarcastic and comical manner, I do not mean to wipe out the potential psychological impact on the teenage male involved. I do mean to wipe out the illegality, or at least the felonious nature of these acts. Ask any male, and he would have been thrilled if a hot teacher came on to him. If I had teacher sex when I was underage, it would have been the crowning achievement of my childhood.

In My Kingdon, this would be a facts and circumstances matter with the judge reviewing all aspects of the case, including consent, undue influence, and psychological ramifications. The psychological damage done by these acts is far, far, less than the damage that can be done by parents to their children. Again, in my humble opinion. Out of no intent or desire, but simply because parents are not given a handbook on how to raise children, they fuck up the minds of their children much more than a hot teacher ever could. No one has ever been accused of being a serial killer because he banged his teacher, but many have become serial killers because of the way they were raised.

Leave the female teachers alone and go catch some real bad guys.

CHAPTER 30
MAKING IT PERSONAL
(It Is My Book, You Know)

DESPITE HAVING TO DEAL WITH a world full of humans (imagine what He has to deal with on other planets), God has had time to relax and enjoy Himself. Most humans have no idea what He does when he's not commanding shit, parting seas, and rolling His eyes over barnacle penis studies. Here's an inside glimpse of God 2.0.

SURVIVOR

Survivor is my all-time favorite TV show. Well, except for *Star Trek*—the original, of course. I never watched the original season of *Survivor* but heard about these idiots on some island eating rats. Really? Get a fucking life. I actually tuned in for the rat episode and saw some really skinny people noshing on something only cats should enjoy. I could not possibly figure out how people would enjoy watching this shit on TV. I would rather watch reruns of *Leave It to Beaver*. But several weeks later, a woman I worked with showed me the front page of the newspaper with pictures and an article about the Final Four in the first season of *Survivor*. She extolled the virtues of the show, and I listened like a rat listens to the cat chasing it. I was always a believer in employee happiness, however, and when she was done, I thought it could be fun to have a *Survivor* pool. There were four people left. There were 50 people in my department. Let's each pick one of them for a small donation, and the ones who pick the winner split the donations. Did I just invent fantasy sports?

No, since I had been playing that for a while, but it seemed like a new iteration of it. So, there were four starving, dirty, and what I thought were incredibly stupid people left. Then I found out the winner would make $1 million. Oops. I am the dumb one. The four were a 70-plus-year-old Navy SEAL, some obnoxious blonde, a gay guy who apparently walked around the island naked, and a hot chick in a bikini. (Would I hang out with a naked gay guy for six weeks for a chance to make $1 million? And eat rats? Depends. Hot chick certainly helps to sway my decision.)

So I circulated the rules, put in $5, and picked a winner. I know you have no doubt who I picked. And this is the *only* reason I watched *Survivor*. To root for the hot chick in the bikini. She came in second. Based on my watching of just this one final episode, I was convinced that the gay guy who won it was worthy, and I was fucking hooked. The next night, CBS began rerunning the entire season. Every night. One episode each night. I popped in a VHS tape (this was before DVDs) and taped every episode. I became intoxicated. I got the rat thing. I got the naked thing. I got it all.

So I began to tape every episode. When I was a kid, my fantasy was to be able to watch reruns of *The Man from U.N.C.L.E.* on those tape reels when I retired. Well, now they'd invented VHS, and my fantasy had come true. I guess when you don't shoot for the moon, you have a better chance to get your fantasy than the threesome thing. And yes, I have the box set of the three seasons of *The Man from U.N.C.L.E.* I actually ran into David McCallum, who'd played Illya Kuryakin, a couple of years ago. I was loath to approach him, but finally got the guts to do so. He is more famous now for his role in *NCIS,* and he looked amazing for an 82-year-old man. I finally went up to him and told him that I loved him in *The Man from U.N.C.L.E.* He seemed quite taken aback that I mentioned *The Man from U.N.C.L.E.* and not *NCIS*. I attributed that to him assuming I was much younger than I actually am.

So I now have every episode of *Survivor* on tape, except two. Of course, they have the box set for every season of *Survivor* now, so I can throw my VHS tapes away, but it is a badge of fucking honor. Why did I miss the two episodes?

See, the advent of taping TV shows meant that I did not have to stay home to watch them when they were originally aired. I could tape them and watch them later. Like the New York Jets game I had to tape instead of watch live because I had to accompany the pain-in-the-ass girlfriend to her 15th cousin's wedding on a Sunday afternoon. Did I get any points for that? No. Only a shout to shut up when I cheered a rare Jet touchdown, because she was sleeping by the time I got to watch it.

But why did I miss those two episodes? Well, the goddamn timer on the VCR did not automatically adjust for daylight savings time. Imagine that! How was I supposed to know? I came home from dinner with the wife, chomping at the bit to see what disgusting food they were going to eat that night, and I get the Nightly Fucking News. Damn, nothing else to do for the night but...

It's called making lemonade from lemons.

GOD 2.0

I always wanted to be on the show, but not really. I am not sure I have the fortitude to put up with what they do. Plus, I am extremely un-photogenic and nobody would want to see me on the screen. And, for sure, I could not eat the shit they make you eat for those challenges. Pig guts, all sorts of brains, beetle larvae—and they are moving. So if I were God,

I would lose my sense of taste, fall in love with all manner of bugs, and make an old-guy-friendly version of the game.

And invite some hot chicks in bikinis.

STAR TREK

Alas, most of them are dead. Kirk and Sulu are still kicking, but they hate each other. Almost like *Survivor*, I was not a big fan when it was on prime time. My parents were a tad overprotective and thought I was too young to be scared by the monsters on *Star Trek*. They also thought the Bond movies were too provocative. Like I would have gotten the Pussy Galore innuendo at the age of 10. But in college, there was a TV in the dorm lounge and every night on channel 11 (one of five channels at the time) at 6 PM was *Star Trek*. We all would gather and watch and have a blast. I was into the science fiction part of it, but I slowly began to realize that each and every episode told a very impactful story. Not only was it light years ahead of its time in terms of technology, but the storytelling was second to none. Every single episode was a commentary on society, and most of them were amazingly insightful. You Trekkies out there know what I am talking about. The rest of you, there is a box set for that too.

GOD 2.0

Simply put, I would recreate the original *Star Trek*; bring back Bones, Scotty, and Spock from the dead; and make it the longest-running TV series in the history of TV.

NEW YORK JETS WIN ANOTHER SUPER BOWL...FINALLY

Hopefully by the time I am done writing and editing this book, I can delete this section.

There are some things even God can't accomplish.

CHAPTER 31
PONTIFF-ICATION
(A God's Gonna Do What a God's Gotta Do)

Of course, I have to wait until the final chapter to consider my own worth. I needed to do all the good the previous chapters allowed me to do first, but now that all is right with the world, I can focus on what is probably my biggest issue with the world—organized religion. I do not necessarily believe there is no higher being or thing, just that it is not the traditional definition of God. You know, all powerful, all knowing, all good, all ecclesiastical (don't ask), and by my account, all fucked up.

The one thing that must be remembered throughout this discourse is that, while my research has been "thorough," it has not been exhaustive. But it doesn't really matter, as I read the internet with a grain of salt anyway. Ultimately, My logic concludes that "thorough" is enough and even if it were deemed "inadequate," I would still say the same shit.

Much of the following reciting (and trampling) of the history of the Catholic Church has been derived from a book titled the *Vatican Billions* by Avro Manhattan. It also includes stuff from the internet. We all know the veracity of that. Avro has a strongly biased view against the Catholic Church, which is easy to recognize. The internet was random. I have recited much of what Avro believes without caveats that might impeach his views. The internet supplements that from both sides. I take what everybody says with a grain of salt. I invite you to do the same. Especially with what I have to say.

My personal religious beliefs are based upon, not a religious upbringing I rebelled against, but rather the lack of a serious religious upbringing. After I never attended church as a kid, Mom wanted me to get some form of religious education when I was in high school.

Thanks, Mom.

I ended up getting confirmed as a Presbyterian when I was 16. I found Sunday School to be boring, but there were a couple of cute chicks there, so that is how I found redemption. My aunt was very religious and did take me to church when I visited her and my grandparents back then. No cute chicks there, but one day I actually shook the hand of Richard Nixon before he was president.

Or a crook.

I was basically left to my own devices for my religious beliefs, or lack thereof, and fell prey to my overwhelming sense of logic. I guess by my own definition of my beliefs, one could call me agnostic. Belief that there is something there, I just have to wait until I die to find out. That sucks. It is one of the reasons religion does make sense. It gives you a reason to believe and provides an image, albeit ghostly, of what it is you believe in. But you can't feel it, smell it, or touch it. So, it remains a fleeting concept.

I don't hate religion for religion's sake. Religion has done a tremendous amount of good in the world, helping the poor and needy, providing comfort and solace to those in need of emotional support, even acting as a social network (let's face it, before internet dating, one of the best ways to meet someone to date was church). My grandfather used to say that there are no atheists in foxholes or on deathbeds. I get that. If you think death is imminent, you will reach out for something to believe in. It has a huge benefit in those situations.

What I don't like is what organized religion has become. I am going to pick on the Catholic Church as it is the biggest and perhaps most abusive (in more ways than one) religion, but my rant pertains to all religions that have accumulated wealth. And that wealth has, in many instances, been accumulated through deceit, dishonesty, and outright thievery.

SALVATION SELLS

My grandfather's words were apparently not original as from early on in Christianity, it appeared that salvation sells. Let's face it. Assume you lived in the 9th century or so. You raped and pillaged the villages and stole from the peons. You are about to die, you have been a schmuck all your life, and you know it. Some guy in robes comes up to you and says, "If you repent all your sins and ask forgiveness, you can go someplace cool when you die." Maybe you were not a believer and figured that you were going no place, so who cares. Or maybe you were worried because of the schmuckiness. Either way, you are going to die, and you really don't know what is in store. It could be nothingness, or it could be hell or heaven. So you have a choice. You can leave your worldly possessions to the shitty son or the bitchy wife, or you can roll the dice. I mean what do you have to lose? If there is nothingness after you die, so what, you are dead. If the Robes were fucking with you, and they are enjoying your riches, why do you care—you can't. But, if by some strange reason the Robes are legit, do you really want to fuck up heaven?

PA BROOK

So you are on your deathbed and say, "Screw the gay son and cheating wife, and, shit, the animal shelter doesn't need *that* much money." You (gulp) give it all (or maybe just a portion) to the church. You take your last breath with the possibility that you may be banging 72 virgins for the rest of eternity. It's better than taking your last breath wondering what your cheating wife is going to be doing with all the money you stole from the peons who served you while you were alive.

So there it goes. And this story repeats itself literally millions of times. Who can blame the dying? I'm jealous I hadn't figured out this racket first. That is exactly what the Catholic Church did. Again, I am not singling out Catholicism. This is a trait in all organized religion. This includes temples, mosques, shrines, obelisks, etc. Organized religion. I am using the Catholic Church as my proxy.

I would have a lesser reaction if the wealth gained through the promise of an afterlife was consistently and righteously used for the purpose it was promised—to help the poor. Or if there really were 72 virgins there. But it wasn't. And there aren't. Mmm, but can we say that for certain?

Look at the Vatican and other scared grounds. There are thousands of art treasures there worth millions, if not, dare I say, billions of dollars. Why not sell a couple and feed the poor living on the streets. Imagine what a piece of art from the Vatican walls would fetch. Advertise it with a ticket to heaven and put it on eBay. As they say...Priceless!

Even if one is not on his or her deathbed, heaven sounds pretty nice. If you can afford a piece of your wealth even though death is not imminent, it sounds like a reasonable bet. Beats the shit out of betting on the New York Jets every weekend. *Voila!* The every week contribution. Envelopes, so no one knew what his neighbor was contributing, but

IF I WERE GOD

everyone felt guilty that he may not be contributing as much. Genius.

So, what's wrong with this picture? The guys in the robes are con artists. They put forth something that was not a certainty as a certainty and got really, really good results. Salvation sells. If I had no one to leave my meager book sale profits to, I would buy into the concept of repentance and fork over my coins to the church. Why not?

I do not wish to cast aspersions on the entire population of organized religion. There are an overwhelming number of good people doing good things. If there wasn't the church, even more people would go hungry and more people would have no place to sleep. On balance, charity provides a significant benefit to society, and the religions are very much at the heart of that.

But that does not excuse those dudes in the robes. Write a check in my name, and you will go to heaven. What a racket.

Here is an indisputable parcel of logic that I bestow upon my religious brethren. Not all religious brethren, but primarily those who believe in Adam and Eve and that God made everything in six days. We have no way of knowing whether that is true or not. Logic begs to differ with it, but God, by definition, is not logical. The other alternative still leaves a lot to be desired as well. Even if you are Darwinian and believe in the evolution of life. That man walked out of the ocean one day as the descendent of fish or whatever. Even if you subscribe to that vision of our past, even if you go back to the big bang theory, we are still missing the ultimate answer. The big bang theory suggests that it all started from a black hole or we sprang into existence or some piece of dust was the original source of all of this. Even that begs the question: where did that black hole or piece of dust come from? Even I, the quintessential non-religious dude, can't answer that question.

The logic is coming.

To finally debunk those who believe in the Adam and Eve story, I offer you the following. If Adam and Eve were truly the first two human beings and everyone else that has ever lived sprang from them...

Why do we all speak different languages? I don't care what the Bible says. The Robes wrote it. Why would I make life so difficult?

If we all started from the same place, why don't we all speak the same? I could understand that some dialects arose as folks moved around and took up shop in other areas of the world, but Chinese and English are not exactly dialects of the same language.

How can we all have sprung from the same bosom and have no fucking idea what most of our brothers and sisters are saying?

VATICAN BILLIONS AND OTHERS

Now for some history. Again, I invite you to take everything with a grain of salt or two, do your own research, and come to your own conclusions. You probably have already come to your own conclusions without the research. I won't let that stop me.

The early church acted upon and practiced the tenets of Jesus, with its members giving their possessions to the church for the good of the poor. This began an accumulation of wealth, which was justified since it was to be used in the service of religion. Christianity was actually respectable.

But then the "Others" arose. Christianity was at odds with

IF I WERE GOD

paganism, which to my very unreligious and feeble mind can only be described as non-Christianity. So you had the Christians and the pagans/non-Christians/others. As paganism took hold, Christians began to get persecuted. It wasn't pretty.

Then in the 300s, the Roman Emperor Constantine recognized Christianity. This gave the church the backing of the state. The result was carte blanche to expand its base, and ultimately, its power and wealth. The church took full advantage. Paganism was dealt a death blow and its wealth was transferred to the Catholic Church.

The Others were toast.

The legacies of the pious; the gifts of land, estates, and goods from newly converted, highly placed pagans; and the givings of repentant sinners all contributed within a few centuries to make the church the custodians of earthly riches far beyond their initial dreams. But the church seemed to have lost its mission of serving the poor.

In the 8th century, the church came under pressure and pilferage from outside sources, and its power and wealth began to wane. To combat this, the brilliant pope at the time orchestrated the receipt of a letter from St. Peter. For those of you who do not know who St. Peter was, he was like the main dude. If Jesus was the Son of God, Peter was akin to the Grandson of God, or maybe the Nephew of God. But he was big time and the first pope. And he had been dead for centuries.

Despite being in the ground for a while (good thing he wasn't cremated), all of a sudden a letter from St. Peter arrives from heaven. Delivered in person by the dead Grandson. This is big shit! The letter basically said, if you believe in God, your sins will be forgiven. Imagine that fucking séance. This created a groundswell of good feeling about the church, and many of those who were straying were reined back in. And with it, all their wealth.

It was the most brilliant fund-raising event ever!

Until the next one.

Remember Emperor Constantine recognized Christianity and was responsible for the church's accumulation of wealth in the 4th century. About 400 years later, another dead dude becomes relevant again. In the Donation of Constantine, supposedly written in the 300s, the emperor apparently had granted immense possessions and vast real estate to the church. But no one took notice at the time. Now, in the 700s, this document showed up. Oops. In addition, this "Donation" put the pope above kings, emperors, and nations, and made the pope the legal heir to the Roman Empire. Now that's a fucking donation. One piece of paper. Forged. The kings, emperors, and nations all believed it.

I've got some real estate...

WE'RE NOT DONE

Not that the church really needed it, but a new way of extorting—pardon me, collecting—money was excommunication. Or rather escape from excommunication. Excommunication means relieving people of their rights to be Catholic. Potentially condemning them to hell. It was to be avoided. People were excommunicated for various and sundry infringements upon the church. Such infringements were at times almost randomly assigned to extract the most amount of fear and "payments of forgiveness" possible. If you screwed up, you can pay to avoid hell. Just pay for your current sins. Ah, but that was not enough.

Who knew what action or non-action might be deemed worthy of excommunication in the *future*? In order to prevent even the most religious and esteemed of the populace from that possibility, one only had to purchase insurance against being exed.

These were some pretty smart motherfuckers.

But wait, fear of being excommunicated yourself was not good enough. If your neighbor was excommunicated, you could then also be excommunicated. Guilt by association. But wait, you could buy insurance to protect you from that as well.

"15 minutes can save your ass from hell."

But excommunication wasn't reserved for mere humans. Caterpillars, grasshoppers, and flies were also subject to excommunication. What do they have to offer the church? Ah, but the brilliance of the Robes comes into play again. It's not what these bothersome insects can offer the church, it's what those bothered by them can offer the church to get rid of, or excommunicate, them. And it worked, as grateful residents showered the church with tithings in order to rid themselves of the pests.

I wonder whether the bugs went away.

INDULGE ME

An indulgence is a way to reduce the penance a sinner must make in order to be forgiven. Or something like that. I'm not a fucking theologian, so don't go tweeting that I don't have it right. I'm close enough for this discussion.

An indulgence is kind of like saying a few Hail Marys after confession.

Anyway, the church got into the habit of issuing indulgences as a way to help sinners be forgiven. Originally it was used in its correct context and very sporadically. Ah, but then there was money to be made. Let's sell these fuckers. So indulgences went on eBay.

Imagine being a sinner and fearful of going to hell. But you are not ready to die and leave all your worldly possessions to the church to prevent that. You are going to continue living with all this guilt and fear.

"Not so," said the bishop. "I can provide you with the ability to lift the guilt and provide for the penance you are seeking."

"OMG," said the sinner. "What do I have to do for that?"

"Become BFFs with God and buy an indulgence."

Damn, thought the sinner. *I can go do horrible shit all day and just buy an indulgence to be forgiven. I like this!*

Voila! Another motherlode for the church.

As the power of the church and the pope expanded, some interesting excesses took place. Apparently, one pope designed a papal crown with an immense number of jewels on it. It was very heavy, but undeterred, the pope decided to wear it. All the time. Then, one particularly long, hot day, he had an apoplectic fit, literally dying from the weight of the crown.

I hope he gave away all his wealth to the church before he bit the bullet.

Another rather studly pope is thought to have had more than 100 illegitimate children. That's one way to make sure the religion expands. The only thing abstinent in his life was sleep.

Then there was the pope who decided to annex all of America, once it was discovered. He actually assigned it to Spain and Portugal. Interestingly, the American Revolution and its subsequent liberation led to a major milestone in the

IF I WERE GOD

history of the church—the separation of church and state, a concept the Catholics hated, since they deemed themselves both church and state.

SANITY RETURNS, BUT ONLY TEMPORARILY

In the mid-1800s, Italy proclaimed itself a republic and deposed the pope as king. That is like saying "Fuck you" to God. Seriously. Who has balls that big? Even if you don't believe, what if you are wrong? You really wanna take this kind of chance? Guess so, because they did.

This led to Italy reclaiming vast real estate that the church claimed it owned and the shuttering of the Catholic presence in Italy to inside the walls of the Vatican. A pope didn't poke his head outside for several decades. The church never relinquished its claim on the land. It just shut up about it.

Eventually, another brilliant mind emerged from the church, and a treaty was negotiated whereby the church would renounce its ownership of the land that had been taken in return for a substantial payment of money. Let me get this straight. The country of Italy, with a rather large army, I am sure, takes land from the church, which then goes and hides for decades. After a period of time, the church comes out and says, "Hey, you guys with the bazookas, you can keep the land you took from us. But we have been playing nice for a while. We didn't part any seas or make it rain for 40 days. Can you throw us a bone?"

Sure. In return for getting nothing, Italy paid the church 1.75 billion lira. Now that's a guilt trip.

This propelled the church into a new realm of moneymaking. A legitimate one. Investing.

But then World War II created a black mark against the church as it backed Nazi Germany in spirit, if not in public. The church was concerned about the Russians, who were endangering religion and, therefore, the fortunes the church had. Politically, perhaps it made sense, but it was boldly hypocritical for the humanitarian reasons that the church purportedly exists. This is a much debated topic that I will leave for others. Suffice it to say, the church made another decision to increase/protect its coffers at the expense of its prime directive.

HOLY MONEYMAKER, BATMAN!

Not to be outdone by indulgences and excommunication extortion, Holy Years have been another marketing bonanza for the church. The Bible calls for one every 50 years. Originally they were designed to include forgiveness of sins and the granting of pardons. These special Years would mean the freeing of slaves, forgiveness of debts, and generally, God doing some extra-special miracles. They created opportunities for those of faith to participate at a deeper level than in other years.

And with deeper pockets.

The forgiveness of sins and granting of pardons can make people particularly grateful. Forgiving those who need forgiveness and have money, the church can have a Holy (Shit! of a) Year. Which is why these Holy Years, or Jubilees as they are also called, have become more popular. There have been several "interim" Holy Years in the 20th century. In addition to the regularly scheduled Holy Years in 1950 and 2000 there were Holy Years in 1925, 1933, 1966, 1975, and 1983. Either people were really fucking up more than in the past and needed significantly more forgiveness, or God was just bored and wanted to do some cool miracles.

Or maybe the church figured out just how big a cash cow these Years were, and just scheduled a few more. That's called good business!

IF I WERE GOD

The 21st century did not leave the church wanting. In 2016, the pope celebrated the Extraordinary Jubilee of Mercy.

The church is not alone in its lust for money or power. Many have used or misused what they had. One particular story had some wealthy monarch decide he wanted to take over the church. He didn't do anything violent, like storm the Vatican. He simply purchased the pope-ship for his son. I feel certain that the bishops/cardinals/whoever were in charge of picking popes used the sales proceeds for the good of the church and its constituents. Certain.

Unfortunately, little Antonio died after becoming pope. Undaunted and fortunate to have a second son in tow, Dad purchased another pope-ship. Oops, son #2 kicked the bucket too. He, of more money than God, did have a third son, but he was only 14. Fuck it! Son #3 became the family's pope #3, the youngest pope ever. This one had assassins coming after his ass.

Thanks, Dad.

He managed to escape them and ran off to screw a bunch of women for many years. Still as the pope. He finally decided to settle down and get married. Now that's called redefining a position. Ah, but he did have to resign from being pope before getting married.

So he sold his pope-dom to the highest bidder.

NOT THAT THERE IS ANYTHING WRONG WITH IT

Of course, I have to go here. And I do not pretend that this only occurred in the Catholic religion. It will occur wherever there are restrictions on lifestyle that draw certain types into that lifestyle or exclude others from it. The issue, of course, is the denial, and maybe even worse, the pompousness to continue to deny when there was no doubt. When you convince rich people to give you their millions when they are about to die because you put heaven in front of them, you think you can talk anyone into or out of anything.

Even convincing the world that pedophilia does not exist among the Robes, when the evidence is overwhelming. The Robe said, "Joe, you can go to heaven and enjoy a better life than you can imagine after you die. I can't prove it to you, but if you give me all your money, I will make it happen." *Voila!* A 13th-century equivalent of a check appears with lots of zeros in it.

Now Head Robe tells everyone that his Worker Robes did not do that horrible thing. Initially, everyone believed Head Robe. It was understandable because of how easily salvation sells. Zeros had appeared on a check because a Robe (not even Head Robe) said something was true. At first, denial worked because no one could imagine that a man of God could do something so despicable to children. But when the evidence became overwhelming, the church, without batting a homosexual eyelash, continued to deny. "Not me. Must be the demonic Jews making up shit."

As of a 2012 article, sexual abuse cases have cost the Catholic Church more than $3 billion. They cost, on average, $1 million per victim. Let me put on my CPA hat. That comes to 3,000 victims.

Pause.

3,000.

Children.

And that is just those who have come forward and been acknowledged. There likely are hundreds if not thousands more who have been given hush money that we will never know about. So every Catholic who has contributed to the church now knows that a portion of their contribution has gone to efforts to cover up and then pay for pedophiles. Who would ever give another dollar to the church?

Statute of limitations on sexual abuse cases are preventing many cases against the church from being pursued. Various states are extending the statute of limitations on sex abuse cases to permit victims to come forth and sue despite the length of time since the abuse. Vatican sources have said that the church has spent $100,000 to $1,000,000 in New York to keep the current statute of limitations in place. This would prevent lawsuits that occurred prior to the expiring of the statute of limitations from being litigated.

Vatican sources themselves.

So, lobbying to prevent cases being brought to light means even more of your contribution is being used to cover up pedophiles.

With so much money being diverted to pedophile cover-up, some dioceses reverted to borrowing. Many municipalities have issued municipal bonds for the benefit of religious groups. The church basically enjoys borrowing at municipal rates, even though it pays no taxes and is not supporting the general public.

Many dioceses have declared bankruptcy because of the sex scandals. Or from mismanagement. Or from fraud. The church has tried to hide assets as ingeniously as the divorcing husband hiding assets from the pissed-off wife. Or the money-laundering drug dealer. I understand trying to protect yourself, but if you swear to live by a higher standard by being a believer and follower of God, then you must live your life that way. Don't hide the money, offer it up. Don't hide the pedophiles, force them out.

Who is really representing the teachings of God?

HOLY SEE, HOLY DO

Let's take a look at Catholic Church finances. This will be fun if you like a lot of numbers. If you haven't noticed, I do.

The Catholic Church has many parts. At the top is the pope and the Holy See. The Holy See is akin to the office of the president of the Catholic Church. Or in this case, the office of the pope.

Why See? What about Taste? Or Hear? That has a ring to it. Ugh.

The Vatican is its own country and has its own money and laws. It came about when the Italians and the church settled their differences early in the 20th century. The Vatican and the Holy See are separate and distinct entities for operational as well as financial purposes. The Holy See is an episcopal designation, while Vatican City is primarily a political and diplomatic one.

Does anyone really give a Goddamn?

Under the Holy See are several other layers of organization. Dioceses divided into parishes. Independently run, their finances are completely unknown except by those on the inside. The Holy See earns revenue from gifts to the pope, publication sales and ad revenue, fees for ceremonies, sale of videocassettes, and earnings received from the Vatican Bank (see below).

Sounds like Amazon.

Vatican City is separate from the Holy See, as noted above, and operates like a government. It is the world's smallest sovereign nation. Vatican City makes much of its revenue from tourism and from entities wishing to pay money for access to the City. Like having the Rolling Stones play at your birthday party.

The Vatican is thought to own more than 18,000 works of art valued in the billions (as of a 1986 article). The Holy See also owns 30 buildings in Rome (as of 1986) and elsewhere in Italy, many in prime locations. The value of this real estate is unknown.

In 2012 when Italy proposed to tax the Catholic Church on its properties, it was estimated that the church owned 110,000 properties worth 9 billion euros. *In Italy alone.* The tax would have brought in an estimated 720 million euros to the general government coffers of Italy.

Holy See!

VATICAN BANK

The Vatican Bank manages money like any other bank. It is privately held and run by a CEO who reports to a committee of cardinals and the pope. The pope has dictator-like power. The bank only accepts deposits from Catholic institutions and individuals who are tied to the church.

The bank has faced numerous scandals over the years, including $1.4 billion in what may have been loans to dummy companies that almost brought the bank down and resulted in a presumed fake suicide (aka murder) of its president.

As of December 31, 2014, the bank had $6 billion euros in total assets. Its annual report notes there were 15,181 customers with the vast majority of assets from institutions. Remember, the $6 billion only pertains to the Holy See, not the thousands of dioceses that have their own assets and income. The bank does not accept customers unless they are related to the Holy See.

The Holy See's revenues include the net profits of the bank, which are donated to the Holy See. The bank made 69 million euros in 2014.

PA BROOK
In 2012, Vatican City made $27 million.

Gee, a government making money. I have a new source of revenue for them. Consulting for all the other governments.

The Holy See lost $18 million.

Vatican City's first client.

ECONOMIST STUDY
The American Catholic church is estimated to have spent $170 billion in 2010. This estimate was derived by adding up publicly available budgets and/or reports of expenditures for various Catholic institutions. For those that were known to exist but had no publicly available information, estimates were formed. This would purport to be a minimum number, since there is a large amount of money spent that is not reported anywhere.

Here comes my CPA hat again. Spending at least $170 billion in the United States means spending a lot more than that around the world. Shall we double that? $340 billion, a conservative estimate. Since this is just expenditures, we assume revenues are greater. This makes the Catholic Church the largest non-governmental institution in the world.

MORE NUMBERS
There are 1.3 billion Catholics as of 2016.

According to Georgetown University, the average weekly donation of an American Catholic is $10. There are 85 million American Catholics. Where's my abacus? That's $850 million *per week*. And that's less than 10% of the world's Catholics. That's $44.2 billion per year. And that's just the common folk.

One foundation in Pennsylvania includes 138 members

who pledged to donate at least $1 million annually. That's another $138-plus million. And just from one foundation. In one state.

Local and federal governments bankroll Medicare and Medicaid of patients in Catholic hospitals, the cost of educating students in Catholic schools, and loans to students attending Catholic universities. Oh, and the church charges its constituents for these services as well.

WANNA COME UP AND SEE MY ETCHINGS?

A shameless line used to attempt to lure women to apartments where no etchings had gone before. Until now. The church has some etchings. By one person's estimate, the total value of all these "etchings" exceeds $1 billion. This would likely make the church the largest owner of art in the world. It also owns its fair share of real estate. When one thinks of the value of a painting, the painter is a good barometer to use. For a piece of land, we know its location. Add on top of that the value of God.

Normal people pay a lot of money for things owned by famous people. Rich people pay a *shitload* of money for things owned by famous people. Babe Ruth, a fat, drunk, not-very-nice human being hit a baseball a long way. Often. A baseball that a shitty human being autographed can be worth in excess of $100,000 today. That baseball cost probably 25 cents. Imagine the markup on something touched by the pope. Or even a cardinal. Shit, an altar boy can probably get laid even with acne. We all know that you don't have to be "in" a rock band to have groupies lust for you. Just being "associated with" a rock band can get you laid. So anything remotely associated with the Vatican or the pope will have an exponential increase in value over the building owned by me.

And rightly so. Perhaps owning this piece of art will bring

you closer to God. Maybe God will appreciate how much you spent on it. "You got a good deal," God might observe. He would know. And appreciate your keen negotiating skills.

"They will come in handy during pedophile settlement talks."

But they never sell the art to provide for the poor, do they?

Excuses run from, "Well, it was gifted to the church, so it should remain a part of the church," to "I just can't bear to be without my diamond tiara." Certainly the latter is unspoken, but the fact remains that this collection of art and real estate (and I haven't even mentioned investments) that the church has amassed is just sitting there. It is not helping the poor. It is not making the world a better place. A lot of it is not even making the life of a priest any better. It's just sitting there.

It's pretty to look at, but I would rather it be just a tad less beautiful and feed a couple of poor people. It's not that hard. What is hard to believe is that men who supposedly devoted themselves to the teachings of God and the charitable work the church is supposed to do cannot bring themselves to actually do the work of God.

Shame on them.

We are not going to be able to make them sell things, so the next best thing is to...

TAX THE SHIT OUT OF IT

But wait, I'm God, and I can make them sell it. That's no fun. I could send down some lightning bolts, maybe a flood or two. They would eventually get the hint, but this is so much more entertaining. And as God, I need to let humanity finds its way. I can direct, but I won't dictate. But I can give 'em some hints.

IF I WERE GOD

Before we get into taxation, let's discuss the government funding of religious charities.

As we have already memorized, the First Amendment of the Constitution says the following:

"Congress shall make no law respecting an establishment of religion, or prohibiting the free exercise thereof; or abridging the freedom of speech, or of the press; or the right of the people peaceably to assemble, and to petition the Government for a redress of grievances."

We previously discussed the difficulties these guys had with English. We parse through the First Amendment in more detail here. What does "respecting an establishment of religion" mean? I understand "free exercise thereof," in case you think I am the issue. It appears the word "respecting" means concerning, touching upon, in relation to, or with respect to. Ah, that sounds like English.

"Congress shall make no law *with respect to* an establishment of religion, or prohibiting the free exercise thereof;"

Much better. What were these guys smoking?

So now we know that there was a clear intention that Congress not establish a religion. Separation of church and state, while not a concept in the Constitution, was borne from the First Amendment. Its interpretation over the years has evolved, or maybe just changed. There are those who believe church and state should at all times be separated. There are those who believe some crossover is OK. Usually, each party has an agenda.

I do not.

A key question in the debate over separation of church and state is whether the government should fund religious organizations. Religious organizations are nonprofits like other organizations that receive government funding, but they have a very targeted audience and effectively discriminate against nonbelievers. And the First Amendment provides some legislative guns for separation.

Without getting too technical and boring, there is a history of legislation on this with the final result being something along the lines of it's OK to provide government funding to a religion, providing the funding is not going to the betterment of the religious organization or its members. Rather the benefit must be to general society. Research to find a cure for cancer that benefits all of society—good. Why Catholics kill themselves—bad. We already know that answer.

Those virgins.

There is also the argument that government funding of religious organizations raises the issue about the fungibility of money provided to religious charities. Fungible, as in mutually interchangeable. Did you ever wonder about the utility of defining a word by using even more complex words? A rant for another day. Seems there are a lot of them. I smell a sequel. Digression ended.

If religious organizations are able to use government funds for their "secular" or non-religious, charitable activities, money that had previously been used for those activities will be freed to be used for their religious activities. In a real sense, the effect would be the same as that of the federal government directly funding the religious activities. That shoots down 300 years of judicial rulings!

Religious organizations, like other nonprofits, are prohibited from being involved in politics. However, as with the example of the church lobbying to prevent the extension of the statute of limitation in sex abuse cases, this is not always adhered to.

IF I WERE GOD

FINAL JEOPARDY CATEGORY – "THAT'S 12 ZEROS"

Final Jeopardy Answer: "The net worth of the Catholic Church."

"What is, um, it's gotta be a trillion. Right, Alex?"

Even Alex Trebek can't get this one right. Because no one knows. But let's use a little CPA logic, throw in some useless facts (also known as CPA logic), take out my abacus again, and have a little fun.

There is no public information regarding the wealth of the Catholic Church. Part of that is because of the autonomy of all the local pieces of the church. The Holy See and Vatican are completely separate financial entities from individual dioceses, parishes, or whatever. So I need to put my CPA hat on and try to come up with something. I mean, there is a number that is correct, though I don't even think the Catholic Church knows the number. They probably do not want to know it, as it would be embarrassing.

So I will come to the rescue and use some fancy abacus/pro rata/spreadsheet magic to come up with a number. And I am going to do it from two fronts. Neither is necessarily accurate, but neither is necessarily wrong. I encourage everyone to come up with a similar methodology and/or update my numbers.

I came across a list of Catholics by country. It was from the early 2000s, so it may not be as accurate today. But proportionally it may not be far off from today. I also came across an article that noted an estimate of how much the Irish Catholic Church was worth. And keep in mind, Ireland is a small country in the scheme of the world as well as in the scheme of the Catholic Church. Bear with me as my spreadsheet nerdiness takes over. I asked myself, "Self, does it make sense that if the Irish make up a certain percentage of the Catholic population, then perhaps the value of the

Irish Church would make up the same percentage of the total Catholic Church value?" Seems logical.

Now, here is where you have to trust me. I'm the accountant dude. I have banked most of my career on making sure the calculations I make are accurate. Leave the comments regarding why I am now writing books instead of doing more spreadsheets to yourself. So I did a little pro ration/witches brew/Spock mind meld and came to the conclusion that the Catholic Church is worth $1.1 trillion.

If you care to challenge me, the article referred to dove into the value of properties and other assets of the Irish Church. It ended up with an estimate of $4 billion. The list of the Catholic population by country noted the number of Catholics in Ireland was 4.2 million, and the total of the list was 1.1 billion Catholics in the world. In Ireland, that's like $1,000 per Catholic. I am not sure what that means. Perhaps that each Catholic in Ireland has given the Church $1,000 over theirs and their ancestors' lifetime. Or maybe not. We got 1.1 billion Catholics each worth $1,000 to the church. $1.1 trillion. As in $1,100,000,000,000. Now I can be off by $100 billion and still the number is mind-boggling. When can you be off by $100 billion and the result is still relevant?

But this was not enough. I found another article that disclosed that the largest diocese in Germany was worth $3.3 billion. I did some more fancy CPA shit; threw in some dog tongue, frog toes, and newt eyes (actual ingredients in Shakespeare's version of a witches brew; what happened to hops and barley?); and came up with $1.2 trillion.

That's $1,200,000,000,000 for the visual crowd.

So with two independent bits of information, I have come to the conclusion that the Catholic Church is worth in excess of $1 trillion.

IF I WERE GOD

Please forgive me, but one more math thing.

Let's say the Catholic Church is worth the lofty $1 trillion. Interest rates are low at the time of this writing. The 30-year US government bond is yielding an almost historic low of 2.5% per year. Assume the church invests in the safest investment in the market, US government bonds, and yields that 2.5%. And let's say the world taxes the income from that very safe investment at the current corporate rate in the US of 21%. What could the tax revenue on investment income produce? We are not asking the Catholic Church to contribute a portion of the money it has raised, whether through legitimate or illicit means, just a portion of the income it earns from those means. Let's do the math.

$1,000,000,000,000 times 2.5% equals $25 billion of income earned, or $25,000,000,000.

$25,000,000,000 taxed at the corporate rate of 21% in the United States equals $5.25 billion of taxes paid, or $5,250,000,000.

I can think of a lot of good that $5.25 billion dollars could do. Can you? Let's have a contest. Send in your idea of how to spend $5.25 billion for the betterment of mankind.

All these zeros are mind-boggling. Like when the government says we have Godzillions of debt, we really have no clue what they are talking about. So let's put this in zeros we can relate to. Say you invested $10,000 in US government bonds and had to pay corporate income tax on the interest you earned. At 2.5%, you earn $250 and pay $52.50 in tax. You get to keep the remaining $197.50 to do whatever you want. Drugs, alcohol, babysitter porn. And you still have the $10,000.

The government is not an efficient provider of benefits to society. Waste is its middle name. But at least it gives them out. What gives the Catholic Church the right to avoid paying taxes on its income when everyone else has to? And they get to hang on to it.

Oh, right. Politicians want to go to heaven.

So, churches and church-affiliated organizations are nonprofit organizations like the Salvation Army, United Way, etc. They are therefore exempt from taxation of their net income, except in instances in which they earn income non-related to their tax-exempt purpose. Also, nonprofits generally are not subject to property tax.

This book is officially a nonprofit endeavor at this point.

There is a distinct advantage churches have over other nonprofits in the United States. They do not have to file information returns with the IRS that disclose a lot of financial and other information that other nonprofits have to file. The IRS also restricts audits of churches. And since it would be difficult and potentially hellish to audit them, it seems they have it made.

Some of us think IRS agents should go to hell anyway.

As we noted, the First Amendment of the Constitution states that "Congress shall make no law respecting an establishment of religion, or prohibiting the free exercise thereof...." While churches are tax exempt, would some level of taxation or even fiscal oversight impair a religion's ability to be freely exercised?

The argument for or against taxation in this context is based strictly on net income and not gross income. There is no desire to put churches in a worse position than other nonprofits.

ARGUMENTS FOR TAXATION

Those who argue for taxation use the following as some of their arguments:

IF I WERE GOD

It is simply the fear of God that has prevented us from taxing Him previously.

Failing to tax churches violates the separation of church and state. By not taxing the church, the state is being unduly influenced by the church. In addition, the decision to not tax religious organizations puts the determination of what is a religious organization squarely in the hands of...the state. Bye-bye separation.

Regarding property taxes, one estimate puts the amount of untaxed property owned by the church at $500 billion in the United States. Another puts lost revenue from untaxed properties in New York City alone at $627 million dollars.

ARGUMENTS AGAINST TAXATION

Those who stand for the status quo cite the following:

Taxing churches violates the separation of church and state.

Wait a minute. Did I just have too much to drink? I thought *failing* to tax churches violates the separation of church and state. Ah, the beauty of that first amendment. The free speech part. We all have a say, and we are allowed to say it. Give me a moment.

This argument is as cogent as the above. By taxing the church, the state is making the church subservient, potentially infringing upon "the free exercise thereof." And who the fuck wants to tax God anyway? Duh.

If churches were forced to pay taxes, some churches would go bankrupt. No, they would spend less. That may affect society, but only if they don't make enough money. The church does.

In separating church from state, one argues that if taxes are levied against churches, then the proceeds from donations are potentially being spent on activities that the donor disagrees with (e.g., wars, abortion, welfare). The church spends money more wisely than the government. Leave it in their hands.

THE NEW IRS

Nonprofit organizations are designed to accumulate donations and spend them on their constituents. Many nonprofits are evaluated on the percentage of revenue that is spent on the mission rather than on administration. The higher the percentage, the more efficient the nonprofit is in executing its mandate. Many nonprofits use this in their efforts to get additional donations, advertising a very high rate of use of proceeds for mission.

Most nonprofit net income comes close to zero. And if it doesn't, the retained amount is usually going to fund a good cause. Perhaps a building is needed, or a new program. We find that most nonprofit professionals are paid less than if they performed the same service in the for-profit world. Some do this out of belief in the cause; others do it because that was what was available when they needed a job. Regardless, the pay is often less.

So most nonprofits spend what they get in donations on the cause. Otherwise, they would not get many more donations. If their donors knew the money they were donating was being spent on lavish buildings, or expensive artwork, or jewelry for key executives, they sure as shit would not be making more donations.

Unless they did not know about it.

Or the cause was salvation.

Aha!

This is where we are. A nonprofit (the church) has carte

IF I WERE GOD

blanche to spend the donations in any way it deems fit, with no accountability. Hookers, drugs, altar boys. Is this not a recipe for abuse?

As God, I would be a bit conflicted here. I kind of like the Robes accumulating all this wealth on my behalf. Feels good to know they care that much. But do they care that much about Me? Hmmm. Let me try to be impartial.

After 17 million years, that is going to be tough.

OK, we are going to try to separate church from state. By making church indistinguishable from any other nonprofit. Therefore, the state cannot exert undue influence on the church. Just the same influence as all nonprofits. Seems reasonable, although I feel some pain about to be bestowed upon My Holy ass.

The basic premise is that nonprofits spend all their donations. What if they don't spend all their donations? What if they took a portion of them and bought stuff? Well, if it was in the furtherance of the cause, no problem. Like buying a house to create a place to live for the homeless.

But what if there is no accountability? What if I buy a picture and hang it in my living room? Maybe the picture inspires me to work harder for the cause. I look at it and think about how I can build a house for the homeless. Aha. I can also come to the conclusion that if I have this really big gold chain I can hang from my neck, then I will be even more inspired to work even harder to help those homeless guys. And Holy shit, a new Mercedes would take me to some Zen/yoga/sacred/divine level of inspiration. I could build that home with my bare hands.

Or hire some atheists, so I can fondle my chain.

So I let man do his thing, and it results in the Catholic Church being worth some unMe-like billions (trillions?).

Putting the donations of others into a huge jewel and art collection instead of using those donations to help those they were designed for.

And now I have to legislate this whole thing.

GOD 2.0

Am I really going to do this? I need my fucking head examined. Yo, Jesus, stop banging that Mary woman you've been hanging out with for just a second and get over here. I need some advice. All those dudes down there think I am all-knowing, but this shit is getting to me. Whaddya think?

"Yo, Dad, I'm on the internet trying to scarf up a date for Saturday night, OK? I bet you never envisioned that shit happening!"

Jesus is no help. Hey, I can't blame the guy. He was crucified. You spend days with your hands and feet with nails in them. You finally die and rise to heaven. I get it, you're going to have fun after that. Just use a condom, Son.

OK, this is an attempt not to cut off my nose to spite my face, but in reality, I have to do it, because it is the right thing to do.

Since the church (again, whichever one you wish to pick or all of them) has accumulated great wealth without paying taxes and without distributing that wealth to its constituents, reparations must be made. So, I decree the following:

First, the church must make an accounting of such wealth. Once that is done, they must distribute 10% of that wealth per year for the next 7 years. They can keep the remaining 30% for now, providing they follow the rest of My rules.

From now on, they must follow the same rules as other nonprofits in the United States with respect to reporting

IF I WERE GOD

and auditing. There will be a cap on undistributed earnings, both for the current year and since inception, which will hold true for all nonprofits. When Jesus is done having fun, I will put him in charge.

I will not get rid of organized religion, just repurpose their focus. I don't envy someone who gives up his life in the service of religion, but that does not give him the right to abuse the system. It is his choice. If he does not like it, get out.

So in summary, the church (and all nonprofits) will be restricted in how much income they can retain both on an annual basis and from inception. In addition, no person of any faith will ever be able to lie, cheat, steal, do anything illegal, mess with the commandments, or harm anyone in any way.

They can pray for the Jets, however.

I am God after all.

* * *

I hope you enjoyed *If I Were God (The World Would Get a Swift Kick in the Butt)* as much as I enjoyed writing it for you. I'm thrilled you are still reading. If you would like to write a review, I would love to hear from you. I won't take it personally either way.

Yes, I will.

FOR MORE LAUGHS

VISIT:

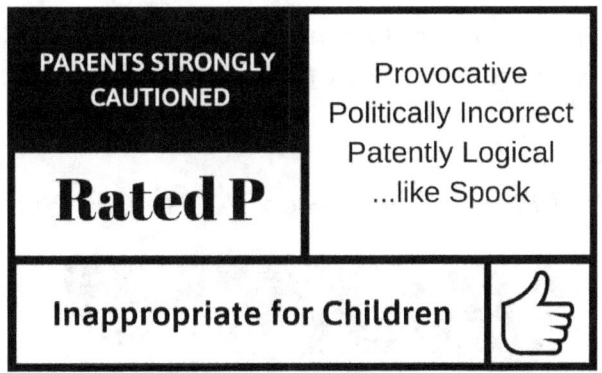

https://pabrook.com/if-you-dare/

OTHER TITLES

Oh Shit! I'm Over 50 and Single

(A Guide for Newly Single Mature Men and the Women Who Want to Understand Them)

Real Places You're Glad NOT to Call Home

MEET THE AUTHOR

PA Brook, Author, Dater and Know-It-All

Making Boring Fun

Trying to put an interesting spin on any topic has always been an interest. I have written dozens of articles for professional and trade publications, and made innumerable presentations in front of dozens, sometimes hundreds, of avid listeners. From writing a Star Trek themed article on investment regulations to using baseball analogies to wake up 700 people at an industry conference, I have always been able to interest an audience and yet get across the technical, sometimes boring, point I needed to make. Perhaps not on the NY Times bestseller list, my titles may sound more interesting than the content, but at least no one snoozes when they read them. Titles include: "WHERE NO (Hedge Fund) MAN (ager) HAS GONE BEFORE" with appropriate references to "Beam me up Scotty" to avoid being photon torpedoed by some nasty Klingon regulator, and "On an Island With the SEC, (Aka Diary of an SEC Exam)," a Survivor based primer on why those Government dudes win every immunity challenge.

My non-writing career has spanned decades, but my thirst for finding an interesting and entertaining outlet for my views has spanned a lifetime. Now I can go from writing about how to save your association by going "Back to the Future" at 1.21 jigawatts an hour to helping single guys in their 50s figure out there is life after divorce.

My first book, *Oh Shit! I'm Over 50 and Single (A Guide for Mature Men and the Women They Date)*, provides an honest and entertaining look at what the hell went wrong and how does one get back into the game. And what made me an expert on that? Not reading psych books, not getting medical degrees, not interviewing thousands of women. How about two divorces, a retirement savings spent on therapy, and dating a thousand women. Okay, not a thousand, but enough to know what worked at that age, at that time. There is no substitute for experience.

WHO WOULD PLAY ME IN THE MOVIE VERSION?

George Clooney is now married, otherwise he would be at the top of my list. Now, since he married a women 16 years his junior, I hope he reads my chapter on dating 30 somethings. It can be pretty awkward when you are the same age as your girlfriend's parents (or your daughter is the same age as your girlfriend), and when you want to go home on Saturday night, her friends are getting ready to go out.

Other choices include:

- William Seymour Hoffman, if he were alive
- Robert Downey Jr., if he were older
- Jeff Probst, because I love Survivor

Let's connect!

Drop by https://pabrook.com/ to check out other entertaining takes on life such as *Mile High Club* and *Holidays on Thin Ice*.

Facebook page: https://www.facebook.com/AuthorPABrook

Twitter: https://twitter.com/@AuthorPABrook/

www.ingramcontent.com/pod-product-compliance
Lightning Source LLC
Chambersburg PA
CBHW070528010526
44118CB00012B/1074